HILDEBRAND'S ROAD-ATLAS
HILDEBRAND'S STRASSEN-ATLAS/HILDEBRAND'S A

CANADA

THE WEST
DER WESTEN/L'OUEST

General Maps 1:7,000,000 • Regional Maps 1:1,500,000
Area Maps and Special Maps (Temperatures, Precipitation) in Various Scales
City Maps • Tables and Charts
Index to Place Names
Mileage Table • Tourist Information.

Übersichtskarten 1:7 000 000 • Regionalkarten 1:1 500 000
Gebietskarten und Thematische Karten (Temperaturen, Niederschläge)
in verschiedenen Maßstäben
Stadtpläne • Tabellen und Schautafeln
Verzeichnis von Orten und Sehenswürdigkeiten
Entfernungstabelle • Reise-Informationen

Cartes générales au 1:7 000 000 • Cartes régionales au 1:1 500 000
Cartes à différentes échelles et Cartes thématiques (températures, précipitations)
Plans de ville • Tableaux et schémas
Index des noms de lieux et des curiosités
Tableaux des distances • Informations touristiques.

KARTO+GRAFIK VERLAGSGESELLSCHAFT MBH, FRANKFURT/MAIN, GERMANY

Title/Titel/Titre
Fotoagentur Helga Lade

HILDEBRAND'S ROAD-ATLAS CANADA – The West
HILDEBRAND'S STRASSEN-ATLAS KANADA – Der Westen
HILDEBRAND'S ATLAS ROUTIER DU CANADA – L'Ouest

Managing Editor/Herausgeber/Editeur
Volker Hildebrand

Publisher/Verlag/Edition
K+G KARTO+GRAFIK Verlagsgesellschaft mbH
Schönberger Weg 15
60488 Frankfurt/Main
Germany

Cartography/Kartographie/Cartographie
Hildebrand Kartographik

Text/Text/Texte
Author/Autor/Auteur: Ellen Knutson
Translation/Übersetzung/Traduction:
Bernadette Boyle, Gabriele Kellermann-Hjort
Lucette Karner
Edited by/Redaktion/Rédaction: Dr. Bernd Peyer,
Andrea Brandhoff, Claudia Antes

Illustrations/Illustrationen/Illustrations
Eckart Müller

Lithography/Lithographie/Lithographie
Haußmann Repro, 64295 Darmstadt

Type Setting/Satz/Composition
Main-Taunus-Satz, 65760 Eschborn

Printed by/Druck/Impression
Fortuna Print, Bratislava

ISBN 3-88989-149-7

TABLE OF CONTENTS
INHALTSVERZEICHNIS/TABLE DES MATIERES

TABLE OF CONTENTS
INHALTSVERZEICHNIS/TABLE DES MATIERES

ROAD ATLAS

General Maps

Regional Maps

Area Maps

City Maps

Special Maps

Tables

ABBREVIATIONS

REGIONS · REGIONEN · RÉGIONS

CAN - Canada :

PROVINCES
AB - Alberta
BC - British Columbia
MB - Manitoba
NB - New Brunswick
NFL - Newfoundland
NS - Nova Scotia
ON - Ontario
PE - Prince Edward Island
PQ - Quebec
SK - Saskatchewan

TERRITORIES
NT - Northwest Territories
YT - Yukon Territory

US - United States:

AK - Alaska
ID - Idaho
ME - Maine
MI - Michigan
MN - Minnesota
MT - Montana
ND - North Dakota
NH - New Hampshire
NY - New York
OH - Ohio
PA - Pennsylvania
WA - Washington
WI - Wisconsin

PARKS, RESERVATIONS, etc ·
PARKS, RESERVATE, usw ·
PARCS, RÉSERVES, etc

N.W.R.	- National Wildlife Refuge/Naturschutzgebiet/ Réserve naturelle
N.S./Nat'l.S.	- National Seashore/Nation. Küstenschutzgebiet/ Réserve naturelle de mer
N.F./Nat'l.For.	- National Forest/Nationalwald/ Forêt nationale
N.R.A./Nat'l.Rec.A.	- National Recreation Area/Nationales Erholungsgeb./Zone nationale de récréation
S.R.A./St.Rec.Area	- State Recreation Area/Staatl. Erholungsgebiet/ Zone publique de récréation
S.B./St.Beach	- State Beach/Staatsstrand/Plage publique
N.M./Nat'l.Mon.	- National Monument/National Denkmal Monument national
N.B./Nat'l.Battlef.	- National Battlefield/Nationales Schlachtfeld/ Champ national de bataille
H.P./Hist.Pk.	- Historical Park/Historischer Park/ Parc historique
H.M./Hist.Mon.	- Historical Monument/Historisches Denkmal/ Monument historique
M.P./Mem.Pk.	- Memorial Park/Gedenkstätte mit Park/ Parc commémoratif
I.R./Ind.Res.	- Indian Reservation/Indianerreservat/ Réserve indienne
M.R./Mil.Res	- Military Reservation/Militärgebiet/Réserve militaire
I.P.P.	- International Peace Park/Internationaler Friedenspark/Parc International de la Paix
N.A.	- Natural Area/Naturgebiet/Zone naturelle
N.H.P.	- National Historic Park /Historischer Nationalpark/ Parc national historique
N.H.S.	- National Historic Site/Nationale historische Gedenkstätte/Lieu commémoratif national
N.P.	- National Park/Nationalpark/Parc national
N.W.A.	- National Wildlife Area/Nationales Wildnisgebiet/ Zone giboyeuse nationale
P.F.	- Provincial Forest/Provinzialer Wald/Forêt provincial
P.H.A.	- Provincial Historic Area/Provinziales historisches Gebiet/Zone historique provinciale
P.H.S.	- Provincial Historic Site/Provinziale historische Gedenkstätte/Lieu commémoratif historique
P.P.	- Provincial Park/Provinzialer Park/Parc provincial
P.R.A.	- Provincial Recreation Area/Provinziales Erholungs- gebiet/Zone provinciale de récréation
W.H.S.	- World Heritage Site/Weltkulturerbe/Site naturel universel

FURTHER ABBREVIATIONS ·
WEITERE ABKÜRZUNGEN ·
AUTRES ABRÉVIATIONS

B.	- Beach/Strand/Plage
Cr.	- Creek/Bach/Ruisseau
Cy.	- City/Stadt/Ville
Ft.	- Fort
Hts.	- Heights/Höhen/Sommets
Hwy.	- Highway
Int.	- International
L.	- Lake/See/Lac
m	- metres/Meter/mètres
Mt., Mtn.	- Mount, Mountain/Berg/Mont
Mts.	- Mountains/Gebirge/Montagne
Nat., Nat'l.	- National
Pk.	- Peak/Gipfel/Cime
Prov.	- Provincial
R.	- River/Fluß/Rivière
Rec.	- Recreational
Res.	- Reservation, Reservoir/Reservat, Stausee/ Réserve, Lac de barrage
Spr., Sprs.	- Spring, Springs/Quelle, Quellen/ Source, Sources
St.	- State/Staat/État

TYPEFACE · SCHRIFTBILD ·
CARACTÈRES DE ÉCRITURE

Alberta	Province / Provinz / Province
District of Keewatin	District / Distrikt / District
Coast Mountains	Mountain range, Landscape / Gebirge, Landschaft / Chaîne de montagnes, Paysage
Prince Edward Island	Island / Insel / Île
Hells Gate	Object of interest / Sehenswürdigkeit / Curiosité

KM

Diagonal list of cities (top-left to bottom-right of the mileage chart):

Anchorage...... Banff...... Boston...... Calgary...... Chicago...... Dawson City...... Edmonton...... Fairbanks...... Flin Flon...... Fort Simpson...... Glace Bay...... Halifax...... Inuvik...... Juneau...... Kamloops...... Kingston...... Lake Louise...... Minneapolis...... Moncton...... Montréal...... New York...... North Bay...... Ottawa...... Philadelphia...... Prince George...... Prince Rupert...... Quebec...... Regina...... Rivière du Loup...... Saint John...... Saskatoon...... Sault Ste. Marie...... Seattle...... Sept Iles...... Spokane...... Thompson...... Thunder Bay...... Toronto...... Vancouver...... Washington...... Whitehorse...... Winnipeg...... Yellow Knife......

distances to Prince Rupert - ferry connection

MILES

NATIONAL PARKS – ACTIVITIES –

National Parks	RV-facilities	Winter camping	Downhill skiing	Cross-country skiing	Ski-touring	Fishing	Boat tours	Rafting	Swimming	Scuba/snorkelling	Sailing	Canoeing	Tennis	Golf	Horseback riding	Picnicking	Group camping	Camping	Pleasure Driving	Bicycling: trail	Nature Programmes	Backpacking	Hiking
1 Kluane	●			●		●		●										●			●	●	●
2 Northern Yukon						●		●														●	●
3 Nahanni						●		●				●						●			●	●	●
4 Wood Buffalo	●			●		●												●			●	●	●
5 Auyuittuq				●		●												●			●	●	●
6 Pacific Rim	●	●		●		●	●		●	●	●	●				●		●	●		●	●	●
7 Mount Revelstoke		●		●		●										●		●	●	●	●	●	●
8 Glacier		●		●	●	●									●	●		●	●	●	●	●	●
9 Yoho		●		●	●	●		●							●	●		●	●	●	●	●	●
10 Kootenay		●		●	●	●		●				●				●		●	●	●	●	●	●
11 Banff	●	●	●	●	●	●			●	●	●	●	●	●	●	●	●	●	●	●	●	●	●
12 Jasper	●	●	●	●	●	●		●	●	●	●	●	●	●	●	●	●	●	●	●	●	●	●
13 Waterton Lakes	●	●		●		●	●		●	●	●	●				●	●	●	●	●	●	●	●
14 Elk Island		●		●		●			●							●	●	●	●		●	●	●
15 Grasslands																●		●	●		●		●
16 Prince Albert	●	●		●		●	●		●	●	●	●		●	●	●	●	●	●		●	●	●
17 Riding Mountain	●	●	●	●		●	●		●	●	●	●	●	●	●	●	●	●	●	●	●	●	●
18 Pukaskwa		●				●			●		●	●				●	●	●	●		●	●	●
19 Georgian Bay Islands									●	●	●	●				●	●	●	●		●	●	●
20 Point Pelee				●					●	●	●	●				●	●	●	●	●	●		●
21 St. Lawrence Islands	●					●			●	●	●	●				●	●	●	●		●	●	●
22 La Mauricie	●	●		●		●	●		●	●		●				●	●	●	●		●	●	●
23 Forillon	●	●		●			●		●	●	●					●	●	●	●		●	●	●
24 Mingan Archipelago							●		●	●						●		●	●		●	●	●
25 Kouchibouguac	●	●		●		●			●	●	●	●	●	●		●	●	●	●	●	●	●	●
26 Fundy	●	●		●		●			●	●	●	●	●	●		●	●	●	●		●	●	●
27 Prince Edward Island		●							●	●	●			●		●	●	●	●	●	●	●	●
28 Kejimkujik	●	●		●		●			●	●	●	●				●	●	●	●		●	●	●
29 Cape Breton Highlands	●	●		●		●			●	●				●		●	●	●	●		●	●	●
30 Gros Morne	●	●		●		●	●		●	●	●	●				●	●	●	●		●	●	●
31 Terra Nova	●	●		●		●			●	●	●	●		●		●	●	●	●		●	●	●

Parks Service Regional Offices

Western Region
Room 520
220 Fourth Avenue South
East
Calgary, Alberta T2P 3H8
Telephone (403) 292-4440

Prairie and Northern Region
457 Main Street
Winnipeg,
Manitoba R3B 3E8
Telephone (204) 983-2110

Ontario Region
111 Water Street East
Cornwall,
Ontario K6H 6S3
Telephone (613) 938-5866

Québec Region
3 Buade Street
Haute Ville
Québec,
Québec G1R 4V7
Telephone (418) 648-4177

Atlantic Region
Historic Properties
Upper Water Street
Halifax,
Nova Scotia B3J 1S9
Telephone (902) 426-3457

The symbols used in the legend apply to maps of all scales.
References in the margin (such as A 1 , etc.) facilitate the locating of towns, places of interest featured in the index.
Die in der Zeichenerklärung dargestellten Signaturen, gelten einheitlich für alle Maßstäbe.
Die Ziffern A 1 , usw. am Seitenrand dienen der Auffindung von Orten und Sehenswürdigkeiten aus dem Register.
L'interprêtation des signes dans le tableau est valable pour la compréhension de toutes les échelles.
Le chiffre A 1 , etc. placé dans la marge sert à retrouver dans l'index les lieux et les curiosités.

Markings at the edge of maps indicate adjoining maps in the following scales :
Die Markierungen am Kartenrand geben den Hinweis auf angrenzende Seiten in folgenden Maßstäben :
Le symbole plac ésur le côté de la carte indique les feuillets correspondant aux Dimensions suivantes :

1 : 7 000 000
1 : 3 500 000
1 : 4 700 000

1 : 1 500 000

1 : 800 000
1 : 500 000
1 : 200 000

Enclosed areas on map indicate that larger-scale maps of this areas are to be found elsewhwere :
Die umrandeten Gebiete in den Karten geben den Hinweis auf Seiten in einen größeren Maßstab für das bezeichnete Gebiet :
Les régions encadrées renvoient à d'aitres cartes dessinées sur une plus grande échelle :

p.p.122/123	1 : 7 000 000
	1 : 3 500 000
	1 : 4 700 000

| p.p.122/123 | 1 : 1 500 000 |

p.p.122/123	1 : 800 000	City & Area Maps
	1 : 500 000	Stadtpläne & Detailkarten
	1 : 200 000	Plans de Ville & Cartes de détaillées

POPULATION OF LOCALITIES · ORTSKLASSIFIZIERUNG · POPULATION DE LA LOCALITÉ

		Inhabitants/ Einwohner/ Inhabitants
VANCOUVER	> 250 000	
Burnaby	> 100 000 – 250 000	
Prince George	> 25 000 – 100 000	
Vernon ○	> 10 000 – 25 000	
Courtenay ○	> 2 500 – 10 000	
Thompson ○	> 0 – 2 500	
Woodridge □	Seasonelly occupied settlement Saisonal bewohnte Siedlung Habitat périodiquement occupé	

TRAFFIC · VERKEHR · TRAFIC

22	Trans-Canada Highway
3	Yellowhead Highway
5	U.S. National Interstate Hwy.
12	U.S. Highway
23	Provincial/State Highway
47	Secondary Provincial/State Hwy.

Free limited access highway
Autobahn mit Anschlußstelle., gebührenfrei
Autoroute avec accés limité, sans péage

Toll limited acces highway
Autobahn mit Anschlußstelle., gebührenpflichtig
Autoroute avec accés limité, à peage

Multilane highway
Fernverkehrsstraße, mehrspurig
Route à grande circulation, à plus. voies

Under construction
In Bau
En construction

Principal through highway
Fernverkehrsstraße
Route à grande circulation

Other through highway
Hauptstraße
Route principale

Through highway, unpaved
Hauptstraße, unbefestigt
Route principale, sans revêtement

Other road
Nebenstraße
Autre route

Other road, unpaved
Nebenstraße, unbefestigt
Autre route, sans revêtement

Trail, Footpath
Pfad, Fußweg
Sentier

12 Distances in kilometres
Entfernungen in Kilometer
Distances en kilomètres

Scenic road
Landschaftlich schöne Strecke
Route touristique

1240 Pass, Height in metres
Paß, Höhe in Meter
Col, Altitude en mètres

11-2 Prohibited Road
Straße gesperrt
Route interdite

Tunnel
Tunnel
Tunnel

Airport, Arodrome
Flughafen, Flugplatz
Aéroport, Aérodrome

Railway
Eisenbahn
Chemin de fer

Ferry
Fähre
Bac

Shipping route
Schiffahrtslinie
Ligne maritime

BOUNDARIES · GRENZEN · FRONTIÈRES

International boundary
Staatsgrenze
Frontière d'État fédéral

Provincial-, State boundary
Provinz-, Bundesstaatengrenze
Frontière d'État fédéral

Time zone boundary
Zeitzonengrenze
Fuseau horaire

SYMBOLS · SIGNATUREN · SIGNE

Banff Place of interest
Sehenswerter Ort
Lieu d'intérêt

Mormon Temple • Object of interest
Sehenswürdigkeit
Curiosités

■ Important building
Wichtiges Bauwerk
Bâtiment important

M̂ Museum
Museum
Musée

Church, Chapel
Kirche; Kapelle
Église; Chapelle

Monastery;- Ruin
Kloster; -Ruine
Monastère;- Ruine

Palace, Castle, Fort; -Ruin
Schloß, Burg, Festung; -Ruine
Palais, château, Fort; -Ruine

Monument, Tower
Denkmal; Turm
Monument; Tour

Lighthouse
Leuchtturm
Phare

Ruine; Cave
Ruinenstätte; Höhle
Ruine; Caverne

Mine
Bergwerk; Mine
Mine

Beach
Strand
Plage

Camping site
Campingplatz
Camping

Camping site, seasonally
4-10 Campingplatz, saisonal geöffnet
Camping, périodiquement

Winter Sports
Wintersport
Sports d'hiver

Golf
Golf
Golf

Panoramic view
Aussichtspunkt
Point de vue

1240 Height in metres
Höhe in Meter
Altitude en métres

PARKS, RESERVATIONS, etc. PARKS, RESERVATE, usw. PARCS, RÉSERVES, etc.

National-,Provincial-,State Park
National-, Provinz-Park
Parc national, -provincial

National-,Provincial-,State Forest/Reserve
National-, Provinz-Wald/Reservat
Forêt nationale, -provinciale/Résreve

Wildlife Refuge
Naturschutzgebiet
Réserve naturelle

Indian Reservation
Indianerreservat
Réserve naturelle

Military reserve
Militärgebiet
Réserve militaire

WATERS · GEWÄSSER · EAUX

Continental Divide
Wasserscheide
Ligne de partage des eaux

Spring, thermal spring, Waterfall
Quelle, Therme. Wasserfall
Source, source thermale, Cascade

Sea, Dam
See, Staumauer
Lac, Barrage

Salt Lake
Salzsee
Lac salé

Periodic lake
Periodischer See
Lac périodique

Priodic river
Periodischer Fluß
Rivière périodique

Swamp
Sumpf
Marais

CITYMAPS · STADTPLÄNE · PLANS DE VILLE

Building, Hotel
Gebäude, Hotel
Bâtiment, Hôtel

Airport, Aerodrome
Flughafen, Flugplatz
Aéroport, Aérodrome

Buildings
Bebauung
Bâtiments

Park, Cemetary
Park, Friedhof
Parc, Cimetière

Green plot
Grünanlagen
Espace vert

Beach
Strand
Plage

Open space
Freiflächen
Espace libre

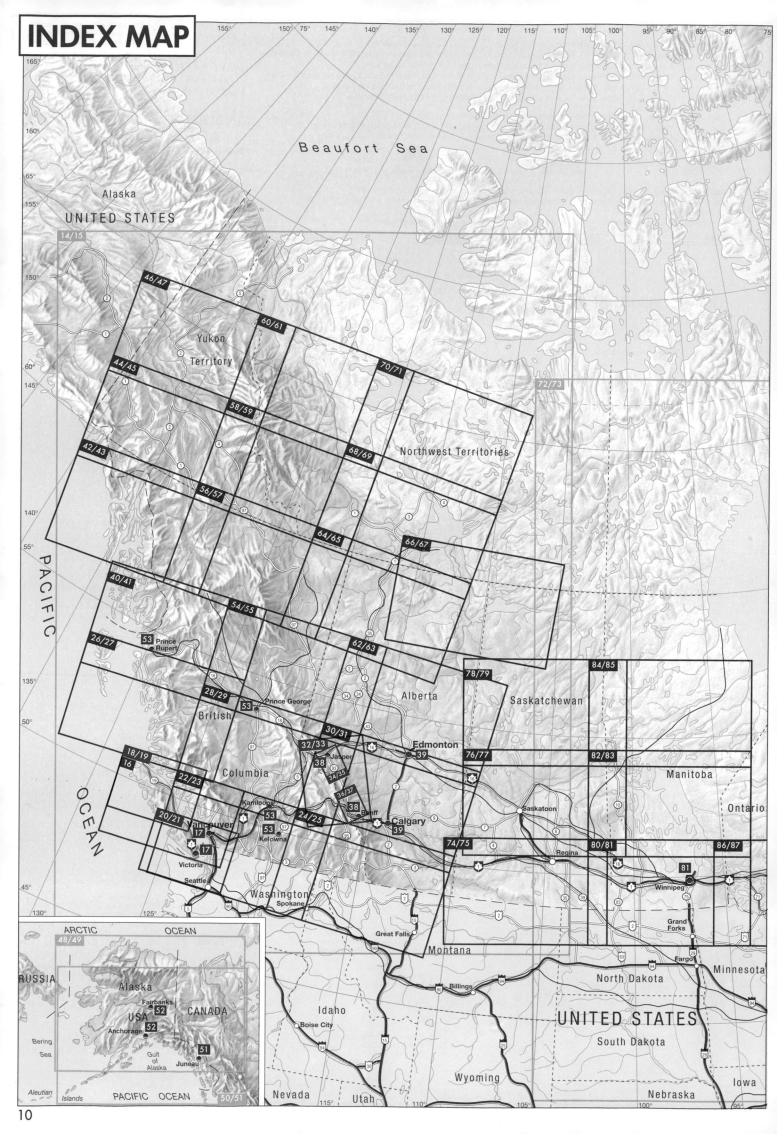

INDEX MAP

Beaufort Sea

Alaska
UNITED STATES

PACIFIC

OCEAN

Yukon Territory

Northwest Territories

Saskatchewan

Manitoba

Ontario

Alberta

British Columbia

Prince Rupert

Prince George

Kamloops

Vancouver

Victoria

Seattle

Washington

Spokane

Great Falls

Montana

Jasper

Edmonton

Banff

Calgary

Kelowna

Saskatoon

Regina

Winnipeg

Grand Forks

Fargo

North Dakota

Minnesota

UNITED STATES

South Dakota

Idaho

Billings

Boise City

Wyoming

Utah

Nevada

Nebraska

Iowa

14/15
46/47
44/45
42/43
26/27
40/41
18/19
16
20/21
17
17
22/23
28/29
53
53
53
60/61
58/59
56/57
54/55
24/25
32/33
38
34/35
36/37
38
30/31
62/63
64/65
66/67
68/69
70/71
72/73
78/79
76/77
74/75
84/85
82/83
80/81
86/87
39
39
81

ARCTIC OCEAN
48/49
RUSSIA
Alaska
CANADA
Fairbanks
52
USA
52
Anchorage
Bering Sea
Gulf of Alaska
Juneau
51
Aleutian Islands
PACIFIC OCEAN
50/51

10

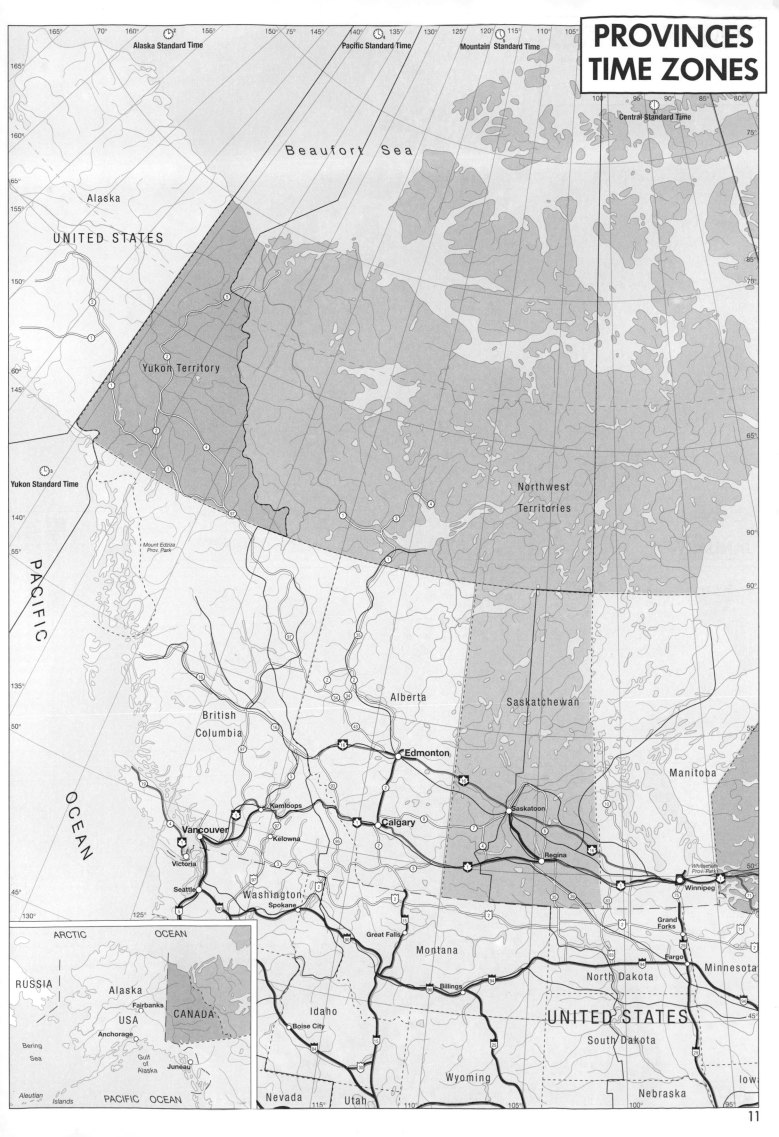

Alaska Standard Time

Pacific Standard Time

Mountain Standard Time

Central Standard Time

Beaufort Sea

Alaska

UNITED STATES

Yukon Territory

Yukon Standard Time

Northwest Territories

Mount Edziza Prov. Park

PACIFIC

OCEAN

British Columbia

Alberta

Saskatchewan

Manitoba

Edmonton

Kamloops

Vancouver

Kelowna

Calgary

Saskatoon

Victoria

Regina

Whiteshell Prov. Park

Seattle

Winnipeg

Washington

Spokane

Grand Forks

Great Falls

Fargo

Montana

Minnesota

North Dakota

Billings

UNITED STATES

Idaho

Boise City

South Dakota

Wyoming

Nevada   Utah

Nebraska   Iowa

ARCTIC   OCEAN

RUSSIA

Alaska

Fairbanks

USA

CANADA

Anchorage

Bering Sea

Gulf of Alaska

Juneau

Aleutian Islands

PACIFIC OCEAN

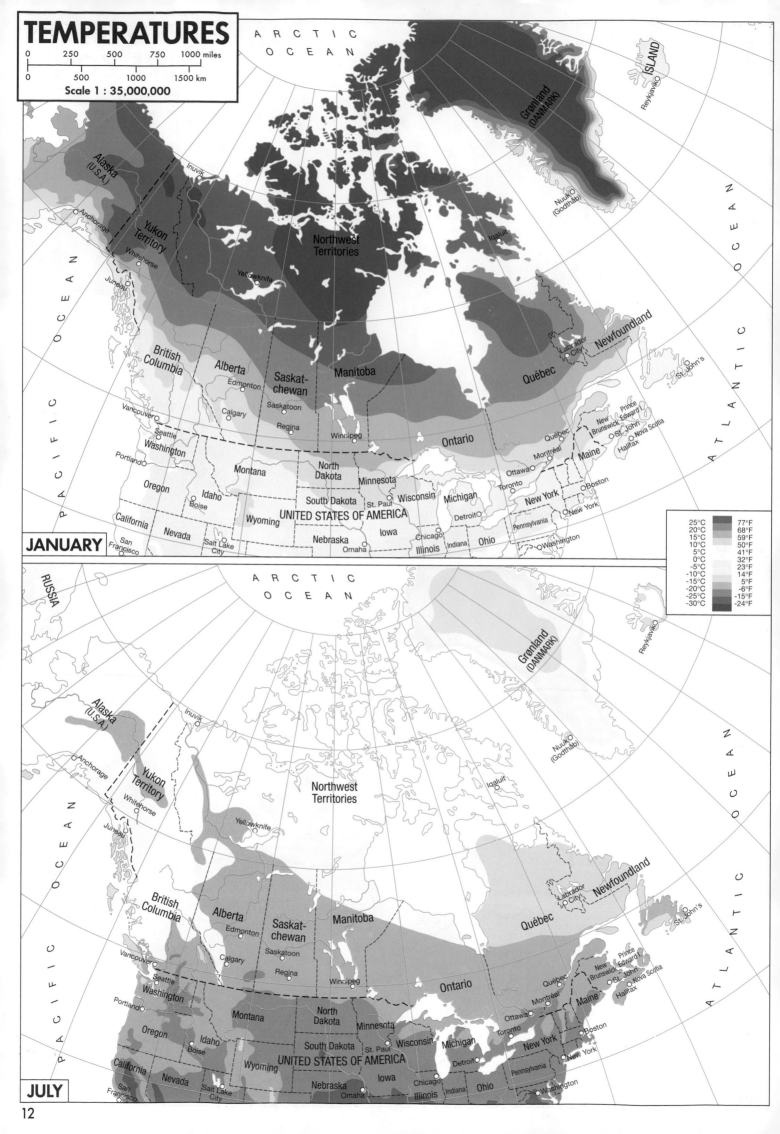

TEMPERATURES

Scale 1 : 35,000,000

°C	°F
25°C	77°F
20°C	68°F
15°C	59°F
10°C	50°F
5°C	41°F
0°C	32°F
-5°C	23°F
-10°C	14°F
-15°C	5°F
-20°C	-6°F
-25°C	-15°F
-30°C	-24°F

JANUARY

JULY

12

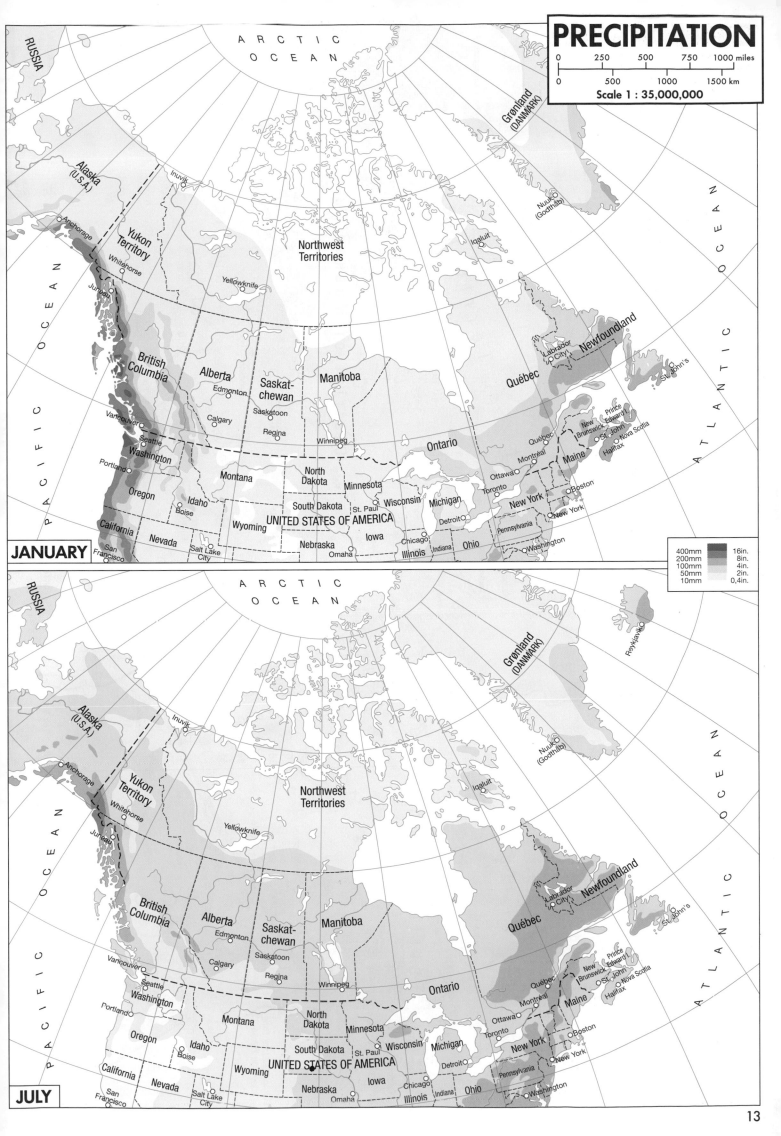

PRECIPITATION

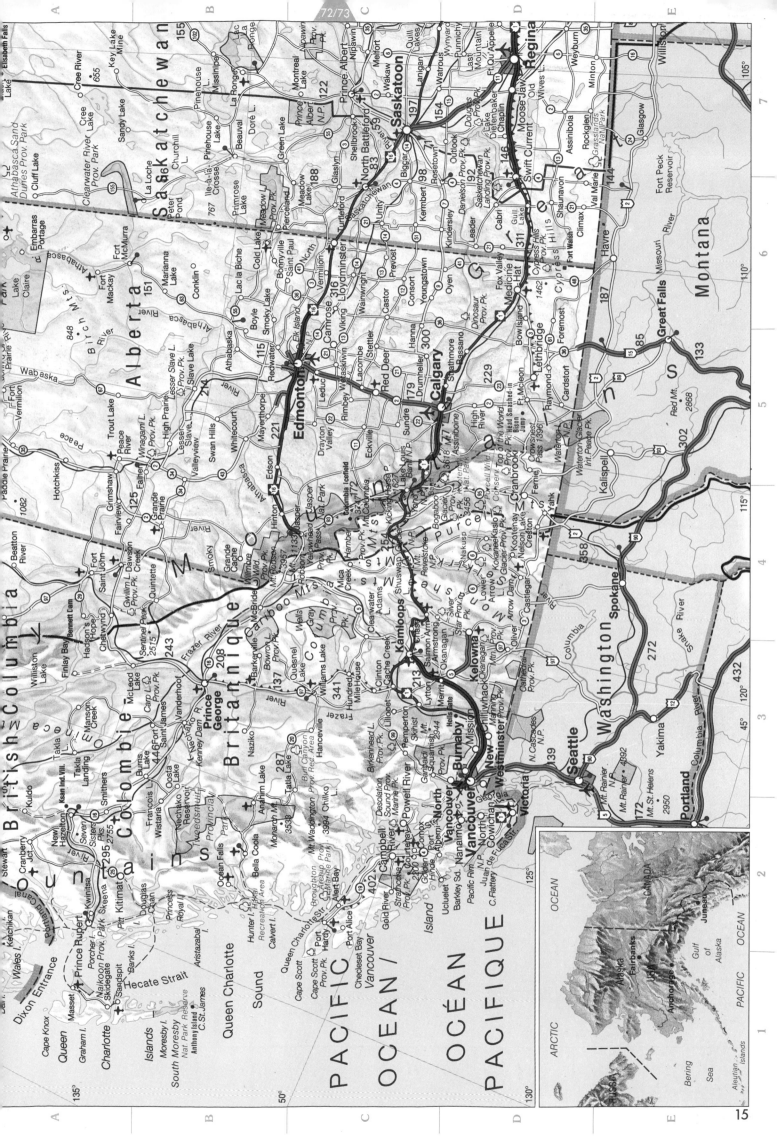

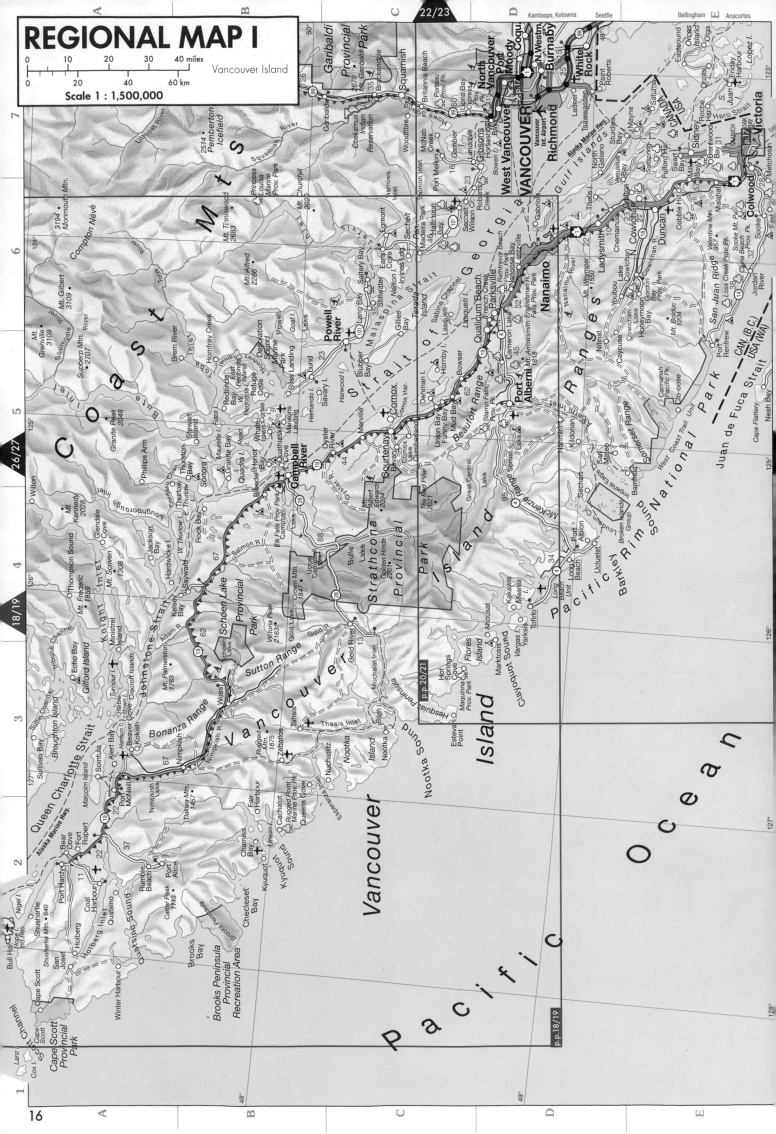

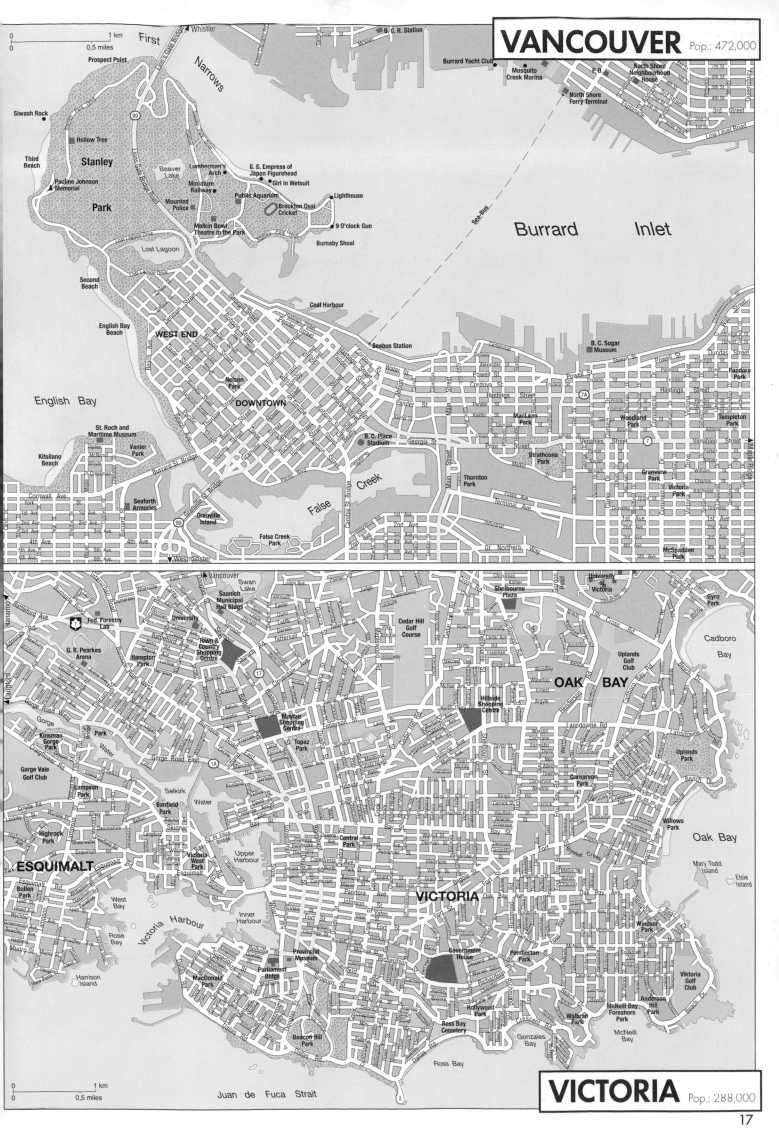

VANCOUVER Pop.: 472,000

VICTORIA Pop.: 288,000

17

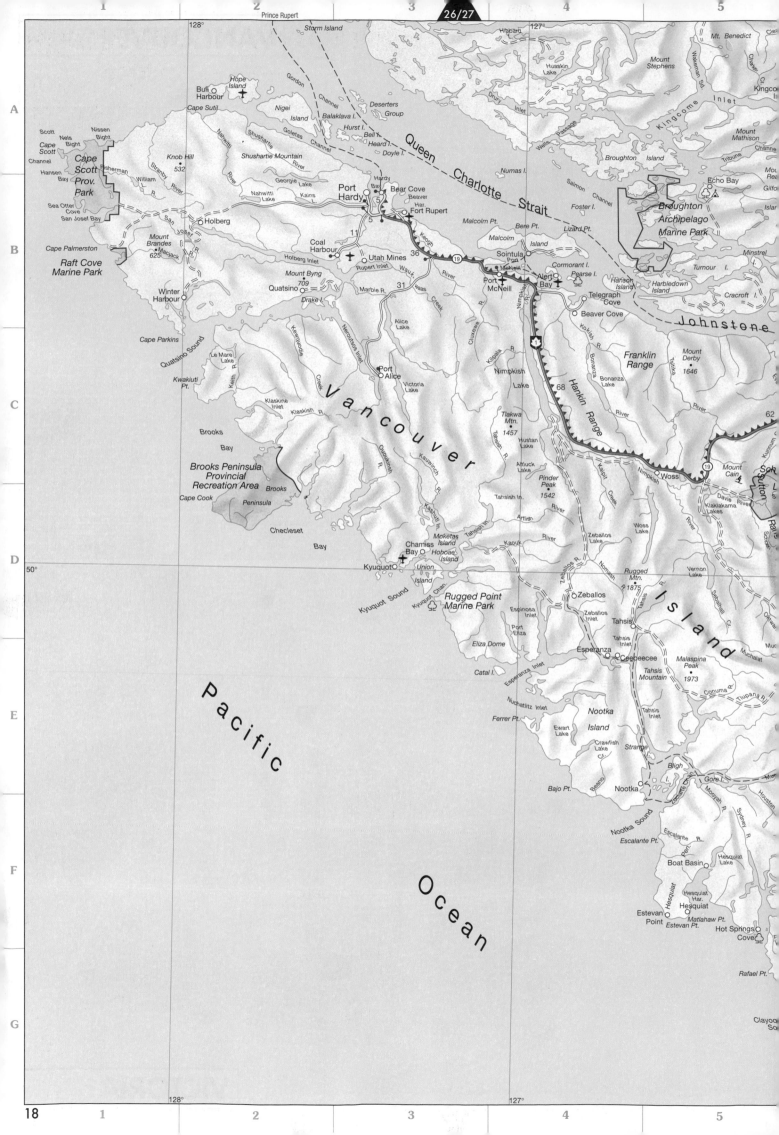

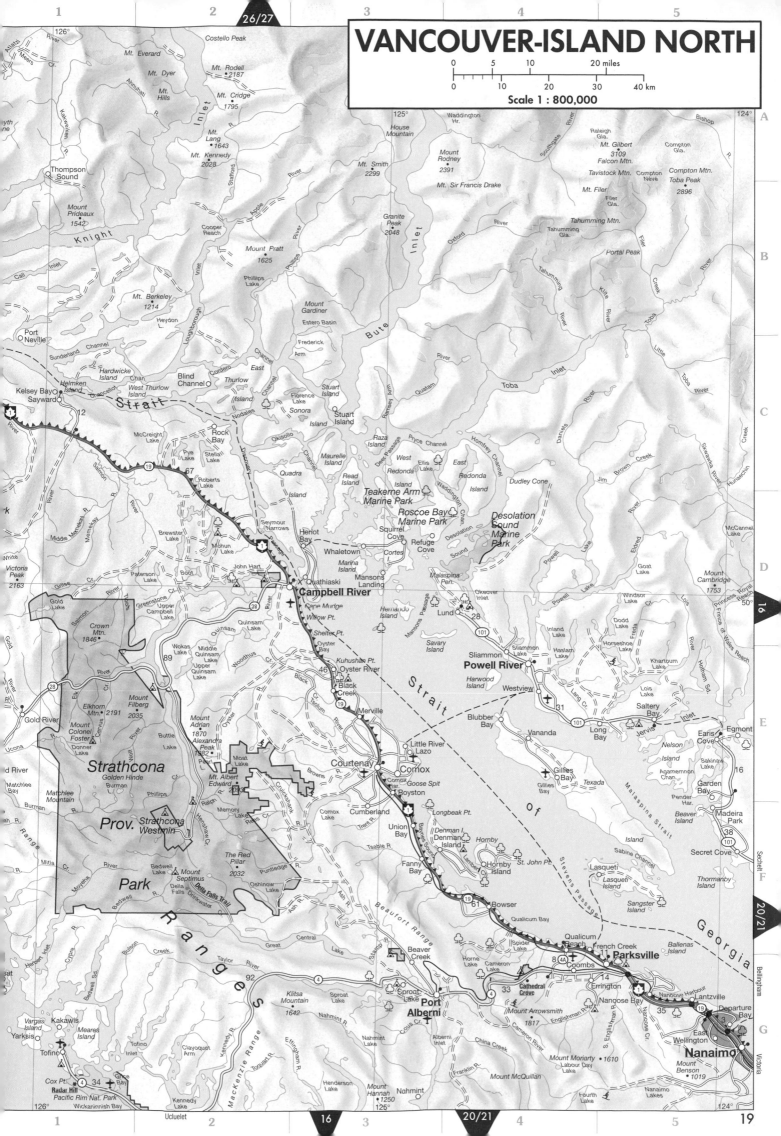

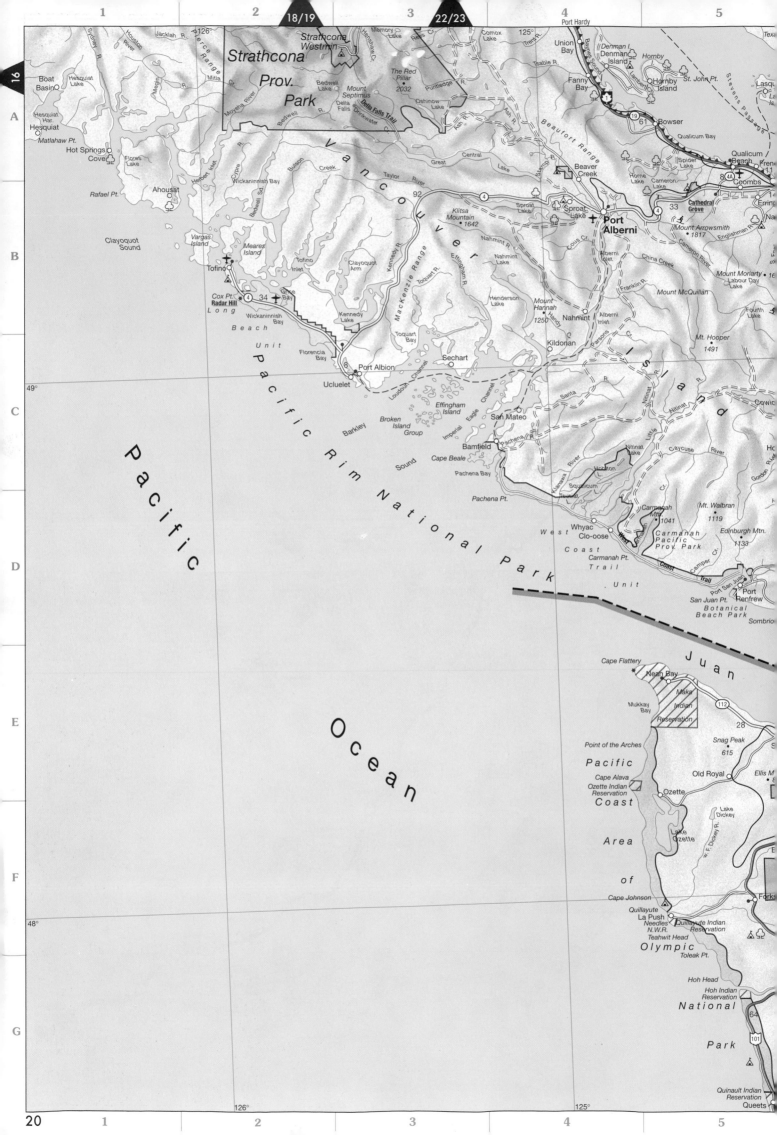

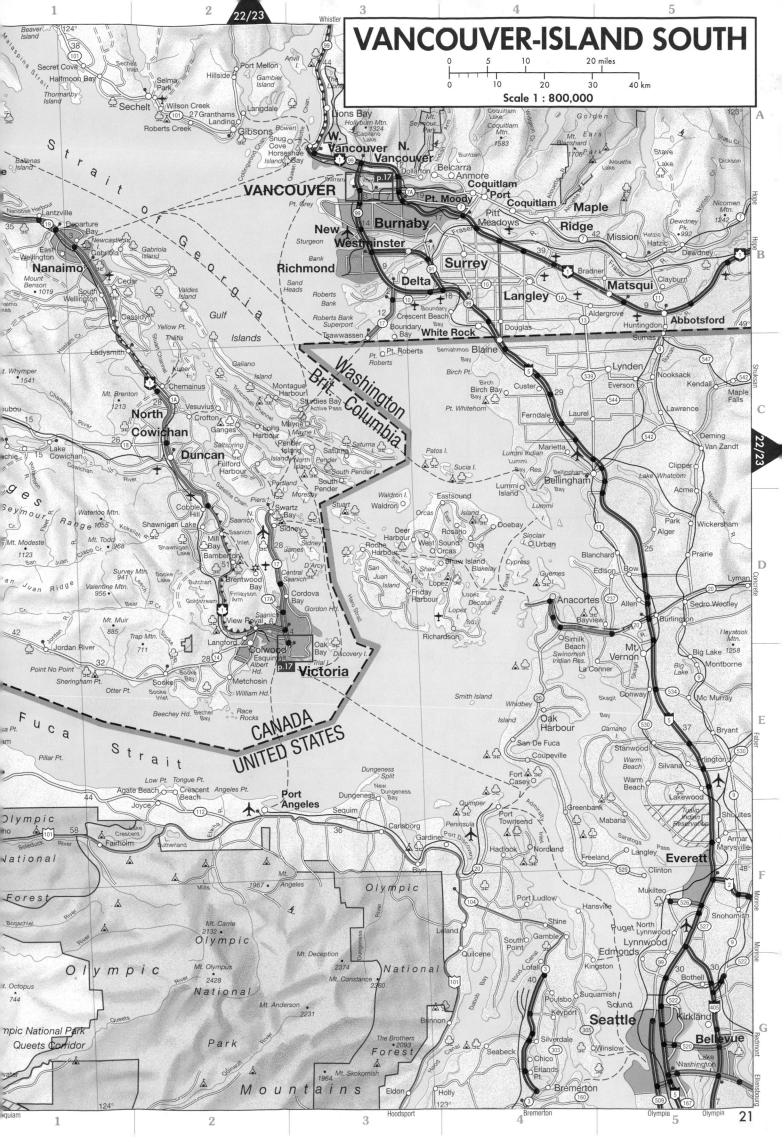

VANCOUVER-ISLAND SOUTH

Scale 1 : 800,000

0 5 10 20 miles
0 10 20 30 40 km

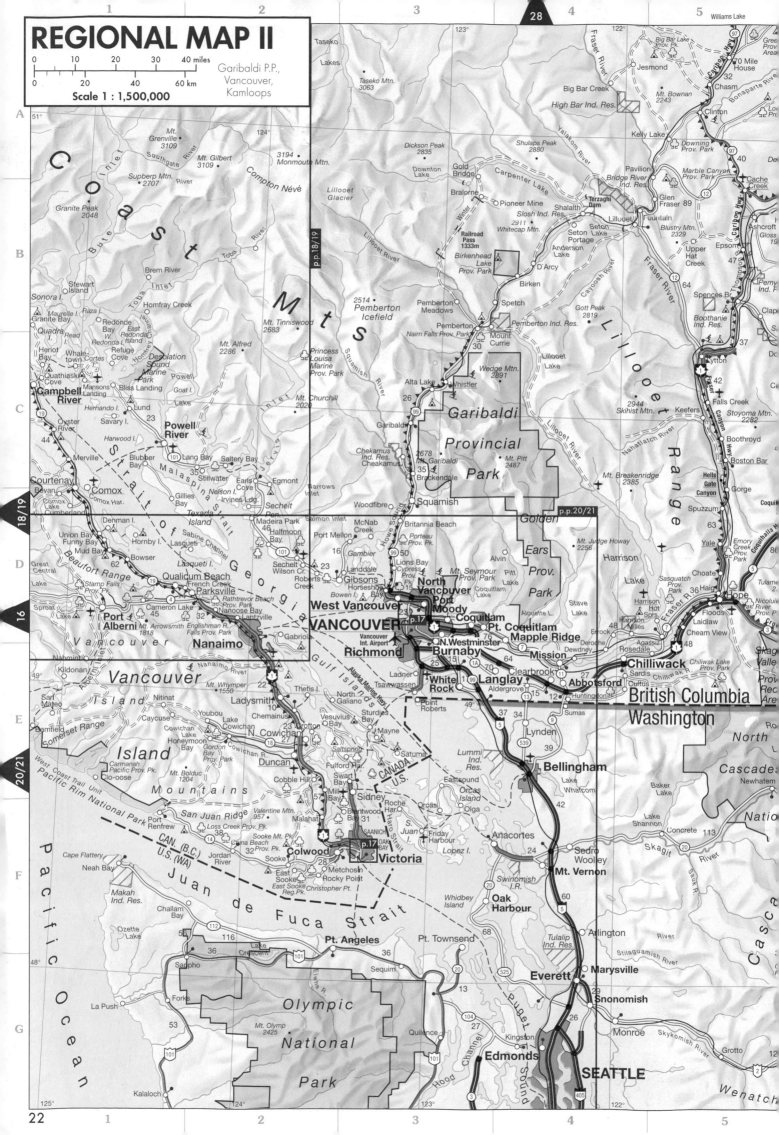

REGIONAL MAP II

0   10   20   30   40 miles
0   20   40   60 km
Scale 1 : 1,500,000

Garibaldi P.P.,
Vancouver,
Kamloops

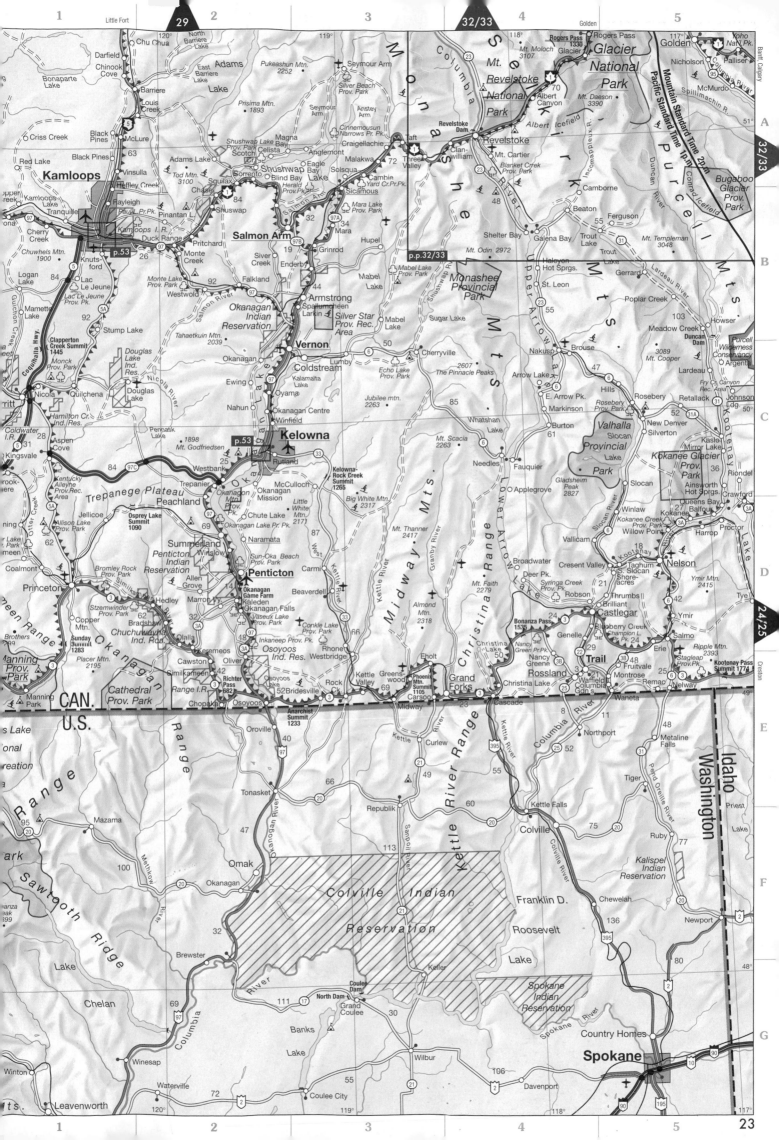

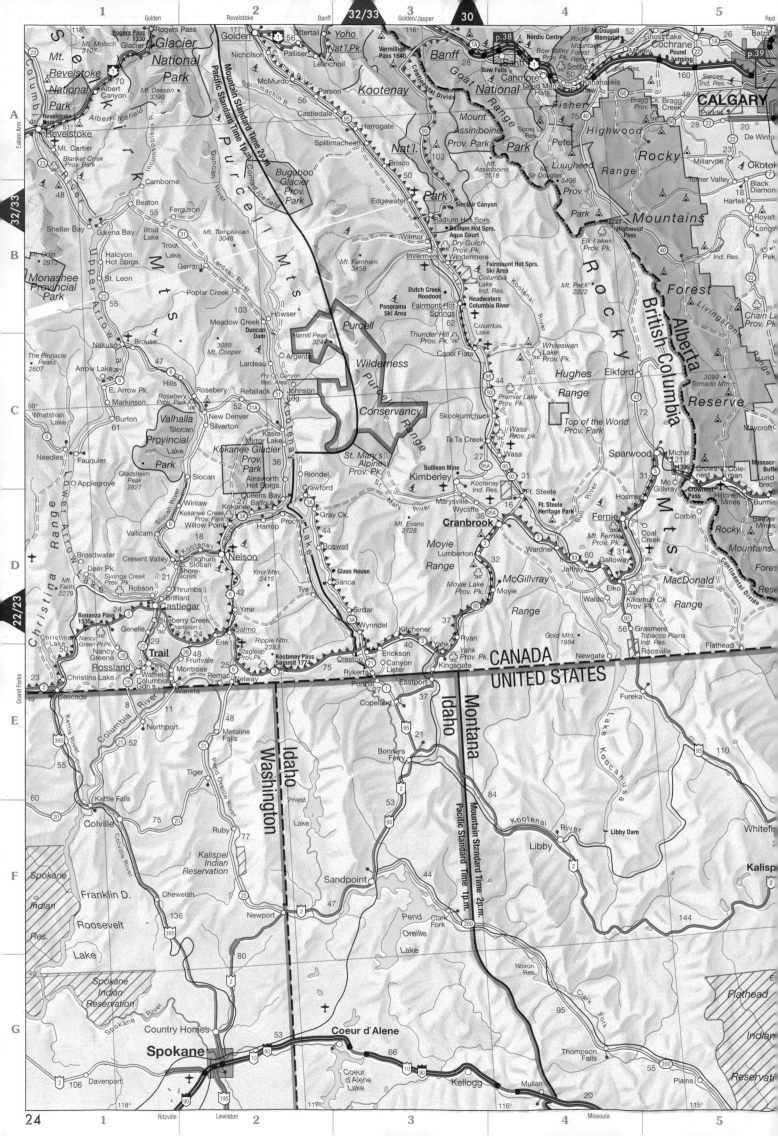

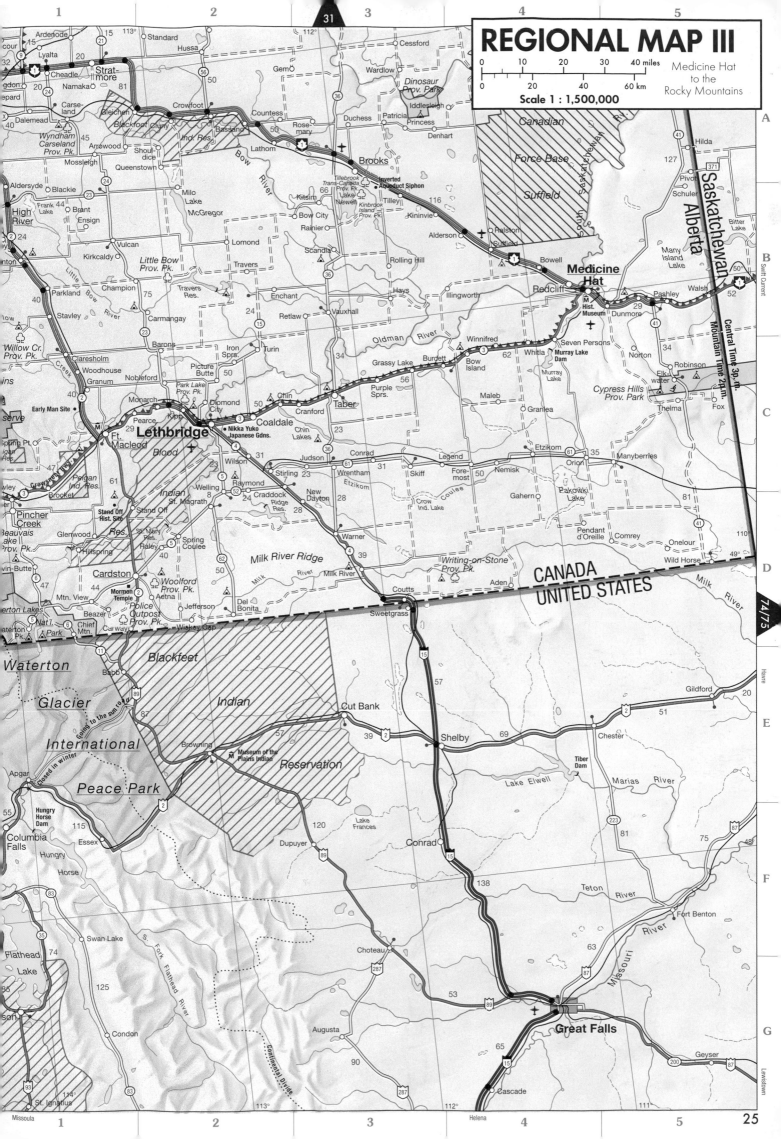

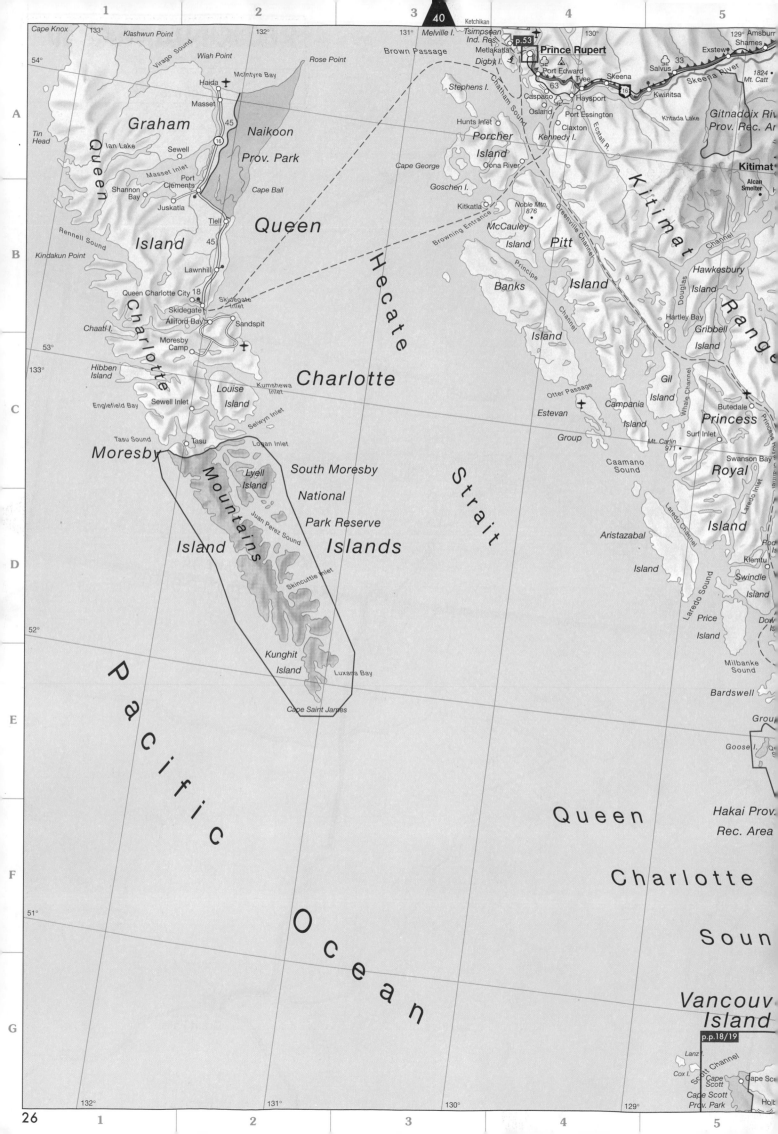

Cape Knox
133°
Klashwun Point
132°
54°
Wiah Point
Virago Sound
McIntyre Bay
Rose Point
131°
Melville I.
Brown Passage
Ketchikan
Tsimpsean
Ind. Res.
Metlakatla
Digby I.
p.53
Prince Rupert
Port Edward
Tyee
129°
Amsburr
Shames
Exstew
Skeena River
Mt. Catt
130°
1824

Haida
Masset

Graham
45

Naikoon
Prov. Park

Tin
Head
Ian Lake
Sewell
Masset Inlet
16
Port
Clements
Cape Ball
Shannon
Bay
Juskatla

Queen

Tlell
45

Island

Lawnhill

Kindakun Point

Rennell Sound

Queen Charlotte City 18
Skidegate
Inlet
Skidegate
Alliford Bay
Sandspit
Moresby
Camp

Chaatl I.
Hibben
Island
133°
53°

Engfield Bay

Louise
Island
Kumshewa Inlet

Sewell Inlet

Selwyn Inlet

Charlotte

Hecate

Stephens I.
Osland
Caspaco
Haysport
Port Essington
Claxton
Kennedy I.
Hunts Inlet
Oona River

Porcher
Island

Cape George
Goschen I.

Kitkatla

McCauley
Island

Noble Mtn.
876
Browning Entrance

Pitt
Island

Banks

Principe

Island

Channel

Otter Passage

Estevan
Campania
Island

Group

Skeena
63
16
Kwinitsa
Khtada Lake

Gitnadoix Riv
Prov. Rec. Ar

Kitimat
Alcan
Smelter

Hawkesbury
Island
Douglas

Hartley Bay
Gribbell
Island

Gil
Island

Butedale
Surf Inlet
Mt. Carlin
971
Princess
Royal
Island

Tasu Sound
Tasu

Moresby

Mountains

Lyell
Island

Logan Inlet

South Moresby

National

Park Reserve

Island

Juan Perez Sound

Skincuttle Inlet

Islands

Strait

52°

Caamano
Sound

Aristazabal

Island

Laredo Channel
Laredo Sound

Price
Island

Swanson Bay

Klemtu
Swindle
Island

Dow
Rod
Is.

Kunghit
Island

Luxana Bay

Cape Saint James

Milbanke
Sound

Bardswell

51°
132°
131°
130°
129°

P
a
c
i
f
i
c

O
c
e
a
n

Q u e e n

C h a r l o t t e

S o u n

Hakai Prov.
Rec. Area

Goose I.
Grou

Vancouv
Island
p.p.18/19

Lanz I.
Cox I.
Scott Channel
Cape
Scott
Cape Scott
Prov. Park
Cape Sco
Holt

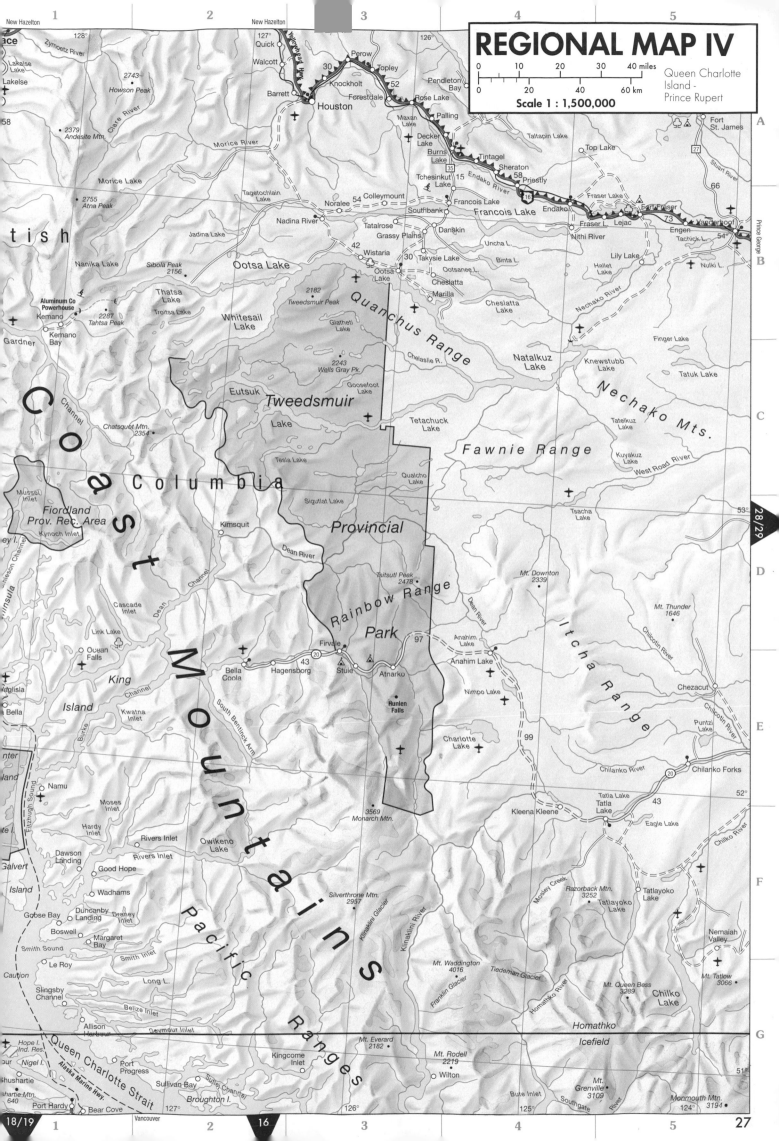

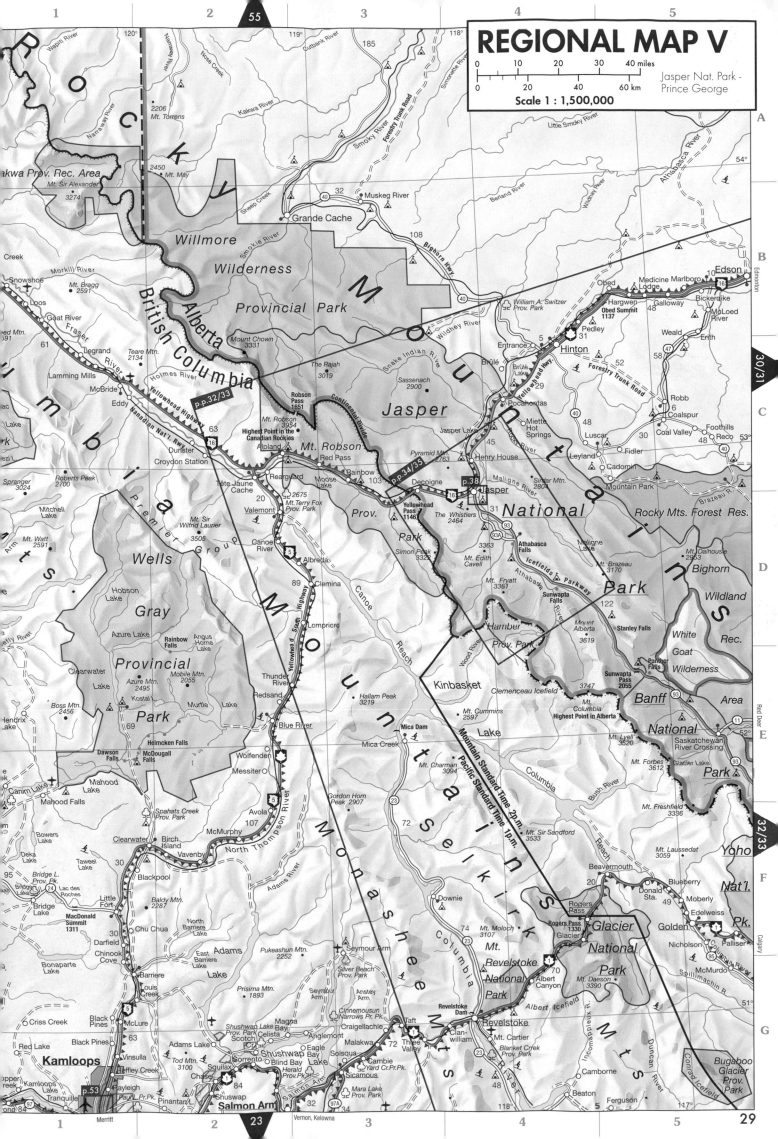

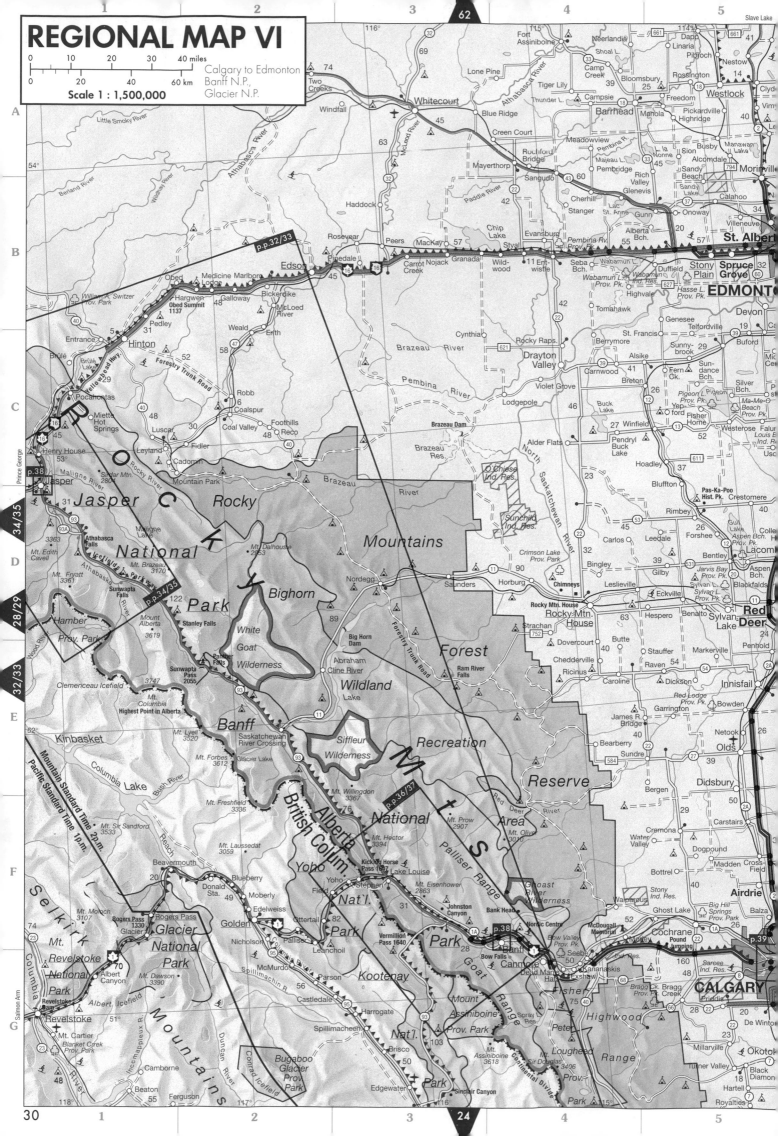

REGICNAL MAP VI

Scale 1 : 1,500,000

Calgary to Edmonton
Banff N.P.,
Glacier N.P.

0 10 20 30 40 miles
0   20   40   60 km

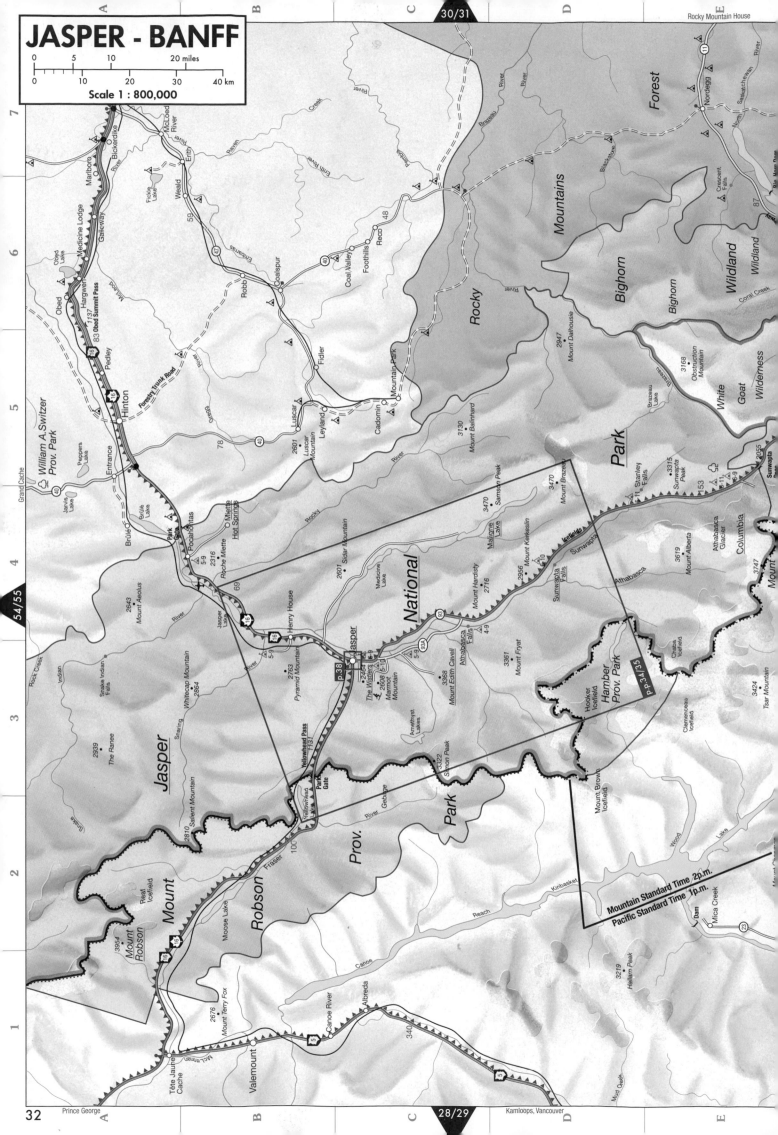

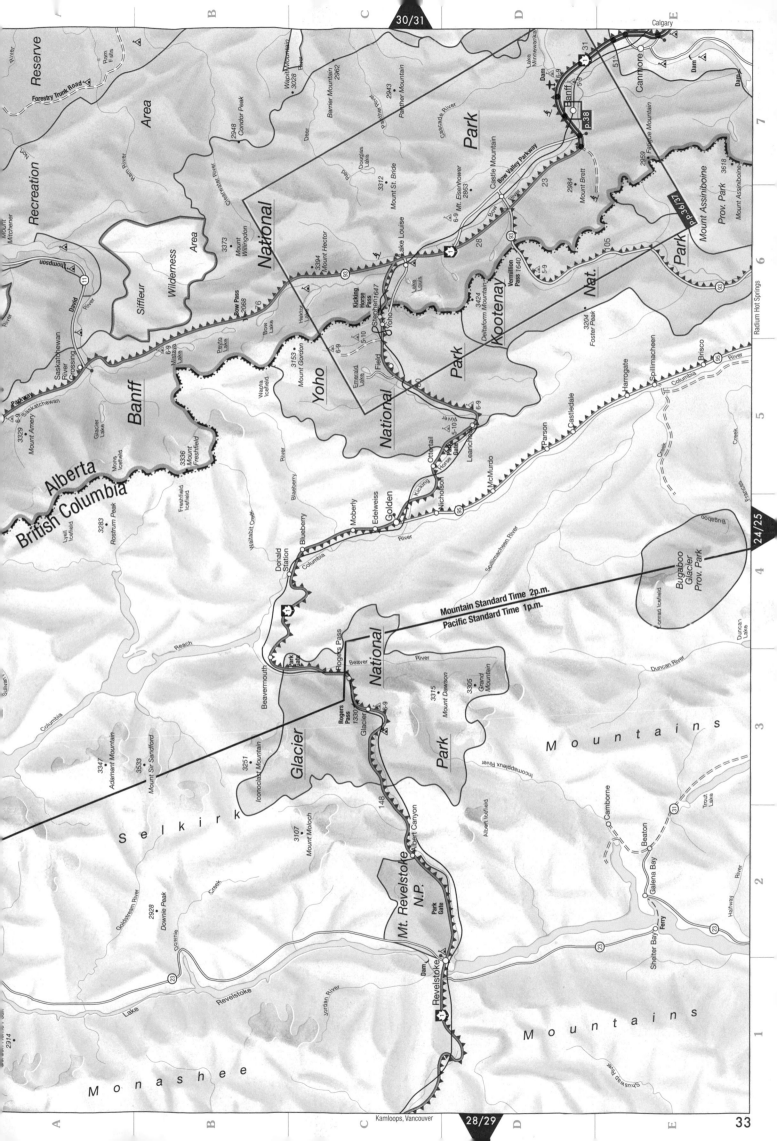

A B 32/33 C D E

7

Roche
Jaques
2316

Miette Range

Edmonton

16
16

Canadian National

Jasper Lake

Talbot
Lake

Capitol Ck

Makwa

Makwa Ridge

Creek

Makwa

Creek

Emir Creek

Merlin Ck

Delphinium

Creek

Rocky

River

River

2654

Ranges

Cinquefoil Ck

Jaques

Emir
Mountain

Range

Mount
Merlin

Merlin Ridge

6

Edna
Lake

Cinquefoil
Mountain

Roche
Jaques

Creek

Jaques

Nashan

Colin Ridge

Merlin
Pass

Range

2820 Sirdar
Mountain

Summit
Lakes

Medicine
Lake

Vine Ck

Creek

2545

2697

Colin

Roche
Bonhomme
2460

2441
Mount
Dromore

Grisette
Mountain

Dromore

River

Maligne

Excelsior
Creek

2628

Park

5

Corral Ck

Moberly
Flats

1676
Morro

Jasper

1169

Maligne
Canyon

Lake
Edith

Lake
Annette

Signal
Mountain
2312

Mount
Tekarra
2694

Excelsior
Mountain

Underground
Stream

The
Watchtower

Curator
Mountain

Range

Cobblestone Ck

River

16

16

The Palisade

Ranges

Pyramid
Lake

Beaver
Lake

Park

Amber
Mountain

Centre
Mountain

4

Chetamon
Lake

Snaring

Cross

Mount
Zengel

Mount
Kinross 2763

Pyramid
Mountain

National

Patricia
Lake

Creek

Cabin
Lake

Tekarra Ck

Wabasso
Lakes

Prairie de
la Vache
1214

Amber

32/33

Buttress
Mountain

Jasper

Mount
Kerr

Cairngorm

Cottonwood

Hibernia
Lake

Jasper

Athabasca

93

Icefields

93

Parkway

3

Victoria

Mount
McKean

Elysium
Pass

Emigrants
Mountain

Mount
Henry

Saturday
Night
Lake

Caledonia
Lake

P.38

5-10

9-5

River

93A

6-9

2

Elysium
Mountain

Minaga

Dorothy
Lake

Creek

Muhigan
Creek

1245

2464
The Wistlers

Whistlers Creek

Indian Ridge

2608

Marmot
Mountain

Marmot
Pass

Portal Creek

The Portal

Lectern
Peak

Aquila
Mountain

Franchère
Peak

Astoria

Cavell
Lake

Angel
Glacier

Mount
Edith 2368

Creek

Yellowhead
Pass

Robson

16

Rockingham

Mountain Time Zone 2p.m.

Pacific Time Zone 1p.m.

Creek

Roche
Noire

Rostrum
Hill

Meadow

Arris
Mountain

Wistler
Pass

Fortalice
Mountain

Mount
Estella

Manx
Peak

Vertex
Peak

Circus Valley

Peveril
Peak

2680

Maccarib
Pass

Chak
Peak

Astoria
Pass

1

Mount

16

Mount
Fitzwilliam
1240

Bucephalus
Peak

Holloway
Rock

Frontier
Peak

British Columbia

Alberta

Kataka
Mountain

Clairvaux

Basilica
Mountain

Curia
Mountain

Baslica

Indian
Pass

Muhigan
Peak

Crescent Ck

Trident
Terminal

Range

Tonquin

Valley

2750
Mount
Clitheroe

Amethyst
Lakes

Mount
Maccarib
2987

Oldhorn
Mountain

Astoria

Beryl

16

Prov.
Park

2350

Clairvaux
Glacier

Meadow
Glacier

Caniche
Peak

Tonquin

The

Moat
Creek

Tonquin Vista
Pass

Tonquin
Hill 2397

Moat
Lake

Tonquin
Pass

The
Ramparts

Moat
Pass

Moat
Ck

Dungeon
Peak

Paragon Peak

Drawbridge
Peak

Redoubt
Peak

Outpost
Lake 2758

Surprise Point

Outpost Peak

Thunderbolt Peak

Campus

Angle Peak

Campus

Eremite
Glacier 2682

Mount
Erebus

Eremite
Mountain

Fraser
Glacier

Alcove
Glacier

Verdant

Angle
Peak

Mount
Glacier

A B 32/33 C D E

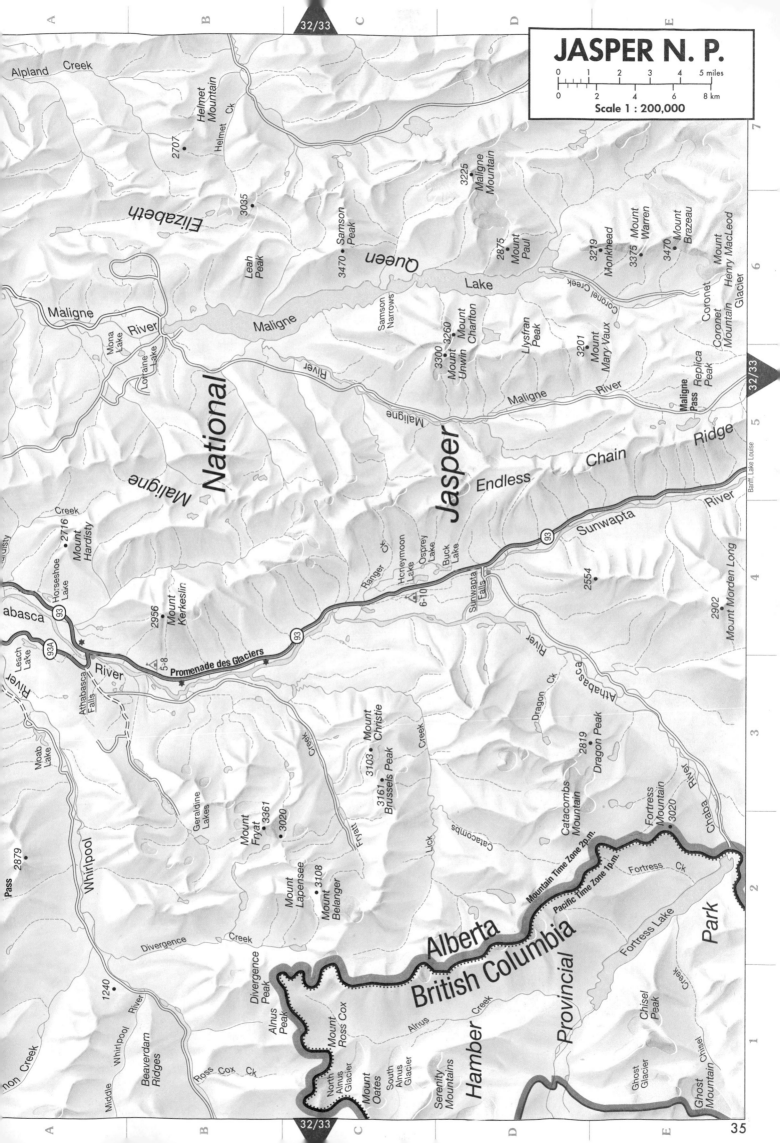

JASPER N. P.

0 1 2 3 4 5 miles
0 2 4 6 8 km
Scale 1 : 200,000

A B C D E

Alpland Creek

Helmet Mountain
Helmet Ck
• 2707

Elizabeth

• 3035

Leah Peak

• 3470 Samson Peak

Queen

Maligne Mountain • 3225

Mount Warren • 1265
Mount Brazeau • 3470

Monkhead • 3219
• 3375

Mount Henry MacLeod

Maligne Lake

Mona Lake
Maligne River
Lorraine Lake

Maligne River

Samson Narrows

Mount Charlton
Mount Unwin • 3260
• 3300

Llysfran Peak • 2875 Mount Paul

Mount Mary Vaux • 3201

Coronet Mount

Maligne River

Coronet Glacier
Coronet Mountain

Replica Peak
Maligne Pass

32/33

National

Maligne

Jasper

Endless Chain Ridge

Mount Hardisty • 2716
Horseshoe Lake
Creek

Ranger Ck
Honeymoon Lake
Osprey Lake
Buck Lake

Sunwapta

Sunwapta River

93

2554 •

Mount Morden Long

abasca
93
Mount Kerkeslin • 2956

6-10

Sunwapta Falls

2902 •

93
93A
Leach Lake
River

△ 5-8
Promenade des Glaciers

Athabasca Falls
River

Athabasca River

Dragon Ck

Dragon Peak • 2819

Moab Lake

Mount Christie
• 3103

Brussels Peak
3161 •

Creek

Fryatt

Lick Creek

Catacombs

Catacombs Mountain

Fortress Mountain • 3020

Chaba River

Geraldine Lakes

Mount Fryat • 3361
• 3020

Whirlpool

Mount Lapensee
Mount Belanger • 3108

Mountain Time Zone 2 p.m.
Pacific Time Zone 1 p.m.

Fortress Lake
Fortress Ck

Park

• 2879
Pass

Divergence Creek

Divergence Peak

Alberta

British Columbia

Provincial

• 1240
River
Whirlpool

Beaverdam Ridges

Middle
non Creek

Ross Cox Ck

Alnus Peak
Mount Ross Cox

North Alnus Glacier
Mount Oates
South Alnus Glacier

Serenity Mountains

Alnus Creek

Hamber

Chisel Peak

Ghost Glacier

Ghost Mountain Chisel Creek

Banff, Lake Louise

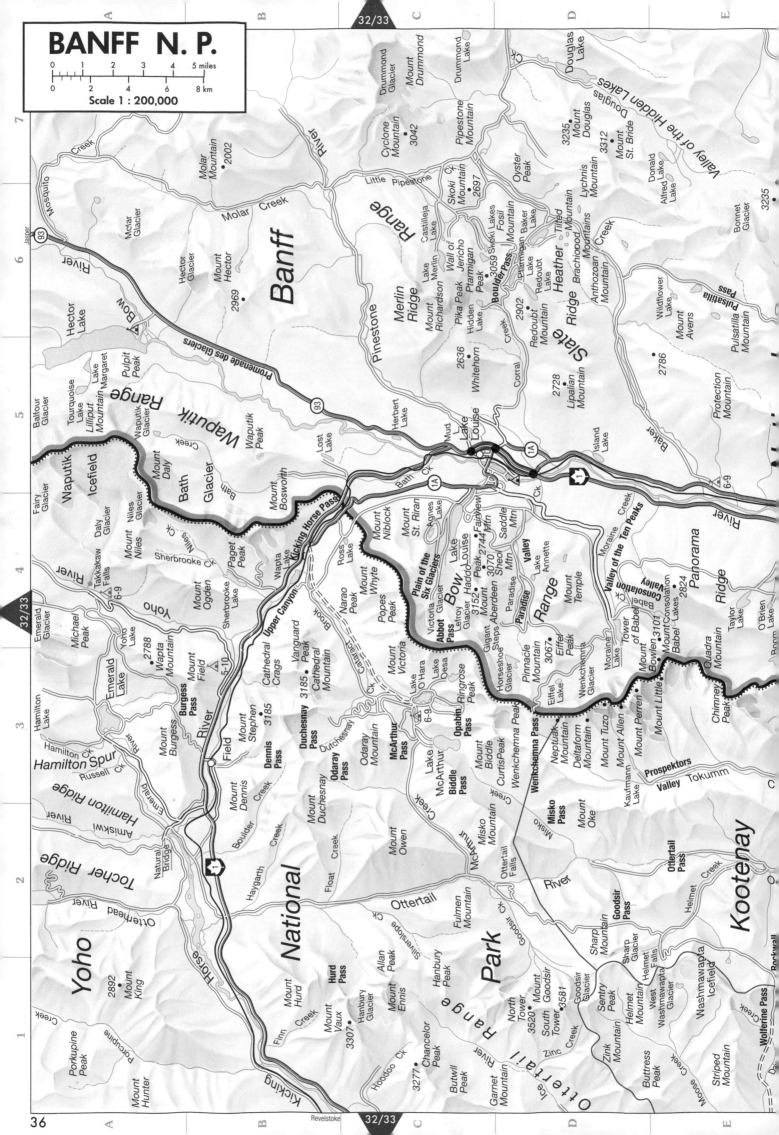

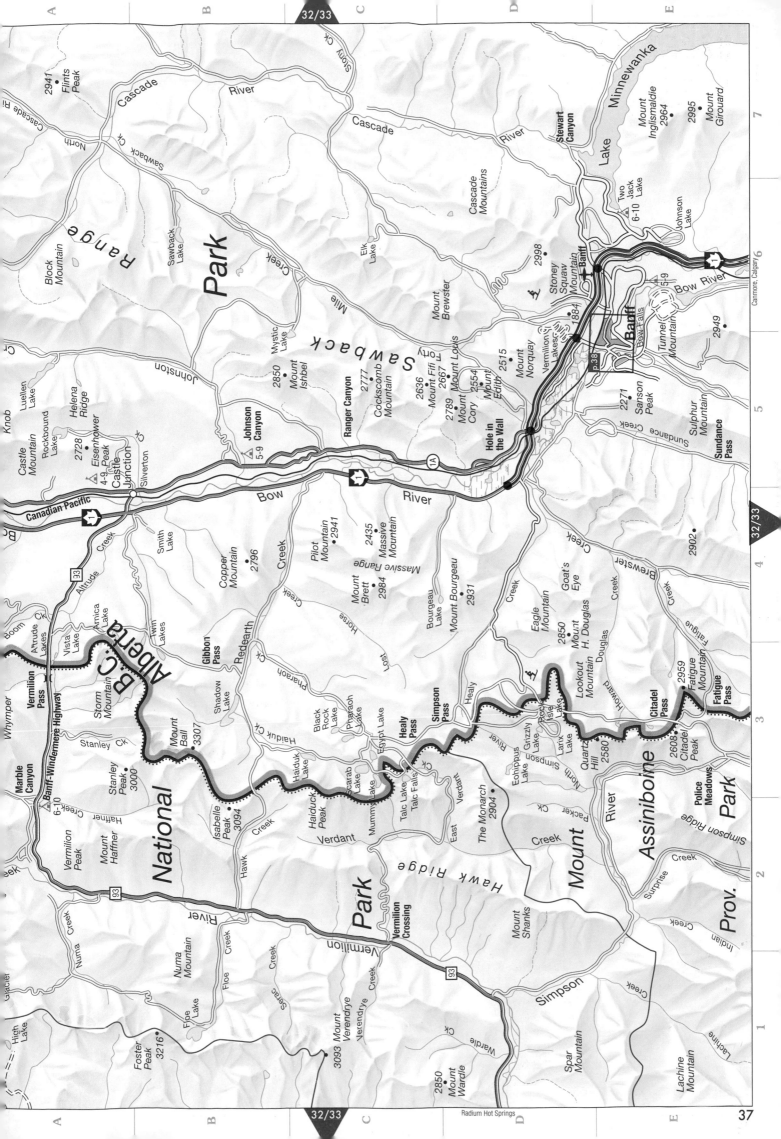

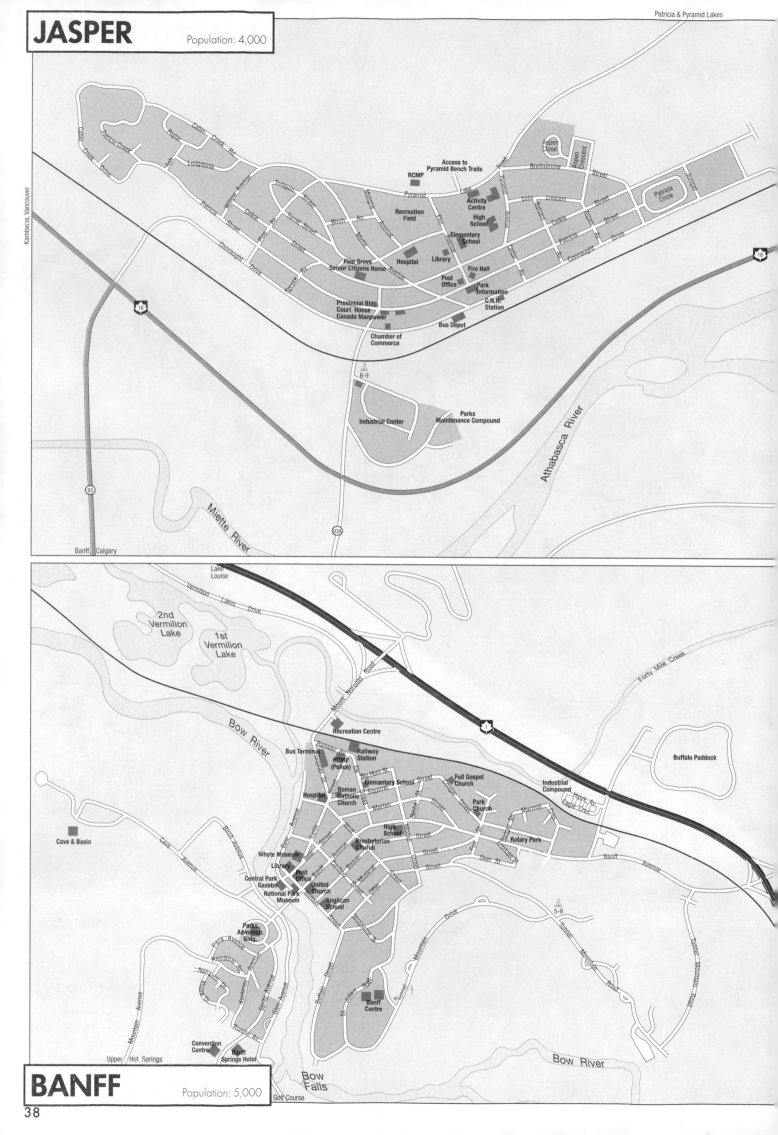

JASPER

Population: 4,000

Kamloops, Vancouver

Patricia Creek

Cabin Creek Dr.

Poplar

Cabin Creek Rd.

Ash

Patricia Drive

Willow Avenue

Lodgepole

Connaught Drive

Tonquin Street

Geikie

Pine Street

Turret Street

Birch Av.

Miette

Maligne Avenue

RCMP

Access to
Pyramid Bench Trails

Pyramid Lake Road

Recreation
Field

Activity
Centre

High
School

Pyramid Avenue

Elementary
School

Pine Grove
Senior Citizens Home

Hospital

Library

Fire Hall

Colin Crescent

Geikie

Cedar Av.

Patricia

Aspen Close

Aspen Crescent

Bonhomme Street

Patricia Circle

Connaught Drive

16

Provincial Bldg.
Court House
Canada Manpower

Post
Office

Park
Information

C.N.R.
Station

16

Bus Depot

Chamber of
Commerce

6-9

Industrial Center

Parks
Maintenance Compound

Athabasca River

93

93A

Miette River

Banff, Calgary

BANFF

Population: 5,000

Lake
Louise

Vermilion Lakes Drive

2nd
Vermilion
Lake

1st
Vermilion
Lake

Bow River

Mount Norquay Road

1

Forty Mile Creek

Buffalo Paddock

Recreation Centre

Bus Terminal

Railway Av.

Railway
Station

RCMP
(Police)

Full Gospel
Church

Caribou Street

Elementary School

Big Horn St.

Squirrel

Park Church

Industrial
Compound

Cave & Basin

Hospital

Roman
Catholic
Church

Marten

Wolf Street

High
School

Rabbit St.

Bear Street

Rotary Park

Hawk Av.

Eagle Cres.

Marmot Cres.

Cave Avenue

Birch Avenue

Whyte Museum

Library

Central Park
Gazebo

Post
Office

National Park
Museum

United
Church

Presbyterian
Church

Beaver Street

Muskrat Street

Otter Street

Anglican
School

Buffalo Street

Deer St.

Antelope St.

Banff Avenue

5-9

Parks
Administr.
Bldg.

Rainbow Av.

Park Avenue

Mountain Avenue

Spray Avenue

Glen Avenue

St. Julien Road

Buffalo Street

Banff
Centre

Tunnel Mountain Drive

Tunnel Mountain Road

Convention
Centre

Banff
Springs Hotel

Upper Hot Springs

Bow
Falls

Golf Course

Bow River

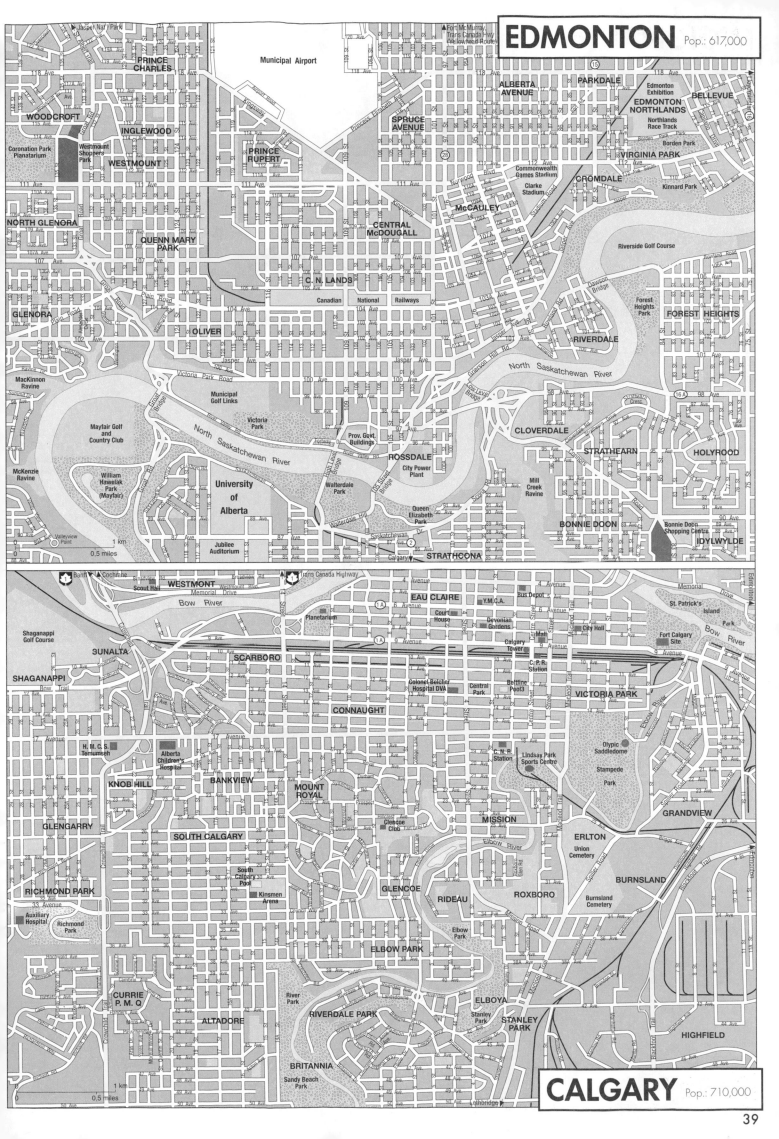

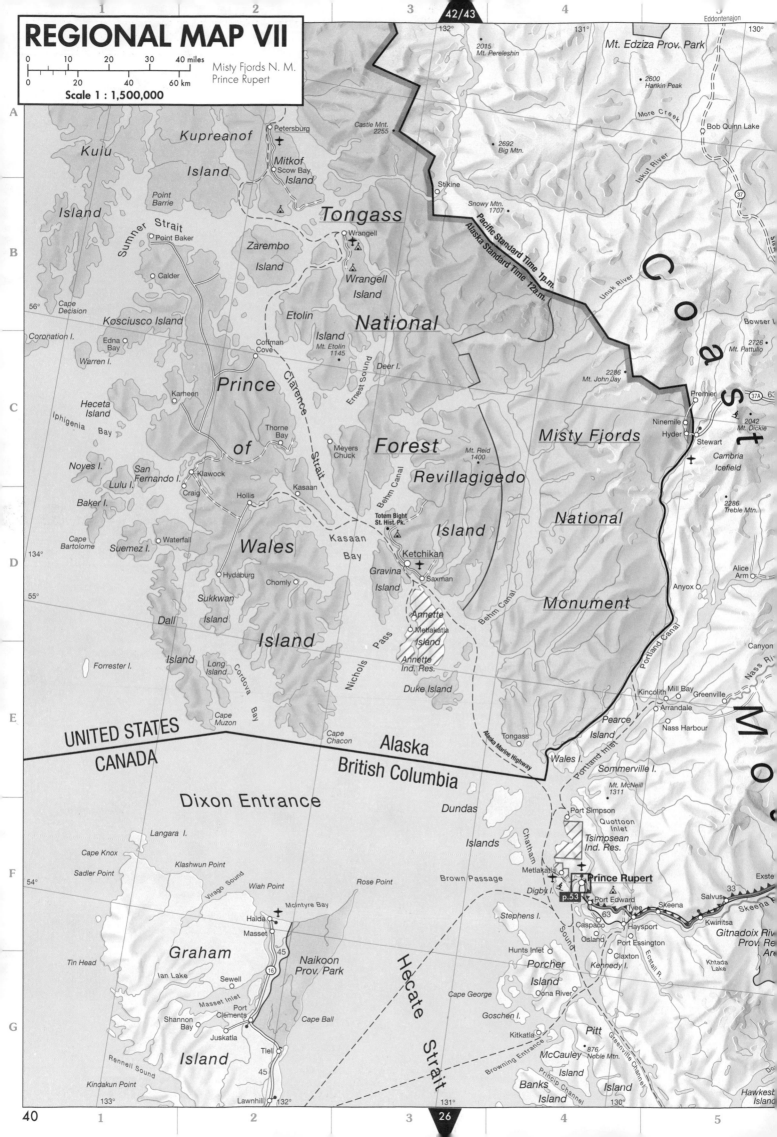

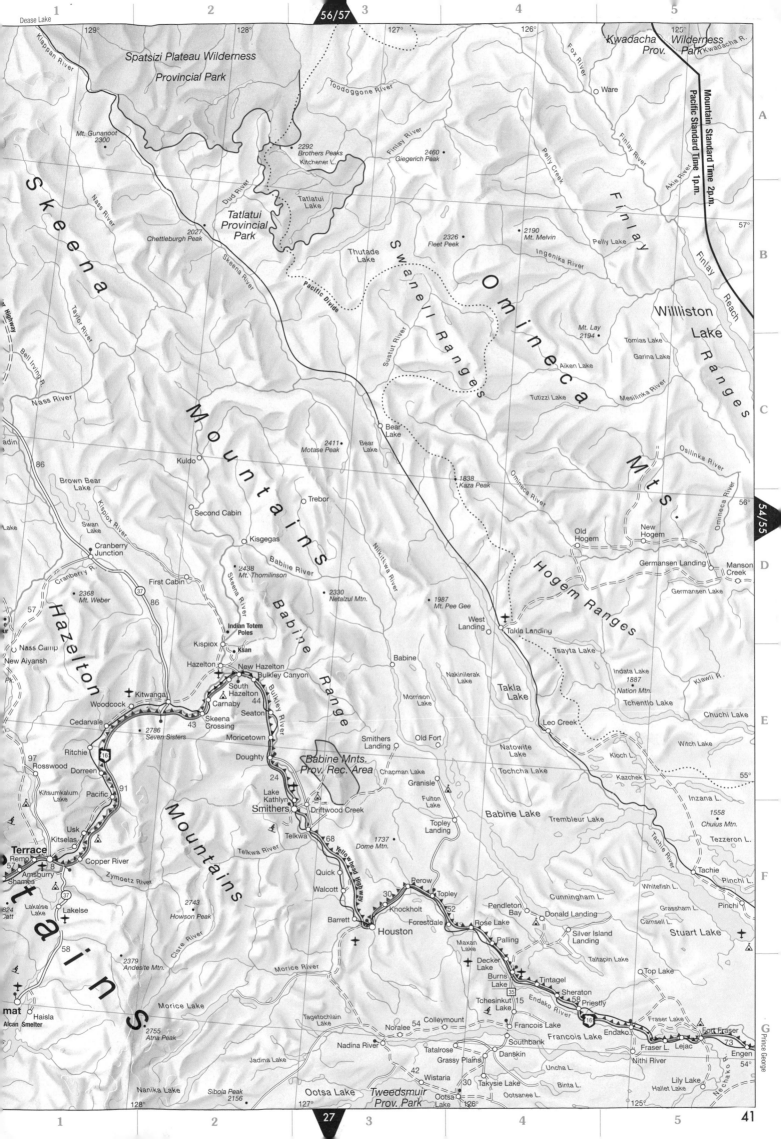

Dease Lake

Spatsizi Plateau Wilderness
Provincial Park

Kwadacha
Wilderness Prov. Park

Kwadacha R.
Akie River

Mountain Standard Time 2p.m.
Pacific Standard Time 1p.m.

Klappan River
129°
128°
127°
126°
125°

Mt. Gunanoot
2300

Toodoggone River

Fox River

Finlay River

Ware

A

Nass River

Taylor River

2292 •
Brothers Peaks
Kitchener L.

Finlay River

2460 •
Giegerich Peak

Pelly Creek

Finlay

57°

Dud River

Tatlatui
Lake

Thutade
Lake

2326 •
Fleet Peak

2190 •
Mt. Melvin

Pelly Lake

Ingenika River

Williston

B

Skeena

Nass River

2027 •
Chettleburgh Peak

Tatlatui
Provincial
Park

Skeena River

Pacific Divide

Swanell Ranges

Sustut River

Omineca

Mt. Lay
2194 •

Tomias Lake

Garina Lake

Mesilinka River

Lake Ranges

C

Bell Irving R.
Highway

Nass River

Aiken Lake

Tutizzi Lake

86

Brown Bear
Lake

Kisplox River

Swan
Lake

Kuldo

Second Cabin

Trebor

2411 •
Motase Peak

Bear
Lake

Bear
Lake

Nikitkwa River

Omineca River

1838 •
Kaza Peak

Mts.

Osilinka River

56°

57

Cranberry
Junction

Cranberry R.

Kisgegas

Babine River

2438 •
Mt. Thomlinson

Skeena River

2330 •
Netalzul Mtn.

1987 •
Mt. Pee Gee

Old
Hogem

New
Hogem

Germansen Landing

Manson
Creek

Hogem Ranges

D

37
86

First Cabin

2368 •
Mt. Weber

Germansen Lake

Hazelton

Nass Camp

New Aiyansh
Pk.

Indian Totem
Poles

Kisplox

Ksan

Hazelton

New Hazelton
Bulkley Canyon

Babine

West
Landing

Talka Landing

Tsayta Lake

Indata Lake
1887 •
Nation Mtn.

Klawli R.

Mountains

Kitwanga

South
Hazelton

Carnaby

44

Bulkley River

Nakinilerak
Lake

Takla
Lake

Tchentlo Lake

Chuchi Lake

Woodcock

Seaton

43

Skeena
Crossing

Morricetown

Morrison
Lake

Old Fort

Leo Creek

E

Cedarvale

2786 •
Seven Sisters

Doughty

Smithers
Landing

Natowite
Lake

Witch Lake

55°

97

Ritchie

16

24

Babine Mnts.
Prov. Rec. Area

Chapman Lake

Tochcha Lake

Kazchek

Kloch L.

Rosswood

Dorreen

Lake
Kathlyn

Granisle

Fulton
Lake

Kloch L.

Inzana L.

Kitsumkalum
Lake

Pacific

91

Smithers

Driftwood Creek

1558 •
Chuius Mtn.

Usk

Telkwa

68

Babine Lake

Trembleur Lake

Tezzeron L.

Kitselas

Terrace

1737 •
Dome Mtn.

Topley
Landing

Tachie River

Tachie

Remo

Amsbury
Shames

8

Copper River

Quick

Perow

Cunningham L.

Whitefish L.

Pinchi L.

37

Lakalse
Lake

Lakelse

2743 •
Howson Peak

Walcott

30

Topley

Pendleton
Bay

Donald Landing

Grassham L.

Pinchi

824
Catt

58

2379 •
Andesite Mtn.

Clore River

Barrett

Knockholt

52

Forestdale

Rose Lake

Silver Island
Landing

Camsel L.

Stuart Lake

mat

Haisla
Alcan Smelter

Morice Lake

Morice River

Houston

Maxan
Lake

Palling

Decker
Lake

Taltapin Lake

Top Lake

2755 •
Atna Peak

Tagetochlain
Lake

Burns
Lake

35

Tintagel

Sheraton

58

Priestly

2156
Sibola Peak

Noralee

Colleymount

54

Tchesinkut
Lake

15

Endako River

16

Fraser Lake

Fort Fraser

Nanika Lake

Jadina Lake

Nadina River

Tatalrose

Grassy Plains

Danskin

Southbank

42

Wistaria

Francois Lake

Endako

Fraser L.

Lejac

73

Engen

54°

30

Takysie
Lake

Binta L.

Nithi River

Lily Lake

Ootsa Lake

Tweedsmuir
Prov. Park

Ootsa
Lake

Uncha L.

Ootsanee L.

Hallet Lake

128°
127°
126°
125°

1
2
3
4
5

F

G

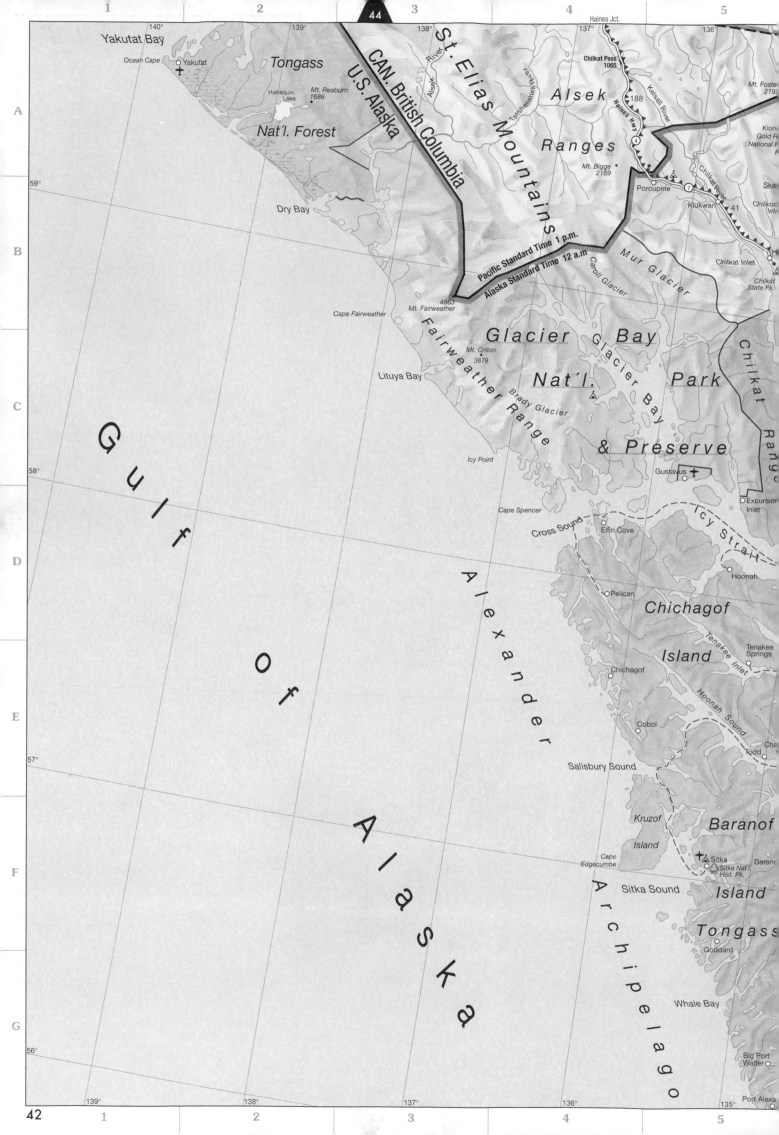

Yakutat Bay

Ocean Cape   ⊕ *Yakutat*

Tongass

140°

139°

138°

137°

136°

Haines Jct.

Chilkat Pass
1065

Mt. Foste
2192

St. Elias Mountains

Alsek

Harlequin Lake

Mt. Reaburn
1686

Alsek River

Tatshenshini River

Ranges

188

Kelsall River

Haines Hwy

Klon
Gold R
National I

Nat'l. Forest

Mt. Bigge
2159

CAN. British Columbia
U.S. Alaska

7

Chilkat River

Ska

59°

Porcupine

Klukwan   41

Chilkoo
Inlet

Dry Bay

A

Chilkat Inlet

Pacific Standard Time 1 p.m.
Alaska Standard Time 12 a.m.

Mur Glacier

Chilkat
State Pk.

H

B

Cape Fairweather

4863
Mt. Fairweather

Caroll Glacier

Glacier   Bay

Mt. Crillon
3879

Glacier Bay

Nat'l.   Park

Chilkat Range

Lituya Bay

Fairweather Range

Brady Glacier

△

& Preserve

58°

Icy Point

C

Gustavus   ⊕
○

○ Excursion
Inlet

G

Cape Spencer

Cross Sound

Icy Strait

u

○ Elfin Cove

○ Hoonah

l

○ Pelican

D

f

Chichagof

o

Tenakee Inlet

○ Tenakee
Springs

f

Island

○ Chichagof

Hoonah Sound

A

l

e

x

a

n

d

e

r

57°

○ Cobol

Cha

Todd
○

E

Salisbury Sound

A

Kruzof

Baranof

l

Island

a

⊕ △ *Sitka*

Baranc

Cape
Edgecumbe

s

Sitka Nat'l.
Hist. Pk.

k

Sitka Sound

Island

a

F

Tongass

A

r

c

h

Goddard ○

i

p

e

Whale Bay

l

a

g

o

56°

Big Port
Walter ○

Port Alexa

139°

138°

137°

136°

135°

G

Gulf

of

Alaska

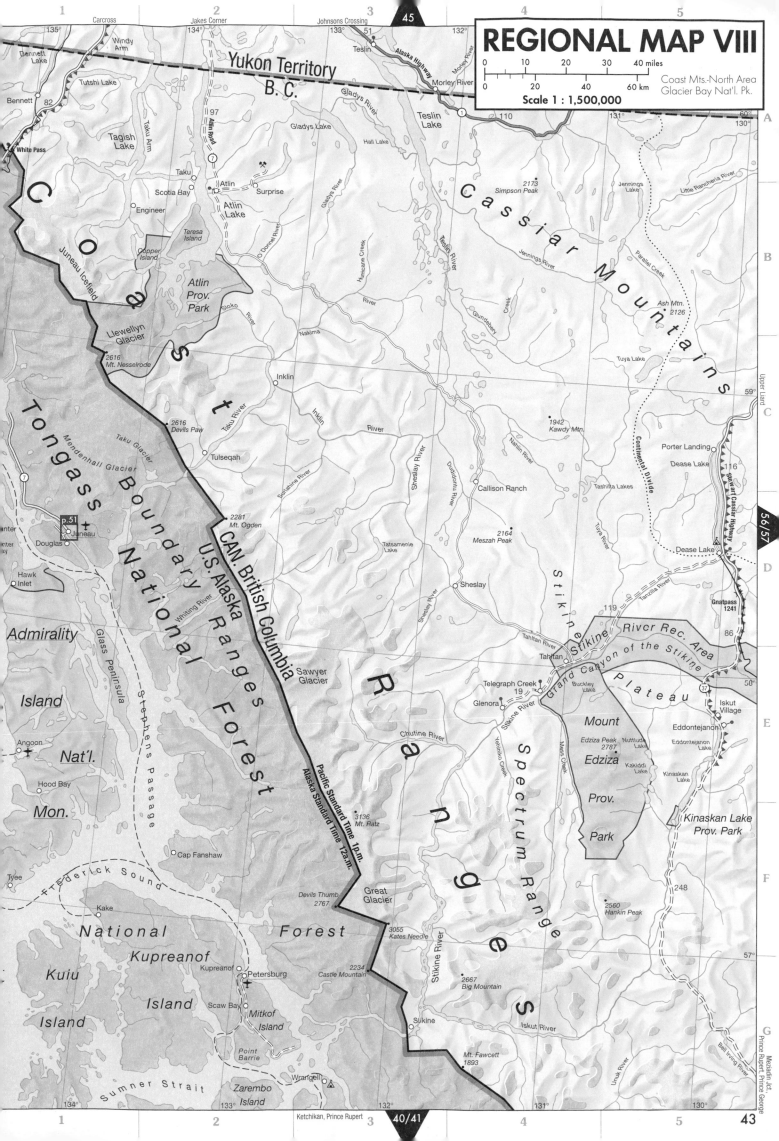

REGIONAL MAP VIII

0 10 20 30 40 miles
0   20   40   60 km
Scale 1 : 1,500,000

Coast Mts.-North Area
Glacier Bay Nat'l. Pk.

Carcross   **Jakes Corner**   **Johnsons Crossing**

135°   134°   133°   51   132°   131°   130°

Windy Arm

Bennett Lake

Tutshi Lake

Bennett 82

White Pass

Tagish Lake

Taku Arm

Taku

Scotia Bay

Engineer

Atlin

Surprise

Atlin Lake

Copper Island

Teresa Island

Yukon Territory
B.C.

Gladys River

97

Atlin Road

7

Atlin Prov. Park

Sloko River

Nakima

Gladys River

Gladys Lake

Hall Lake

River

Hurricane Creek

Teslin

Morley River

Alaska Highway

Morley River

Teslin Lake

1

110

Simpson Peak
2173

Jennings River

Jennings Lake

Little Rancheria River

Cassiar Mountains

Glundeberg Creek

Creek

Ash Mtn.
2126

Tuya Lake

Parallel Creek

60°

A

B

C

59°

Coast

Juneau Icefield

Llewellyn Glacier

2616
Mt. Nesselrode

2616
Devils Paw

Taku Glacier

Mendenhall Glacier

Inklin

Inklin

River

Taku River

Tulsequah

Sortlahine River

Sheslay River

Duddiontu River

Nahlin River

Kawdy Mtn.
1942

Callison Ranch

Tashilita Lakes

Upper Liard

Porter Landing

Dease Lake

116

Stewart Cassiar Highway

Continental Divide

Tongass

7

p.51
Juneau

Douglas

Hawk Inlet

Admiralty

Glass Peninsula

Whiting River

Stephens Passage

Boundary

2281
Mt. Ogden

U.S. Alaska Ranges

CAN. British Columbia

Tatsamenie Lake

Meszah Peak
2164

Sheslay

2164

Dease Lake

119

86

Gnatpass
1241

Tanzilla River

Tahltan River

Stikine

River Rec. Area

Grand Canyon of the Stikine

50°

D

E

Island

Angoon

Nat'l.

Hood Bay

Mon.

National

Sawyer Glacier

Ranges

Chutine River

3136
Mt. Ratz

Telegraph Creek
19

Glenora

Stikine River

Yehniko Creek

Buckley Lake

Plateau

Tahltan

Stikine

Mount

Edziza Peak
2787

Nuttlude Lake

Kakiddi Lake

Edziza

Prov.

Park

Mess Creek

Eddontejanon

Eddontejanon Lake

Kinaskan Lake

37

Iskut Village

Kinaskan Lake Prov. Park

56/57

F

57°

G

Pacific Standard Time 1p.m.
Alaska Standard Time 12a.m.

Forest

National Forest

Kupreanof

Kupreanof

Petersburg

Scaw Bay

Mitkof Island

Devils Thumb
2767

Great Glacier

3055
Kates Needle

2234
Castle Mountain

Stikine River

Spectrum Range

2667
Big Mountain

2560
Hankin Peak

248

s

Kuiu Island

Tyee

Kake

Cap Fanshaw

Frederick Sound

Point Barrie

Zarembo Island

Wrangell

Sumner Strait

134°   133°   132°   131°   130°

Mt. Fawcett
1893

Iskut River

Unuk River

Stikine

Bell Irving River

Meziadin Jct., Prince Rupert, Prince George

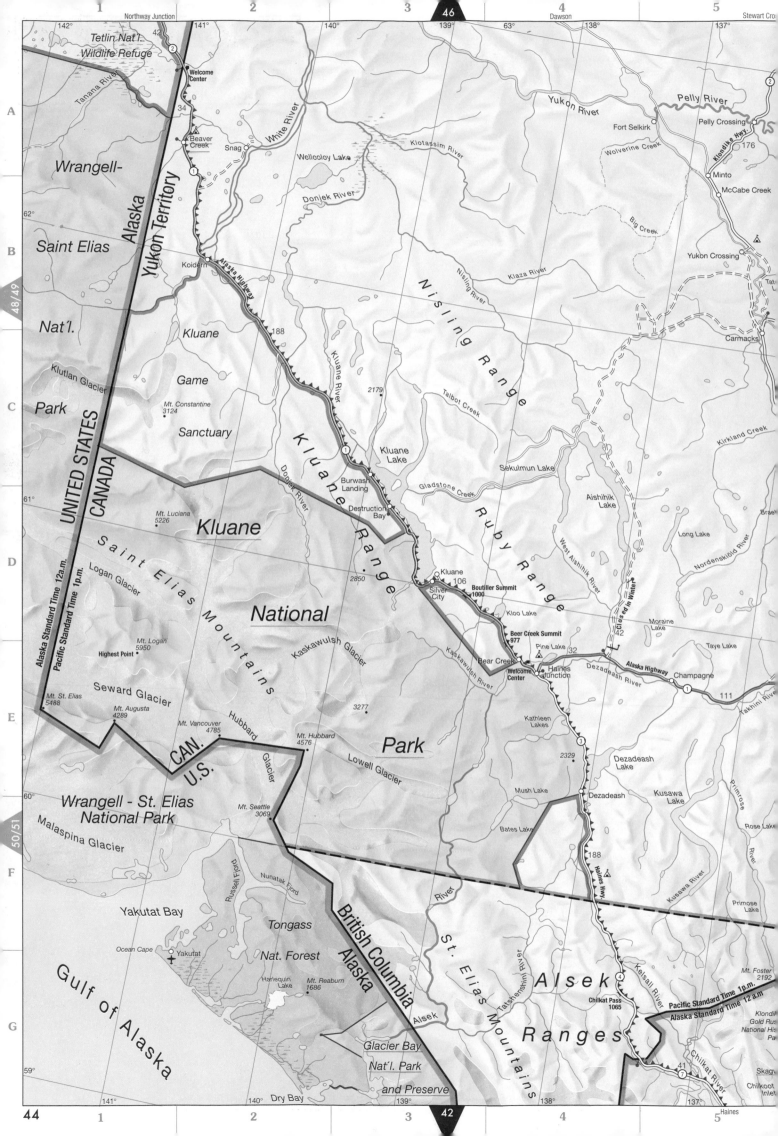

142°   141°   42   140°   139°   63°   138°   137°

Tetlin Nat'l.
Wildlife Refuge

Welcome
Center

34

Yukon River   Pelly River

A

Beaver
Creek

Snag   White River   Wellocloy Lake   Klotassim River   Fort Selkirk   Pelly Crossing

Klindike Hwy.   176

Wrangell-

Tanana River

62°

Minto

Wolverine Creek

McCabe Creek

B

Saint Elias

Koidern   Alaska Highway   Kluane   188   Kluane River   Nisling River   Klaza River   Big Creek   Yukon Crossing

Nat'l.

Kluane

Carmacks

Klutlan Glacier

C

Park

Mt. Constantine
3124   Game   2179   Kluane
Lake   Talbot Creek   Sekulmun Lake   Kirkland Creek

Sanctuary   Burwash
Landing   Gladstone Creek   Aishihik
Lake   Long Lake   Nordenskiöld River   Brae

61°

Mt. Luciana
5226   Destruction
Bay   West Aishihik River

D

Kluane   Kluane   106   Boutiller Summit
1000   Closed in Winter   42   Moraine
Lake   Taye Lake

Saint Elias Mountains   Silver City   Kloo Lake

Logan Glacier   2850

2850   Beer Creek Summit
977   Pine Lake   32

National   Kaskawulsh Glacier   Bear Creek   Pine Lake   Alaska Highway   Champagne

Mt. Logan
5950   Kaskawulsh River   Welcome
Center   Haines
Junction   Dezadeash River   1   111

Highest Point

Seward Glacier   Mt. Vancouver
4785   Hubbard   3277   Kathleen
Lakes   Kakhini River

E

Mt. St. Elias
5488   Mt. Augusta
4289   Mt. Hubbard
4576   Park   2329   Dezadeash
Lake   Taye Lake

CAN.   Glacier   Lowell Glacier   3

U.S.   Mush Lake   Kusawa
Lake

60°

Wrangell - St. Elias
National Park   Mt. Seattle
3069   Dezadeash

Malaspina Glacier   Bates Lake   188   Kusawa River   Primrose
Lake

F

Russell Fjord   Haines Hwy.   Rose Lake

Nunatak Fjord   River

Yakutat Bay   Tongass   St. Elias Mountains   Alsek

Ocean Cape   Yakutat   Nat. Forest   Tatshenshini River

Gulf of Alaska   Harlequin
Lake   Mt. Reaburn
1686   British Columbia   Alsek   Ranges   Mt. Foster
2192

G   Chilkat Pass
1065   Pacific Standard Time 1 p.m.   Kelsall River   Klondi
Gold Rus
National His
Pa

Alaska Standard Time 12 a.m.

59°   141°   140°   139°   138°   Chilkat River   Skagw

Alaska Standard Time 12 a.m.
Pacific Standard Time 1 p.m.

Dry Bay   Glacier Bay
Nat'l. Park
and Preserve   41   7   Chilkoot
Inlet

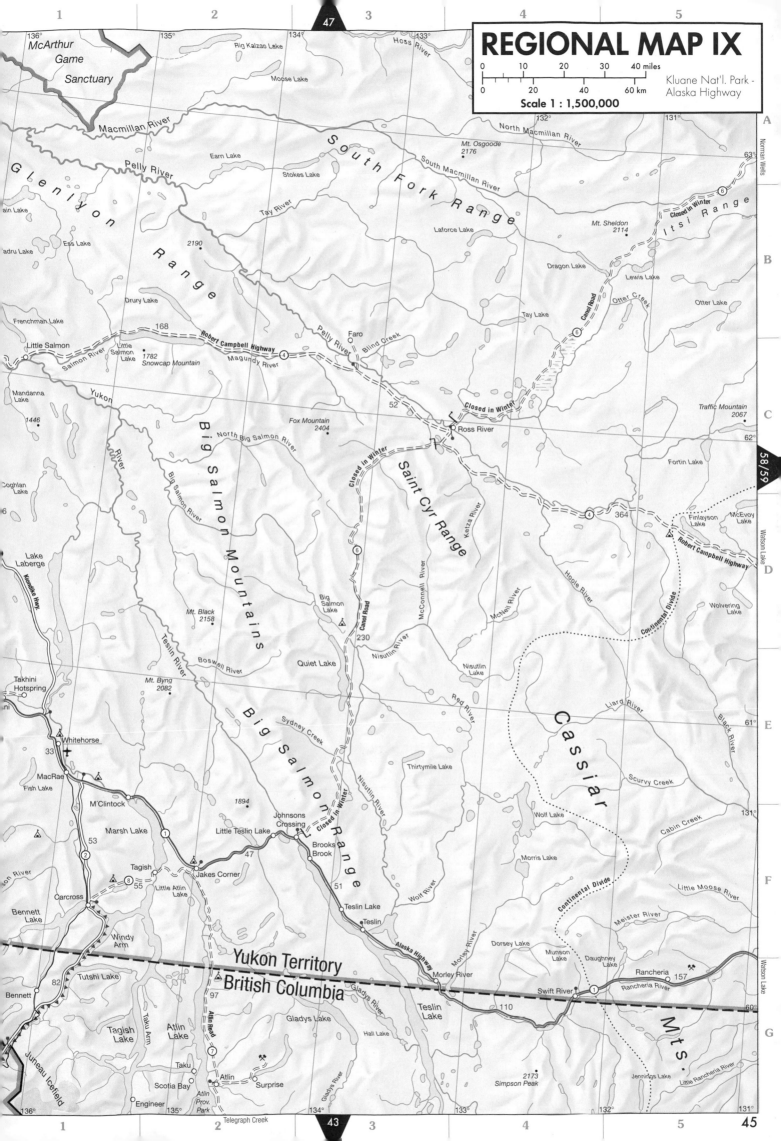

REGIONAL MAP IX

0   10   20   30   40 miles
0   20   40   60 km

Scale 1 : 1,500,000

Kluane Nat'l. Park - Alaska Highway

McArthur Game Sanctuary

Macmillan River

Glenlyon Range

Pelly River

South Fork Range

Big Kalzao Lake

Moose Lake

Hoss River

North Macmillan River

Mt. Osgoode 2176

South Macmillan River

Mt. Sheldon 2114

Itsi Range

Closed in Winter

Norman Wells

Earn Lake

Stokes Lake

Tay River

Laforce Lake

Dragon Lake

Canol Road

Lewis Lake

Otter Creek

Otter Lake

Drury Lake

Frenchman Lake

Ess Lake

Pelly River

Faro

Blind Creek

Tay Lake

168

Robert Campbell Highway

Little Salmon

Little Salmon Lake

Salmon River

1782 Snowcap Mountain

Magundy River

4

Pelly River

52

Closed in Winter

Ross River

Traffic Mountain 2067

Mandanna Lake

1446

Yukon

North Big Salmon River

Fox Mountain 2404

Closed in Winter

Saint Cyr Range

Ketza River

4   364

Fortin Lake

Finlayson Lake

McEvoy Lake

Coghlan Lake

River

Big Salmon River

Big Salmon Mountains

Mt. Black 2158

6

Big Salmon Lake

Canol Road

230

McConnell River

Nisutlin River

McNeil River

Hoole River

Robert Campbell Highway

Continental Divide

Wolverine Lake

Lake Laberge

Teslin River

Boswell River

Quiet Lake

Nisutlin Lake

Cassiar

Mt. Byng 2082

Red River

Liard River

Black River

Takhini Hotspring

Sydney Creek

Thirtymile Lake

Scurvy Creek

Whitehorse

33

MacRae

Fish Lake

M'Clintock

1894

Johnsons Crossing

Nisutlin River

Closed in Winter

Wolf Lake

Cabin Creek

Marsh Lake

1

Little Teslin Lake

Brooks Brook

Morris Lake

Little Moose River

53

2

Tagish

Little Atlin Lake

47

51

Wolf River

Continental Divide

Meister River

Carcross

8   55

Jakes Corner

Teslin Lake

Teslin

Dorsey Lake

Munson Lake

Daughney Lake

Rancheria

157

Bennett Lake

Windy Arm

Alaska Highway

Morley River

Swift River

1

Rancheria River

Yukon Territory

British Columbia

Tutshi Lake

82

97

Morley River

Gladys River

Teslin Lake

110

Watson Lake

60°

Bennett

Tagish Lake

Atlin Lake

Gladys Lake

Hall Lake

Mts.

Juneau Icefield

Taku Arm

Atlin Road

7

Taku

Scotia Bay

Atlin

Surprise

Gladys River

2173 Simpson Peak

Jennings Lake

Little Rancheria River

Engineer

Atlin Prov. Park

136°   135°   Telegraph Creek   134°   133°   132°   131°

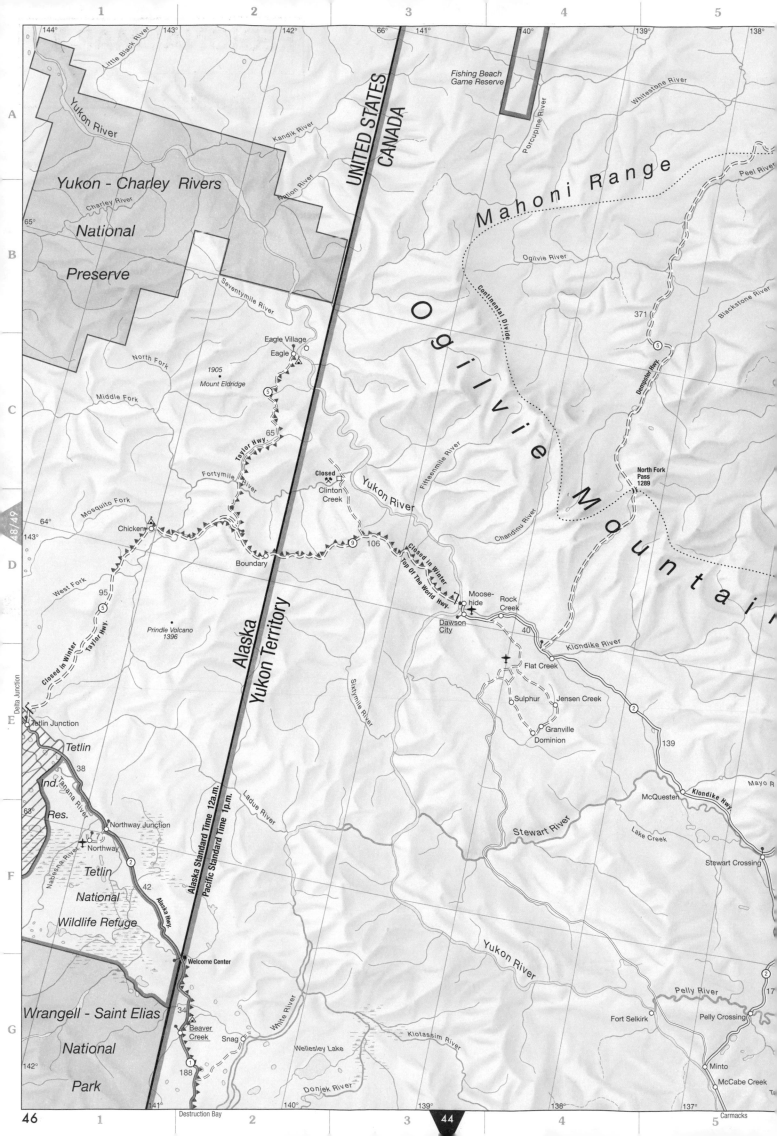

144°   143°   142°   66°   141°   140°   139°   138°

A

Little Black River

Yukon River

UNITED STATES

CANADA

Fishing Beach
Game Reserve

Whitestone River

Porcupine River

Yukon - Charley Rivers

Kandik River

Nation River

Charley River

M a h o n i   R a n g e

Peel River

65°

National

Ogilvie River

B

Preserve

Seventymile River

Continental Divide

Blackstone River

371

O
g
i
l
v
i
e

North Fork

Eagle Village
Eagle

Fifteenmile River

5

Dempster Hwy.

C

Middle Fork

1905
Mount Eldridge

5

65

Taylor Hwy.

M
o
u
n
t
a
i
n

North Fork
Pass
1289

Fortymile River

Closed
Clinton
Creek

Yukon River

Chandinu River

64°
143°

Mosquito Fork

Chicken

9   106

D

Boundary

Closed in Winter

Top Of The World Hwy.

Moose-
hide

Rock
Creek

West Fork

95

5

Prindle Volcano
1396

Dawson
City

40

Klondike River

E

Closed in Winter

Taylor Hwy.

Alaska

Yukon Territory

Flat Creek

2

Delta Junction

Sulphur   Jensen Creek

Tetlin Junction

Granville
Dominion

139

Tetlin

Siskymile River

Mayo R.

38

Tanana River

McQuesten

Klondike Hwy.

Ind.

63°

Res.

Ladue River

Northway Junction

7

Stewart River

Lake Creek

F

Northway

2

Nabesha River

Tetlin

42

Alaska Hwy.

Alaska Standard Time 12a.m.

Pacific Standard Time 1p.m.

Stewart Crossing

2

National

White River

Yukon River

17

Wildlife Refuge

Pelly River

Wrangell - Saint Elias

34

Welcome Center

Fort Selkirk

Pelly Crossing

G

National

Beaver
Creek   Snag

Wellesley Lake

Klotassim River

Minto

Park

142°

1

188

Donjek River

McCabe Creek

Ta

48/49

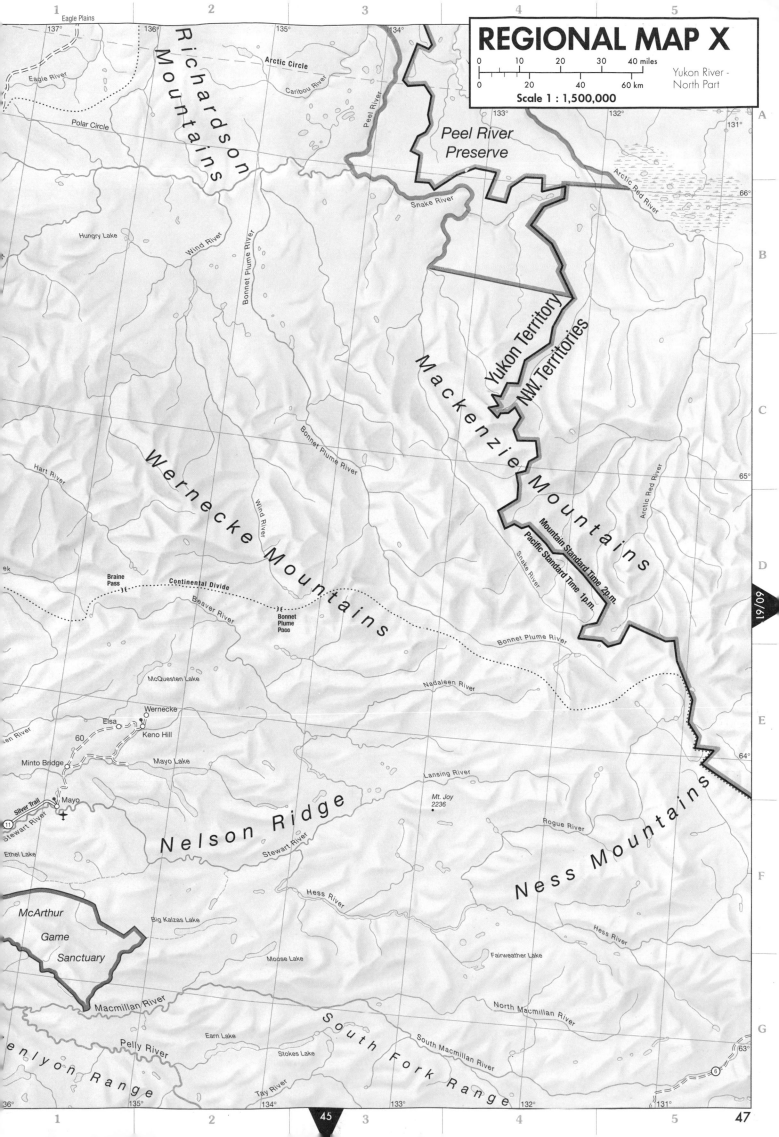

REGIONAL MAP X

0   10   20   30   40 miles

0   20   40   60 km

Scale 1 : 1,500,000

Yukon River -
North Part

Eagle Plains

137°

136°

135°

134°

133°

132°

131°

A

Arctic Circle

Eagle River

Caribou River

Polar Circle

Peel River

Peel River
Preserve

Arctic Red River

66°

B

Richardson Mountains

Hungry Lake

Wind River

Bonnet Plume River

Snake River

Yukon Territory

N.W. Territories

Mackenzie Mountains

C

Bonnet Plume River

Hart River

65°

Wernecke Mountains

Wind River

Snake River

Arctic Red River

D

Braine
Pass

Continental Divide

Beaver River

Bonnet
Plume
Pass

Bonnet Plume River

Mountain Standard Time 2p.m.

Pacific Standard Time 1p.m.

60/61

McQuesten Lake

Nadaleen River

E

ek

Wernecke

Elsa

Keno Hill

60

Minto Bridge

Mayo Lake

Lansing River

64°

en River

Silver Trail

Mayo

Mt. Joy
2236

11

Stewart River

Nelson Ridge

Stewart River

Rogue River

Ness Mountains

Ethel Lake

F

Hess River

McArthur

Game

Sanctuary

Big Kalzas Lake

Hess River

Moose Lake

Fairweather Lake

Macmillan River

North Macmillan River

G

enlyon Range

Pelly River

Earn Lake

South Fork Range

South Macmillan River

63°

Stokes Lake

6

36°

135°

134°

133°

132°

131°

Tay River

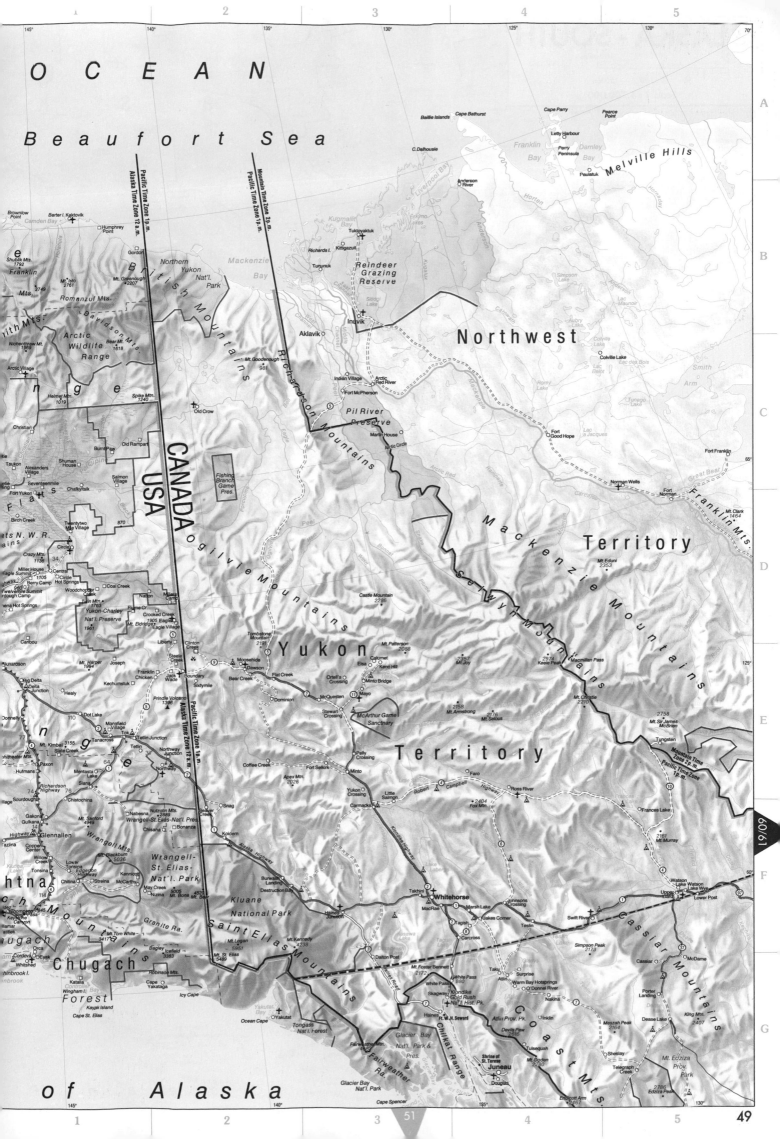

ALASKA - SOUTH

0   50   100 miles
Distances in miles
50   100   150 km
Scale 1 : 4,700,000

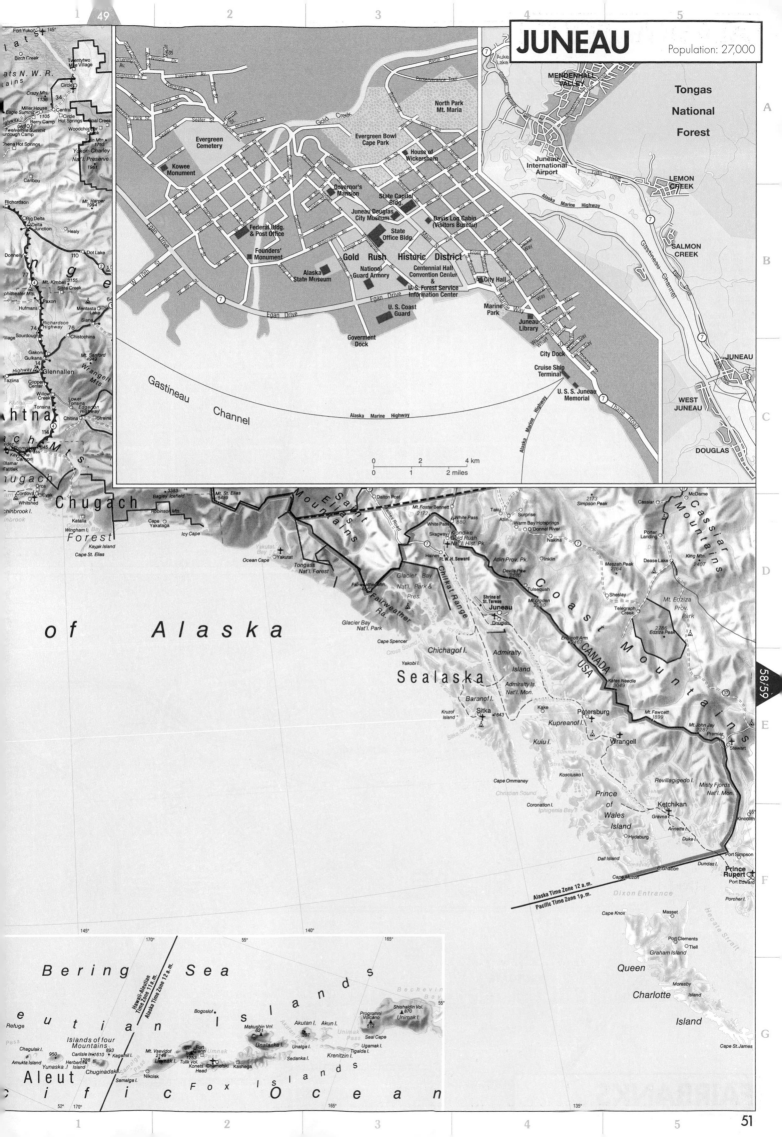

JUNEAU
Population: 27,000

Juneau inset map

Tongas National Forest

MENDENHALL VALLEY

LEMON CREEK

Auke Lake

Juneau International Airport

SALMON CREEK

North Park Mt. Maria

Evergreen Bowl Cape Park

House of Wickersham

Evergreen Cemetery

Kowee Monument

Governor's Mansion

State Capitol Bldg.

Juneau Douglas City Museum

Davis Log Cabin (Visitors Bureau)

State Office Bldg.

Federal Bldg. & Post Office

Founders' Monument

Gold Rush Historic District

Alaska State Museum

National Guard Armory

Centennial Hall Convention Center & U.S. Forest Service Information Center

City Hall

U. S. Coast Guard

Marine Park

Juneau Library

Goverment Dock

City Dock

Cruise Ship Terminal

U. S. S. Juneau Memorial

Alaska Marine Highway

Thane Road

Gastineau Channel

WEST JUNEAU

JUNEAU

DOUGLAS

Gastineau Channel

0   2   4 km
0   1   2 miles

Main map

Fort Yukon 145°
Birch Creek
Twentytwo Mile Village
Circle
Crazy Mts. 1136
Miller House
Eagle Summit 1105
Central
Circle Hot Springs
Coal Creek
Woodchopper
Berry Camp
Twelvemile Summit
Sourdough Camp
Eielson Mtn. 1763
Yukon-Charley Nat'l Preserve 1961

Mt. Harper 1994
Richardson
Big Delta
Delta Junction
Healy
Donnelly
Dot Lake
Mt. Kimbel 2155
Hufmans
Paxon
Amphitheater Mts.
Mentasta Lake
Slana
Richardson Highway
Chistochina
Gakona
Gulkana
Mt. Sanford 4949
Glennallen
Copper Center
Willow Creek
Lower Tonsina
Edgerton Highway
Chitina
Streina
Klutina

Caribou

Tazlina
Valdez
Keystone Canyon
Ellamar
Tatitlek
Chugach Mts.
Cordova
Orca
Eyak
Whitshed
Hinchinbrook I.

Chugach National Forest

of Alaska

Bagley Icefield 3383
Robinson Mts.
Mt. St. Elias 5489
Cape Yakataga
Icy Cape
Kayak Island
Cape St. Elias
Wingham I.
Ocean Cape
Yakutat Bay
Yakutat
Tongass Nat'l. Forest
Fairweather Mtn.
Glacier Bay Nat'l. Park & Pres.
Glacier Bay Nat'l. Park
Cape Spencer
Cross Sound
Chichagof I.
Yakobi I.
Sealaska
Kruzof Island
Sitka 1643
Baranof I.
Cape Ommaney
Coronation I.
Iphigenia Bay

Saint Elias Mountains
Dalton Post
Haines Road
White Pass 880
Skagway
Klondike Gold Rush Nat'l Hist. Pk.
Haines
R. W. H. Seward
Chilkat Range
Shrine of St. Teresa
Juneau
Douglas
Taku
Surprise
Atlin
Warm Bay Hotsprings
Donnel River
Nakina
Atlin Prov. Pk.
Inklin
Tulsequah
Devils Paw 2616
Mt. Ogden 2780
Coast Mountains
Endicott Arm
Admiralty Island
Admiralty Is. Nat'l. Mon.
Kake
Kupreanof I.
Petersburg
Kuiu I.
Kosciusko I.
Prince of Wales Island
Dall Island
Cape Muzon

2172
2173 Simpson Peak
Mt. Foster Bennett 2172
White Pass
McDame
Cassiar
Cassiar Mountains
Porter Landing
Dease Lake
King Mtn. 2407
Meszah Peak 2164
Sheslay
Telegraph Creek
Mt. Edziza Prov. Park
2786
Edziza Peak
CANADA
USA
Kates Needle 3049
Mt. Fawcett 1899
Wrangell
Mt. John Jay 2287
Premier
Stewart
Revillagigedo I.
Misty Fjords Nat'l. Mon.
Ketchikan
Gravina I.
Annette I.
Duke I.
Hydaburg
Port Simpson
Dundas I.
Prince Rupert
Port Edward
Porcher I.

Alaska Time Zone 12 a.m.
Pacific Time Zone 1 p.m.
Dixon Entrance
Cape Knox
Masset
Queen Charlotte Island
Port Clements
Tlell
Graham Island
Moresby Island
Hecate Strait
Cape St. James

Aleutian inset

Bering Sea

Hawaii-Aleutian Time Zone 12 a.m.
Alaska Time Zone 1 a.m.

Islands of four Mountains

Aleutian Islands

Bogoslof
Makushin Vol. 621
Unalaska I.
Unalga I.
Akutan I. Akun I.
Sedanka I.
Seal Cape
Ugamak I.
Tigalda I.
Krenitzin I.
Progromni Volcano
Shishaldin Vol. 870
Unimak I.
Unimak Pass

Chagulak I.
Carlisle Isl. 1610
Yunaska I.
Amukta Island
950
893
1288
Herbert I.
Chuginadak I.
Mt. Vsevidof 2149
Umnak I.
Tulik Vol.
Konets Chernofski Head
Kashega
Nikolski
Samalga I.

Fox Islands

Aleut

cific Ocean

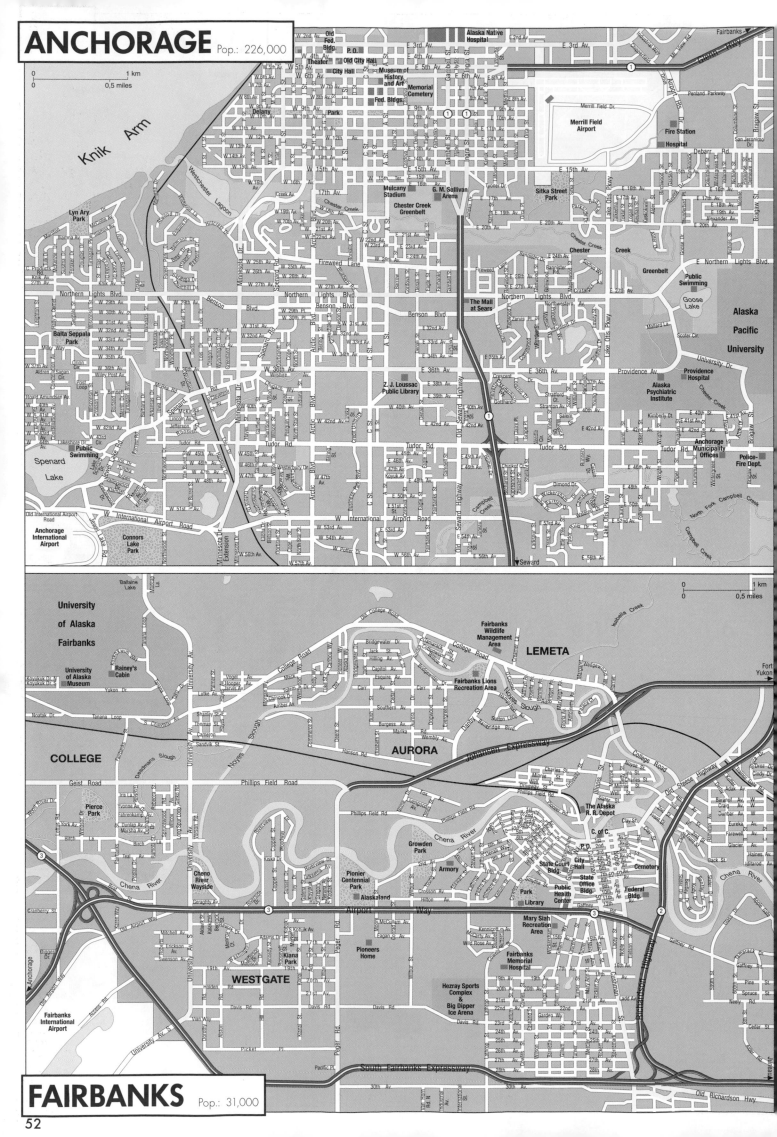

ANCHORAGE Pop.: 226,000

0 1 km
0 0,5 miles

Knik Arm

Westchester Lagoon

Lyn Ary Park

Balto Seppala Park

Spenard Lake

Public Swimming

Anchorage International Airport

Old International Airport Road

Connors Lake Park

Old Fed. Bldg.
P.O.
Theater
Old City Hall
City Hall
Museum of History and Art
Memorial Cemetery
Fed. Bldgs.
Delany Park

Alaska Native Hospital

Merrill Field Airport

Fire Station
Hospital

Debarr Rd.

Mulcahy Stadium
G. M. Sullivan Arena
Chester Creek Greenbelt
Sitka Street Park

Chester Creek

Chester Creek Greenbelt

Public Swimming
Goose Lake

Alaska Pacific University

The Mall at Sears

Northern Lights Blvd.
Benson Blvd.

University Dr.

Providence Av.
Providence Hospital

Alaska Psychiatric Institute

Z. J. Loussac Public Library

Tudor Rd.

Campbell Creek

Anchorage Municipality Offices

Police-Fire Dept.

North Fork Campbell Creek

W. International Airport Road

Campbell Creek

▼Seward

FAIRBANKS Pop.: 31,000

0 1 km
0 0,5 miles

Ballaine Lake

University of Alaska Fairbanks

Rainey's Cabin

University of Alaska Museum

Old College Road

Bridgewater Dr.

College Road

Fairbanks Wildlife Management Area

Isabella Creek

LEMETA

Fort Yukon

Fairbanks Lions Recreation Area

Noyes Slough

COLLEGE

Noyes Slough

AURORA

Johansen Expressway

Old Steese Highway

Geist Road

Phillips Field Road

Phillips Field Rd.

The Alaska R. R. Depot

C. of C.

Pierce Park

Chena River

Cheno River Wayside

Growden Park

Chena River

P.O.
City Hall
State Court Bldg.
State Office Bldg.
Public Health Center

Cemetery

Federal Bldg.

Pioneer Centennial Park

Alaskaland

Armory

Park
Library

Mary Siah Recreation Area

Anchorage

Fairbanks International Airport

Airport Way

Kiana Park

WESTGATE

Pioneers Home

Hezray Sports Complex & Big Dipper Ice Arena

Fairbanks Memorial Hospital

South Fairbanks Expressway

Old Richardson Hwy.

52

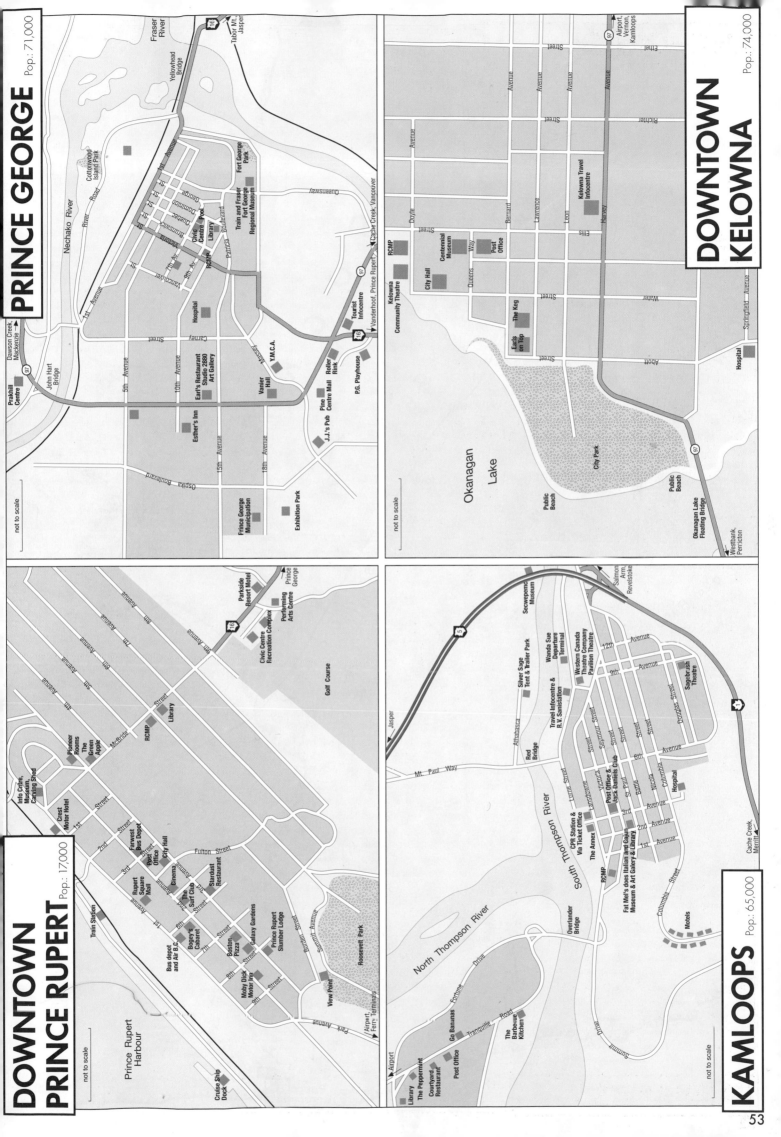

PRINCE GEORGE Pop.: 71,000

Fraser River
Nechako River
Cottonwood Island Park
Fort George Park
16 Tabor Mt., Jasper
Yellowhead Bridge
Queensway

Train and Fraser Fort George Regional Museum
Civic Centre
Pool
Library
RCMP
Hospital
Y.M.C.A.
Vanier Hall
Earl's Restaurant
Studio 2880 Art Gallery
Esther's Inn
Pine Centre Mall
J.J.'s Pub
Roller Rink
P.G. Playhouse
Tourist Infocentre

1st Avenue
5th Avenue
10th Avenue
15th Avenue
18th Avenue
Ospika Boulevard

Prince George Municipality
Exhibition Park

Dawson Creek, Mackenzie 97
Prakhill Centre
John Hart Bridge
97 Cache Creek, Vancouver
Vanderhoof, Prince Rupert 16
Patricia Boulevard

not to scale

DOWNTOWN KELOWNA Pop.: 74,000

97 Airport, Vernon, Kamloops
Ethel
Richter
Street
Avenue

Kelowna Travel Infocentre
Harvey
Springfield Avenue
Hospital
Abbot
Okanagan Lake Floating Bridge
Westbank, Penticton
97

RCMP
City Hall
Centennial Museum
Post Office
Kelowna Community Theatre
The Keg
Earls on Top
Doyle
Bernard
Lawrence
Leon
Queens Way
Ellis Street
Water Street
Abbot

Okanagan Lake
Public Beach
City Park
Public Beach

not to scale

DOWNTOWN PRINCE RUPERT Pop.: 17,000

8th Avenue
7th Avenue
6th Avenue
5th Avenue
4th Avenue
16
9th Avenue

Parkside Resort Motel
Performing Arts Centre
Prince George
Civic Centre Recreation Complex
Golf Course

Info Centre, Museum, Carving Shed
Pioneer Rooms
The Green Apple
McBride Street
RCMP
Library
Crest Motor Hotel
Farwest Bus Depot
Post Office
City Hall
Fulton Street
Cinema
Rupert Square Mall
The Surf Club
Stardust Restaurant
Bogey's Cabaret
Boston Pizza
Galaxy Gardens
Prince Rupert Slumber Lodge
Moby Dick Motor Inn
View Point

1st Avenue
2nd Avenue
3rd Avenue
6th Street
7th Street
8th Street
9th Street
Border Street
Summit Avenue
Park Avenue

Train Station
Bus depot and Air B.C.
Prince Rupert Harbour
Cruise Ship Dock
Roosevelt Park
Airport, Ferry Terminals

not to scale

KAMLOOPS Pop.: 65,000

5
Salmon Arm, Revelstoke
Secwepemc Museum
Silver Sage Tent & Trailer Park
Wanda Sue Departure Terminal
Travel Infocentre & R.V. Sanisation
Western Canada Theatre Company Pavilion Theatre
Sagebrush Theatre
12th Avenue
9th Avenue
6th Avenue
3rd Avenue
2nd Avenue
1st Avenue

Jasper
Mt. Paul Way
Red Bridge
Athabasca
North Thompson River
South Thompson River
Overlander Bridge

Lorne Street
Seymour Street
Victoria Street
St. Paul Street
Battle Street
Nicola Street
Columbia Street
Lansdowne
Douglas Street

CPR Station & Via Ticket Office
Post Office & Jack-Daniels Club
The Annex
RCMP
Fat Mel's does Italian and Cajun
Museum & Art Gallery & Library
Hospital
Motels

1
Cache Creek, Merritt

Go Bananas
The Barbecue Kitchen
The Peppermint
Courtyard Restaurant
Post Office
Library
Tranquille Road
Fortune Drive
Summit Drive
Airport

not to scale

53

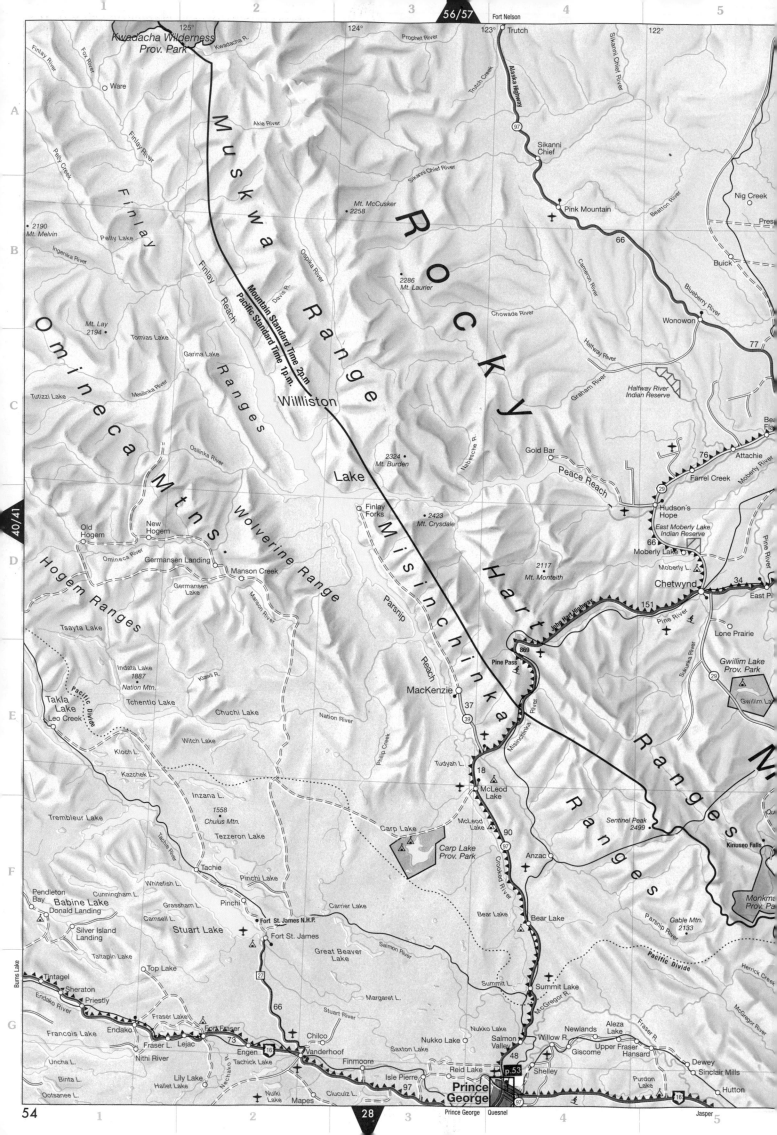

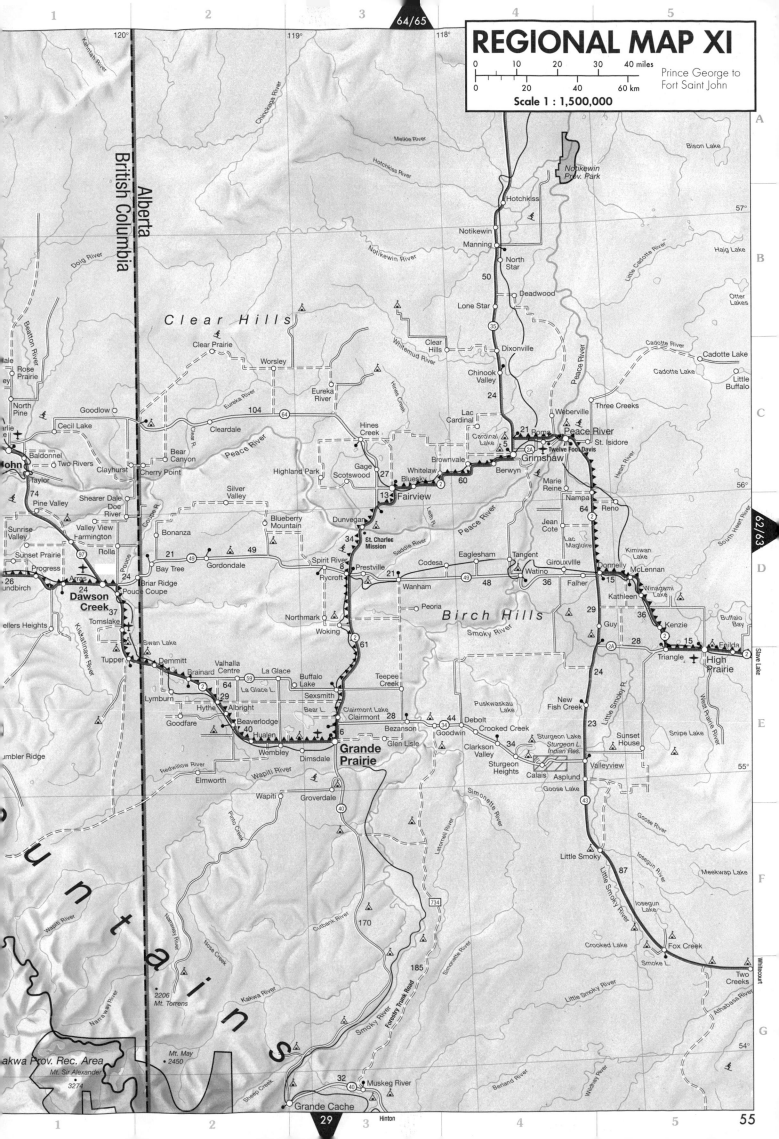

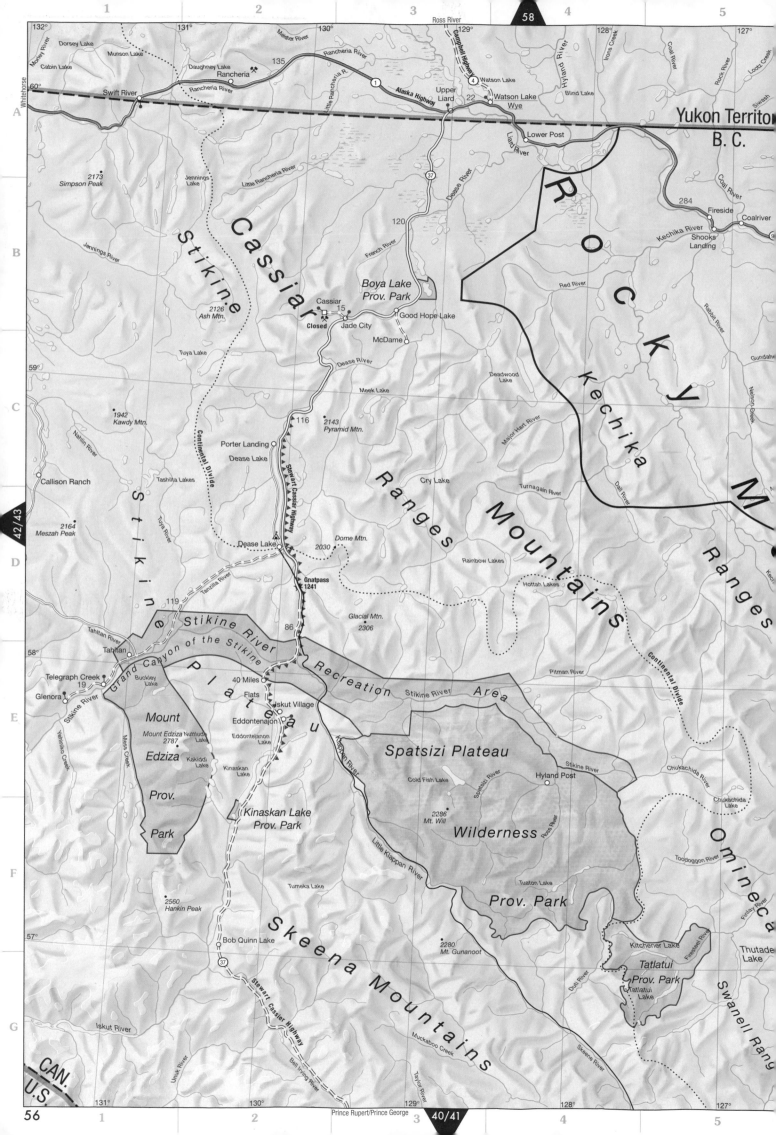

| | 1 | 2 | 3 | 4 | 5 |

Ross River

132° 131° 130° 129° 128° 127°

Morley River
Dorsey Lake
Cabin Lake
Munson Lake

Meister River
Rancheria River

Hyland River

Irons Creek

Coal River

Rock River

Lootz Creek

Siwash

A

Daughney Lake
Rancheria
Rancheria River
Little Rancheria R.
135

Alaska Highway
1

Upper Liard
Liard River
22
Watson Lake
Watson Lake
Wye
Blind Lake

YUKON TERRITORY
B. C.

Swift River
60°

Whitehorse

Lower Post
Liard River

Coal River

Fireside
284
Coalriver

B

Simpson Peak
2173
Jennings Lake

Dease River
120
37

French River

Red River

Kechika River
Shooks Landing

Rabbit River

Gundaha

Jennings River

Boya Lake
Prov. Park

Cassiar
15
Closed
Jade City
Good Hope Lake
McDame

R O C K Y   M

C
59°

Stikine

Ash Mtn.
2126

Tuya Lake

Dease River

Meek Lake

Deadwood Lake

Cry Lake

Nelson Creek

Kawdy Mtn.
1942

116
Pyramid Mtn.
2143

Major Hart River

Kechika

Nahlin River

Porter Landing
Dease Lake

Turnagain River

D

Callison Ranch

Tashilta Lakes

Continental Divide

Dome Mtn.
2030

Rainbow Lakes

Dell River

Ranges

Mountains

Ranges

42/43

Meszah Peak
2164

Tuya River

Stewart Cassiar Highway

Dease Lake
Gnatpass
1241

Hottah Lakes

Glacial Mtn.
2306

Tanzilla River

119

Stikine

E
58°

Tahltan River

Tahltan

Stikine River
86

Stikine River Recreation

Pitman River

Continental Divide

Omineca

Telegraph Creek
19
Glenora

Buckley Lake

Grand Canyon of the Stikine

40 Miles
Flats
Iskut Village
Eddontenajon

Klappan River

Area

Stikine River

Chukachida River

Yehiniko Creek

Mount

Mount Edziza
2787
Nuttlude Lake

Eddontenajon Lake

Spatsizi Plateau

Stikine River

Chukachida Lake

Mess Creek

Edziza

Kakiddi Lake

Kinaskan Lake

Cold Fish Lake

Hyland Post

Spatsizi River

Ross River

F

Prov.

Park

Kinaskan Lake
Prov. Park

Little Klappan River

Mt. Will
2286

Wilderness

Toodoggon River

Finlay River

Swanell Rang

Tumeka Lake

Tuaton Lake

Prov. Park

Kitchener Lake

Friesteel River

Thutade Lake

Hankin Peak
2560

Bob Quinn Lake

Skeena

Mt. Gunanoot
2280

Duti River

Tatlatui

Prov. Park

Tatlatui Lake

57°

37

Iskut River

Stewart Cassiar Highway

Mountains

Muckaboo Creek

Taylor River

Skeene River

G

Unuk River

Bell Irving River

Prince Rupert/Prince George

CAN.
U.S.

131° 130° 129° 128° 127°

| 1 | 2 | 3 | 40/41 | 4 | 5 |

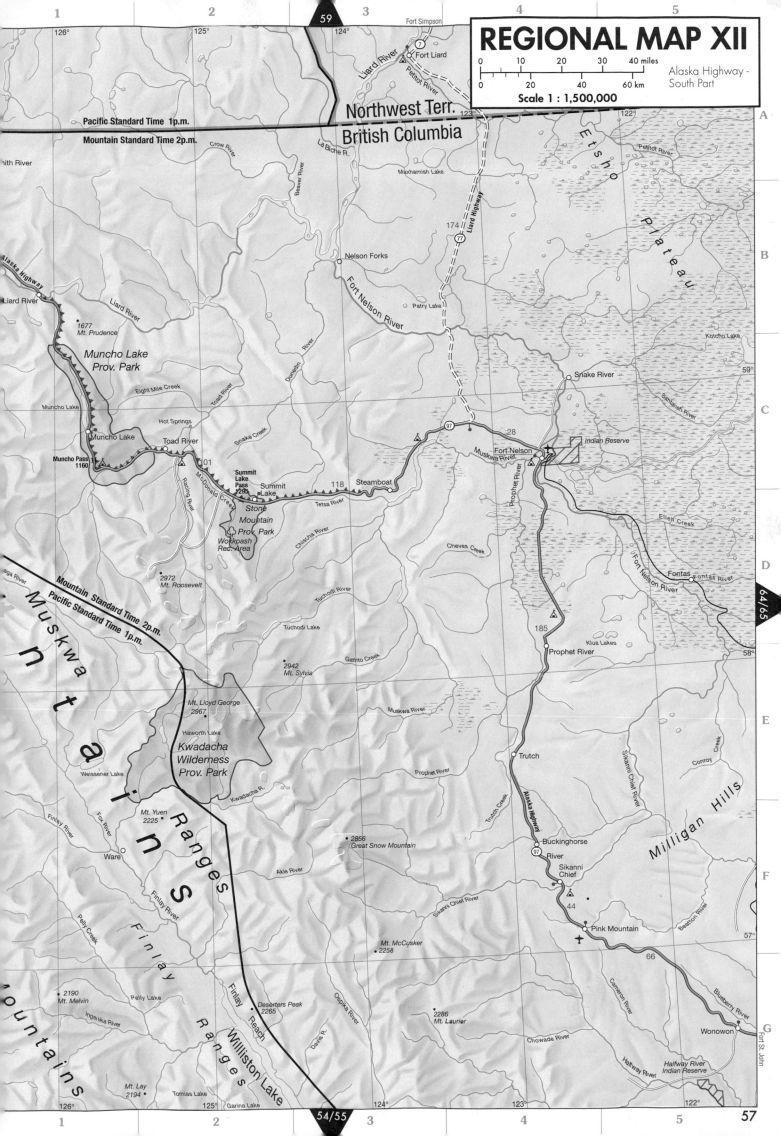

REGIONAL MAP XII

Alaska Highway -
South Part

0 10 20 30 40 miles
0   20   40   60 km
Scale 1 : 1,500,000

Fort Simpson

Fort Liard

Liard River

Petitot River

Northwest Terr.
British Columbia

Pacific Standard Time 1p.m.
Mountain Standard Time 2p.m.

Crow River

La Biche R.

Maxhamish Lake

Etsho Plateau

Petitot River

Beaver River

Liard Highway

174
77

Nelson Forks

Fort Nelson River

Patry Lake

Kotcho Lake

Alaska Highway

Liard River

1677
Mt. Prudence

Liard River

Muncho Lake
Prov. Park

Snake River

Sahtaneh River

59°

Eight Mile Creek

Toad River

Dunedin River

97
28

Muncho Lake

Hot Springs

Snake Creek

Fort Nelson

Indian Reserve

Muncho Lake

Toad River

Muskwa River

Ellen Creek

Muncho Pass
1160

101

McDonald Creek

Summit
Lake
Pass
1295

Summit
Lake

118

Steamboat

Tetsa River

Fort Nelson River

Fontas
Fontas River

Racing River

Stone
Mountain
Prov. Park

Wokkpash
Rec. Area

Chischa River

Prophet River

Cheves Creek

2972
Mt. Roosevelt

Tuchodi River

185

Klua Lakes

Muskwa

Tuchodi Lake

Gathto Creek

Prophet River

58°

2942
Mt. Sylvia

Mt. Lloyd George
2967

Muskwa River

Haworth Lake

Kwadacha
Wilderness
Prov. Park

Prophet River

Sikanni Chief River

Conroy Creek

Weissener Lake

Kwadacha R.

Trutch

Milligan Hills

Finlay River

Fox River

Mt. Yuen
2225

2856
Great Snow Mountain

Alaska Highway

Buckinghorse
River

Sikanni
Chief

Ware

Akie River

Sikanni Chief River

97
44

Finlay River

Pink Mountain

57°

Pelly Creek

66

2190
Mt. Melvin

Pelly Lake

Deserters Peak
2265

Ospika River

Mt. McCusker
2258

Cameron River

Beatton River

Blueberry River

Wonowon

Ingenika River

Finlay Reach

Davis R.

2286
Mt. Laurier

Mt. Lay
2194

Tomias Lake

Williston Lake

Garina Lake

Chowade River

Halfway River
Indian Reserve

Halfway River

Fort St. John

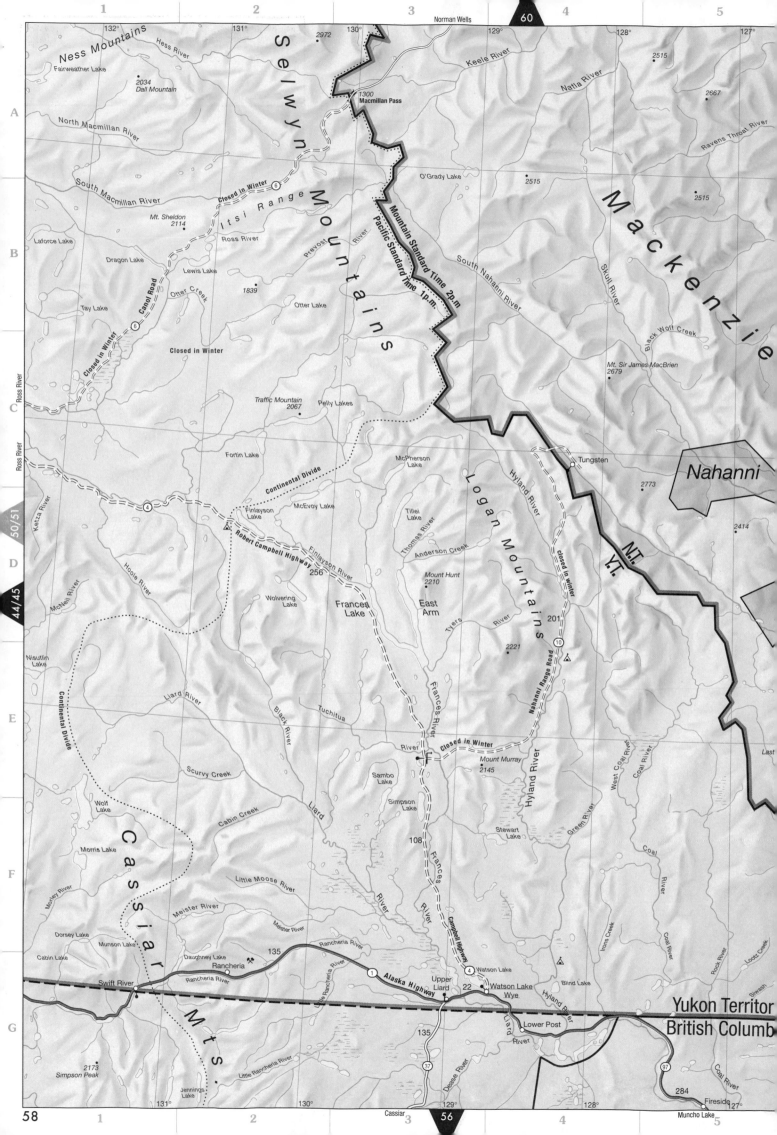

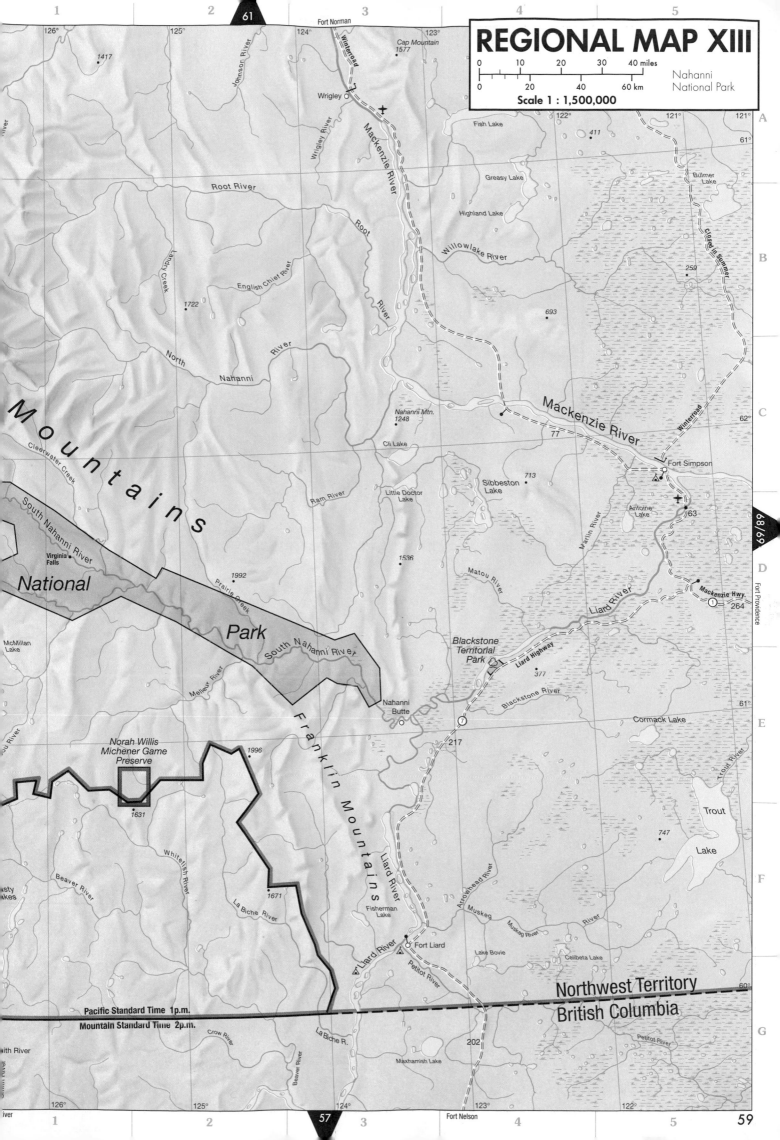

REGIONAL MAP XIII

Scale 1 : 1,500,000

Nahanni
National Park

Fort Norman

Winterroad

Cap Mountain
1577

1417

Johnson River

Wrigley O

Mackenzie River

Fish Lake

411

A

61°

Root River

Greasy Lake

Bulmer Lake

259

B

Wrigley River

English Chief River

Root

River

Willowlake River

693

Landry Creek

1722

North

Nahanni

River

Mackenzie River

Winterroad

77

62°

C

Mountains

Cleerwater Creek

Nahanni Mtn.
1248

Cli Lake

Fort Simpson

Closed in Summer

South Nahanni River

Ram River

Little Doctor Lake

Sibbeston Lake

713

Antoine Lake

63

68/69

Virginia Falls

1992

Prairie Creek

1536

Matou River

Martin River

National

Liard River

Mackenzie Hwy.
264

Fort Providence

Park

South Nahanni River

McMillan Lake

Blackstone Territorial Park

Liard Highway

377

Blackstone River

61°

E

Melieur River

Nahanni Butte

217

Cormack Lake

Trout River

Franklin Mountains

Norah Willis Michener Game Preserve

1996

1631

Trout

747

Lake

Whitefish River

Beaver River

Liard River

F

usty akes

La Biche River

1671

Fisherman Lake

Muskeg

Muskeg River

River

Lake Bovie

Celibeta Lake

ith River

La Biche River

Liard River

Fort Liard

Petitot River

Northwest Territory

60°

Pacific Standard Time 1p.m.

Mountain Standard Time 2p.m.

British Columbia

G

Crow River

202

Beaver River

La Biche R.

Maxhamish Lake

Petitot River

Fort Nelson

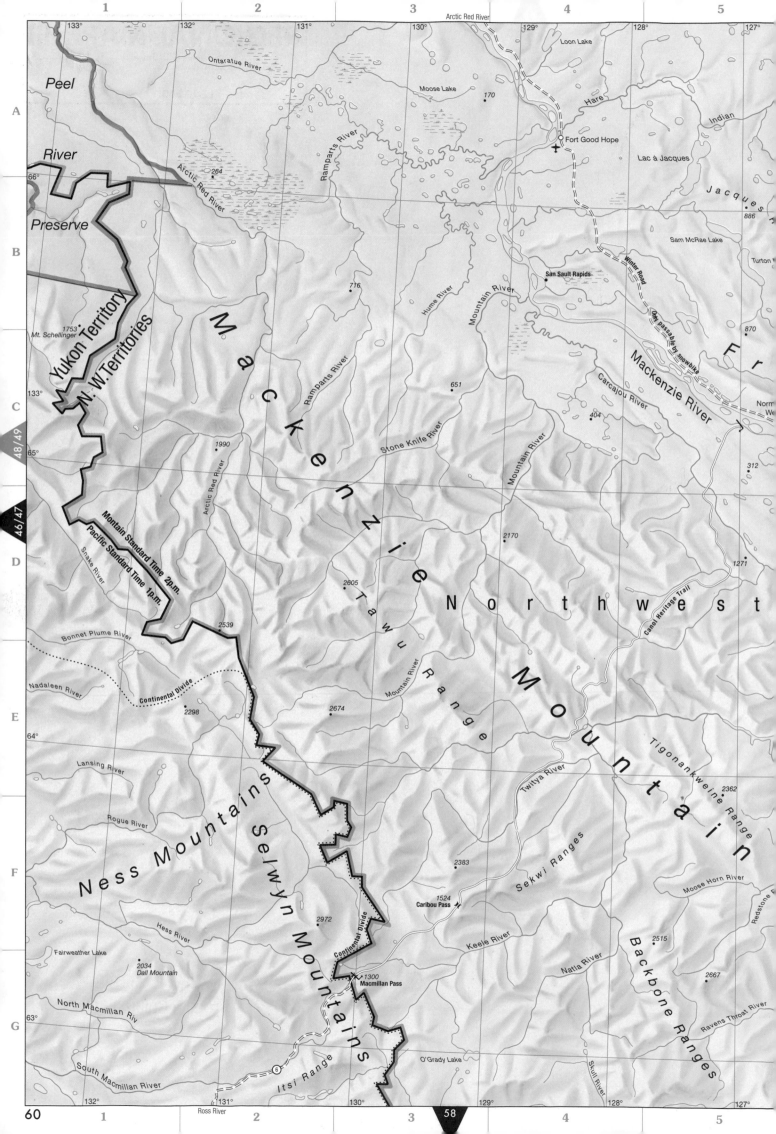

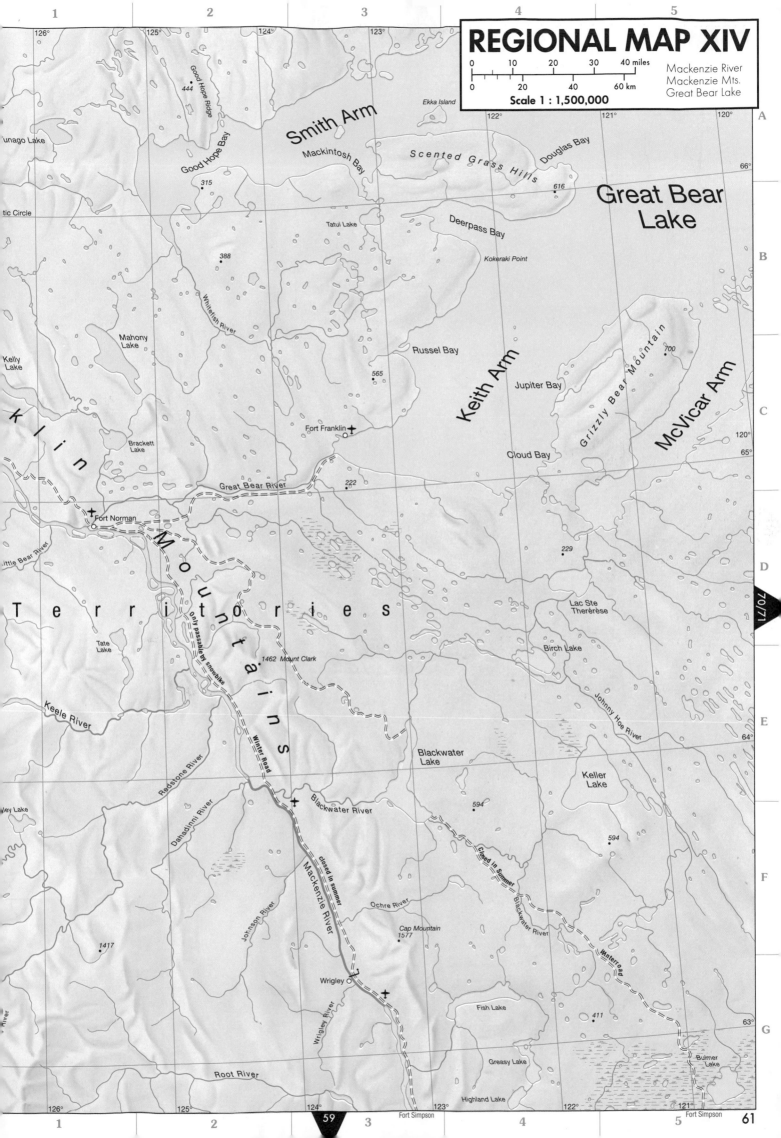

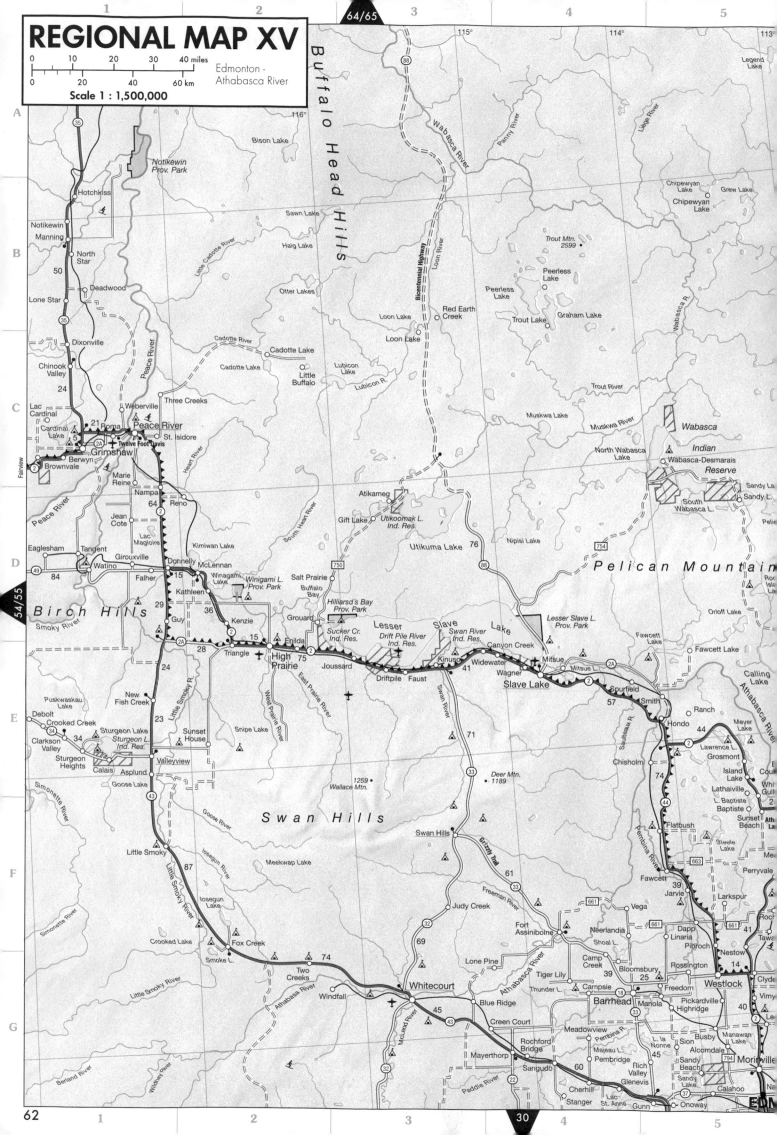

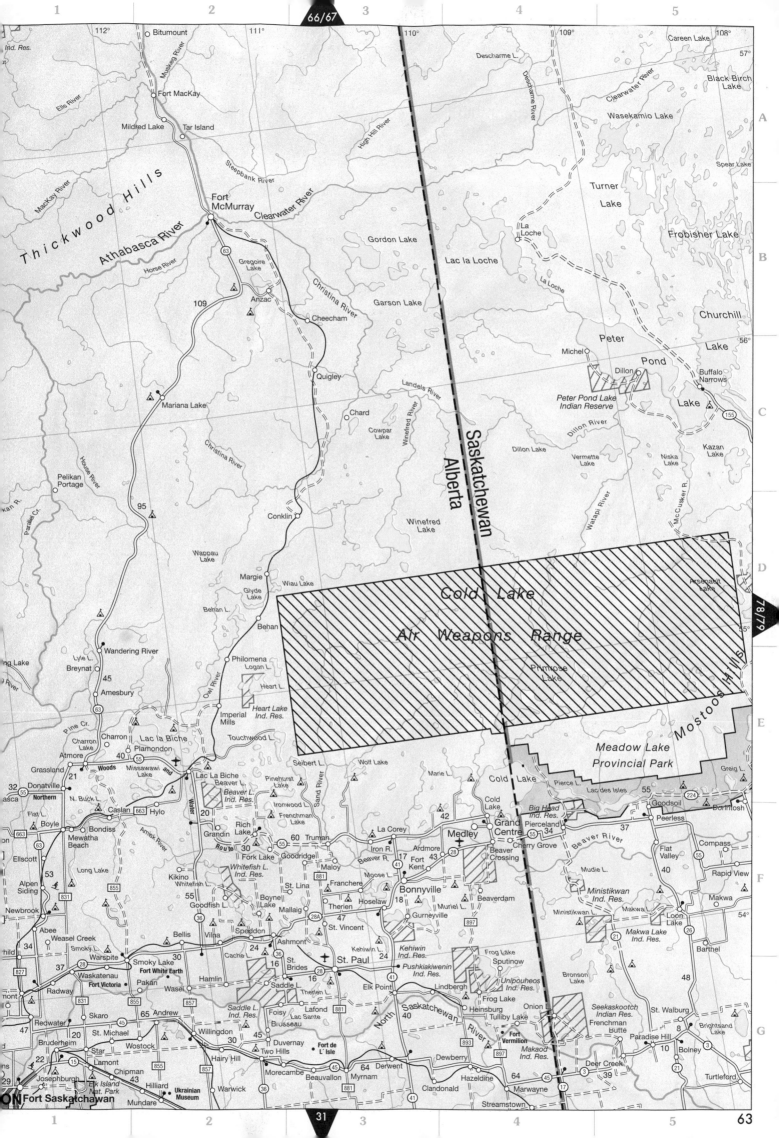

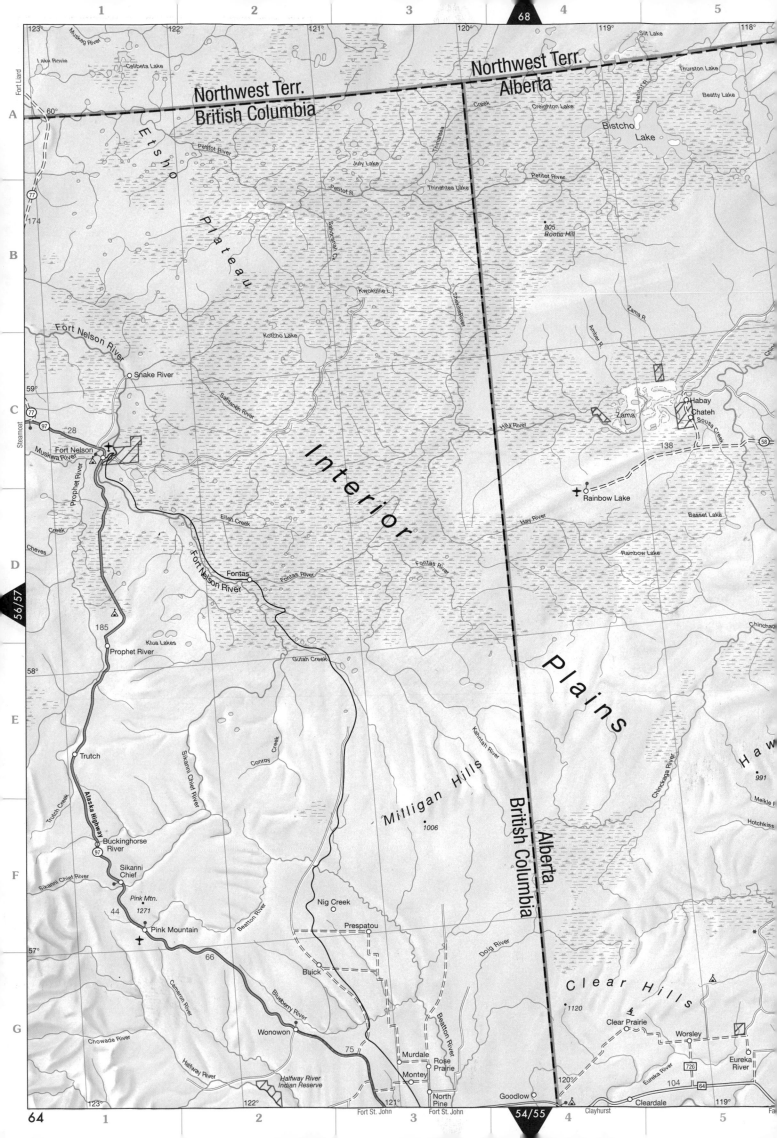

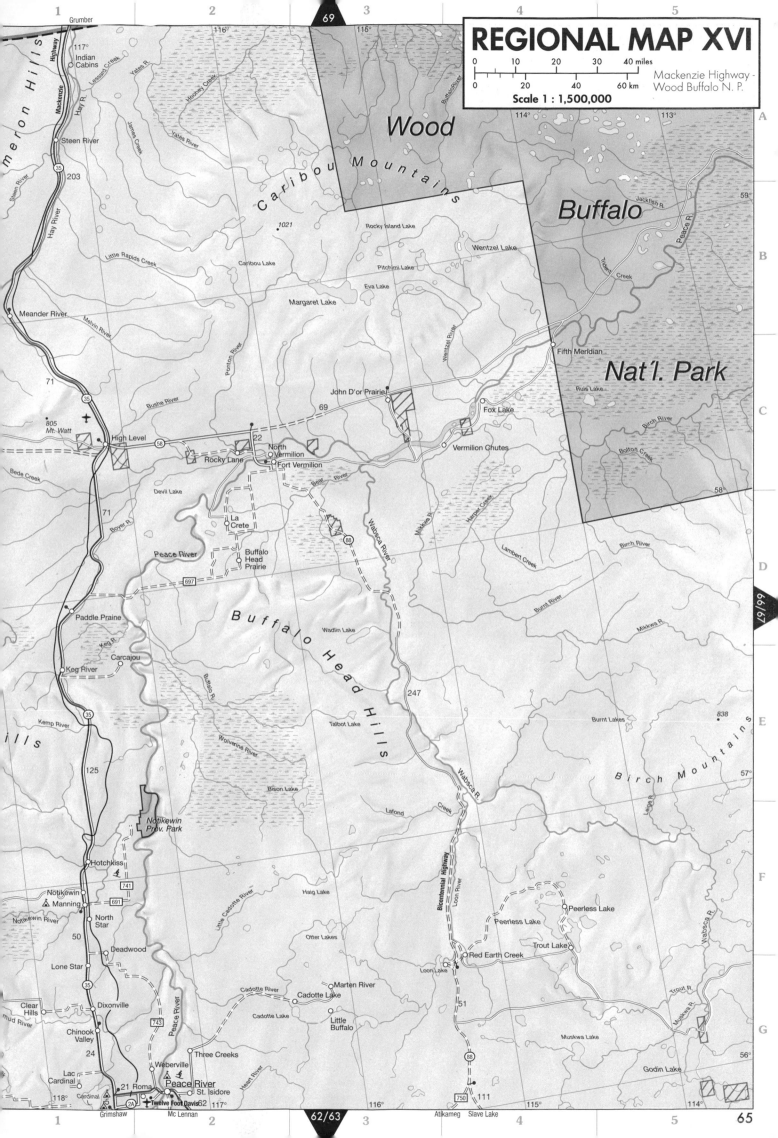

REGIONAL MAP XVI

0 10 20 30 40 miles
0   20   40   60 km
Scale 1 : 1,500,000
Mackenzie Highway -
Wood Buffalo N. P.

Wood

Buffalo

Nat'l. Park

Grumber

Indian Cabins
117°

Mackenzie Highway

Hay R.
James Creek
Lessard Creek
Yates R.
Hooney Creek

Steen River
203
Yates River

Hay River
Little Rapids Creek
Caribou Lake

1021

Rocky Island Lake
Wentzel Lake
Pitchimi Lake

Meander River
Melvin River
Eva Lake

71
Margaret Lake

Ponton River

Bushe River
69
John D'or Prairie
Fox Lake

805
Mt. Watt
High Level
58
North Vermilion
Rocky Lane
Fort Vermilion
Bear River
Vermilion Chutes

Bede Creek
Devil Lake

71
Boyer R.
La Crete
88
Wabsca River

Peace River
Buffalo Head Prairie
697

Paddle Prairie

Keg R.
Carcajou
Keg River

Kemp River

125

35

Buffalo Head Hills

Wadlin Lake

Talbot Lake
247

Wolverine River

Bison Lake

Notikewin Prov. Park

Hotchkiss
741

Notikewin
Manning
691

North Star
50
Deadwood

Lone Star
35

Clear Hills
mud River
Dixonville
743

Chinook Valley
24

Lac Cardinal
118°
21 Roma
Cerdinal
5
2A
Twelve Foot Davis
62
117°

Weberville
Peace River
St. Isidore

Three Creeks
Heart River

Marten River
Cadotte River
Cadotte Lake
Cadotte Lake
Little Buffalo

Haig Lake

Otter Lakes
51

Lafond
Wabsca R.

Bicentennial Highway
Loon River
Creek

Red Earth Creek
Loon Lake
Trout Lake
Peerless Lake
Peerless Lake

Burnt Lakes
838

Birch Mountains

Leje R.

Muskwa Lake
Trout R.
Muskwa R.

Godin Lake

88
750
111

Wentzel River
Fifth Meridian

Ruis Lake
Birch River
Bolton Creek

Mikkwa R.
Harper Creek
Lambert Creek
Birch River
Burnt River
Mikkwa R.

Jackfish R.
Trident Creek
Peace R.

59°

58°

57°

56°

114°
113°

116°
115°

118° 117° 116° 115° 114°

A
B
C
D
E
F
G

1 2 3 4 5

69/67

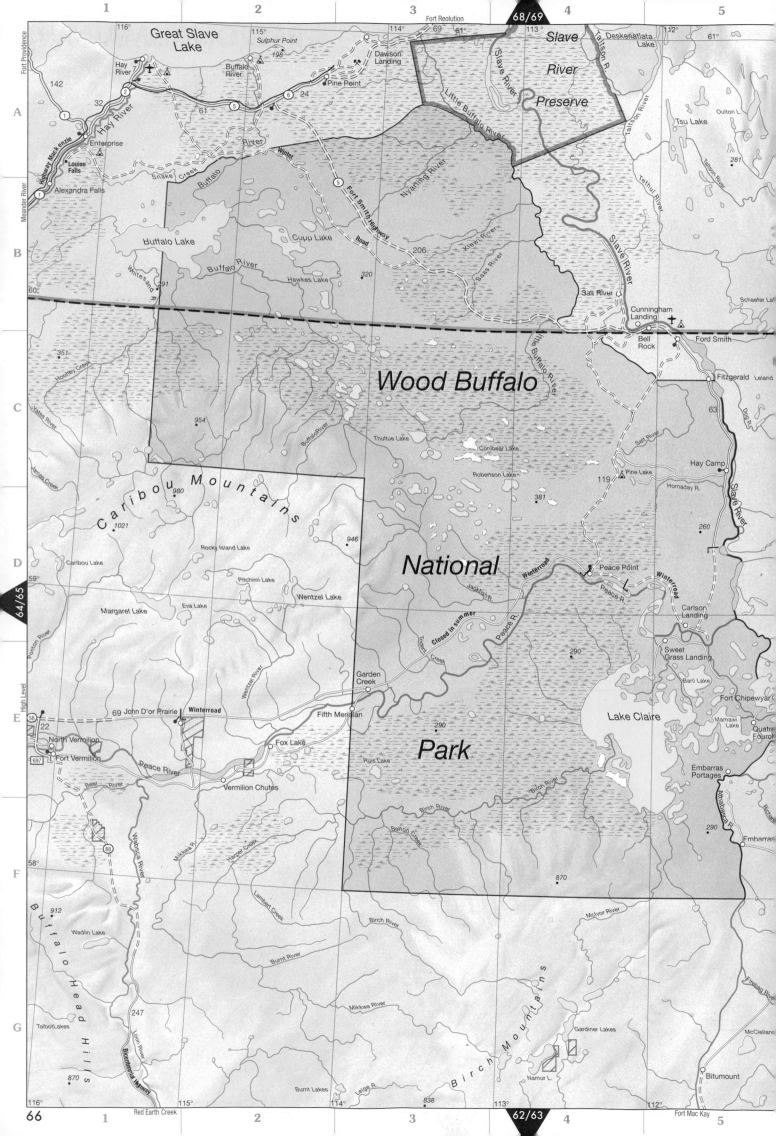

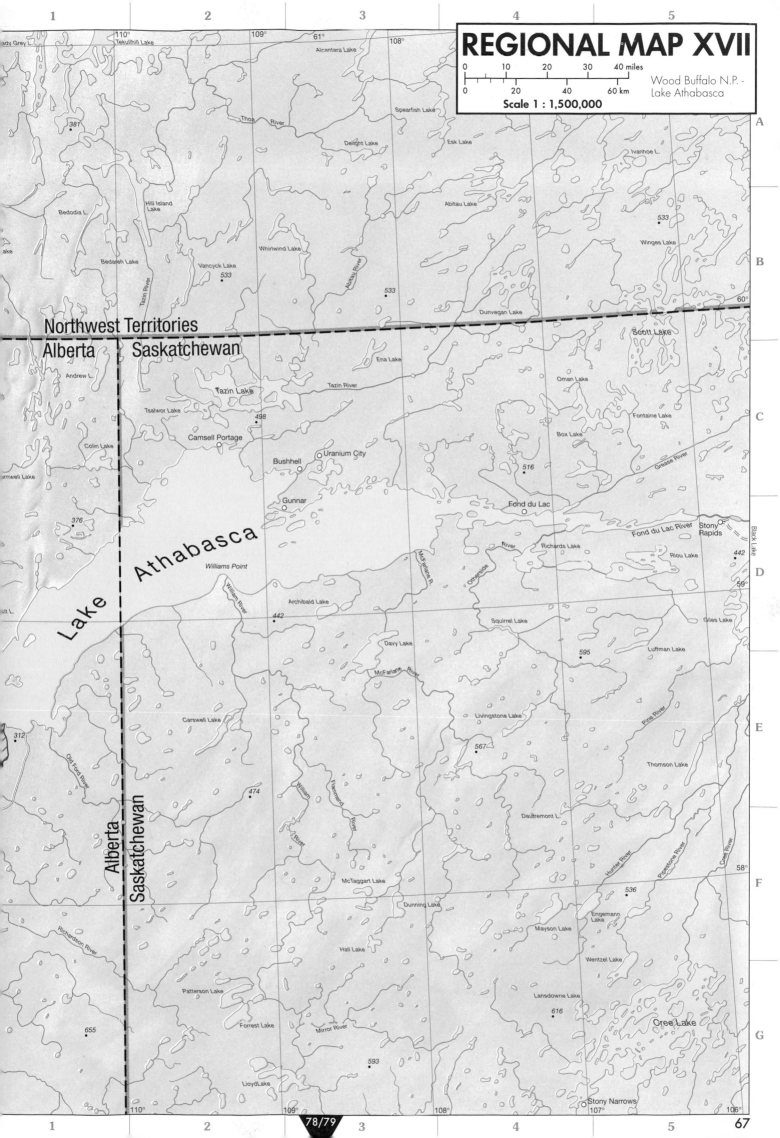

REGIONAL MAP XVII

Scale 1 : 1,500,000

0 10 20 30 40 miles
0   20   40   60 km

Wood Buffalo N.P. -
Lake Athabasca

Lady Grey L.
110°
Tekullhill Lake
109°
61°
Alcantara Lake
108°

Thoa River
Spearfish Lake

381
Delight Lake
Esk Lake
Ivanhoe L.

Bedodia L.
Hill Island Lake
Abitau Lake
533

Winges Lake

Bedareh Lake
Whirlwind Lake
Vancyck Lake
533

Abitau River

Northwest Territories
Alberta Saskatchewan

Andrew L.
Ena Lake
Dunvegan Lake
533
60°
Scott Lake

Tazin Lake
Tazin River
Oman Lake

Tsalwor Lake
498
Box Lake
Fontaine Lake

Colin Lake
Camsell Portage
Bushhell
Uranium City
516
Grease River

Gunnar
Fond du Lac

376
River
Richards Lake
Fond du Lac River
Stony Rapids

Lake Athabasca
Williams Point
William River
Riou Lake
442
Black Lake

Archibald Lake
442
McFarlane R.
Otherside
Squirrel Lake
Giles Lake
59°

Davy Lake
595
Luffman Lake

Carswell Lake
McFarlane River
Livingstone Lake
Pine River

312
567
Thomson Lake

474
William
Flammand River
Dautremont L.

Alberta
Saskatchewan

River
Hunter River
Pipestone River
58°
Cree River

McTaggart Lake
536

Dunning Lake
Engemann Lake

Richardson River
Mayson Lake

Hall Lake
Wentzel Lake

Patterson Lake
Lansdowne Lake

655
Forrest Lake
Mirror River
616
Cree Lake

593
Stony Narrows
107°

LloydLake

122°   121°   120°   119°   118°   117°   116°

Dease Arm

Cape McDonnel

229•

Hornby Bay

Wentzel Lake

Arctic Circle

Echo Bay

Winterroad

438•

Polar Circle

A

Douglas Bay

Scented Grass Hills

616•

Great Bear Lake

McTavish Arm

Richardson Island

503•

66°

Deerpass Bay

Sawmill Bay

Clut Lake

Bish Lake

Kokeraki Point

Point Leith

Leith Peninsula

512•

Grouard Lake

Lever Lake

B

Keith Arm

Jupiter Bay

Grizzly Bear Mountain

700•

McVicar Arm

Hottah Lake

375•

Wopmay Lake

C

Cloud Bay

Bell Island

N o r t h w e s t

65°

716•

Rebecca Lake

229•

Hardisty Lake

D

Lac Ste Therérèse

Etna Lake

Birch Lake

442•

Rae Lake

Johnny Hoe River

Lac Taché

E

Lac Grandin

Faber Lake

64°

Keller Lake

777•

Sarah Lake

Winterroad

594•

Fort Norman

594•

Lac la Martre

F

Closed in Summer

Cartridge Mountain

Big Island

Blackwater River

323•

Lac la Martre ✛

Winterroad

472•

Clive Lake

Bartlett Lake

Weyburn Lake

Fish Lake

411•

123°

G

63°

Greasy Lake

Windflower Lake

Highland Lake

Bulmer Lake

Lac Levis

122°   121°   120°   119°   118°

Fort Simpson

60/61

0   10   20   30   40 miles
0   20   40   60 km
Scale 1 : 1,500,000

Great Bear Lake -
East Area

Samandré Lake

Scotstoun Lake

Redrock Lake

Coppermine River

594

Rockinghorse Lake

588

Itchen Lake

515

Contwoyto Lake

Pellatt Lake

Point Lake

495

Yamba Lake

Rawalpindi Lake

Big Lake

526

Whitewolf Lake

Desteffany Lake

Lac de Gras

T e r r i t o r i e s

Truce Lake

Wirter Lake

MacKay Lake

Snare Lake

Courageous Lake

Jolly Lake

533

Indin Lake

ngray ake

Wecho Lake

Warburton Bay

Mattberry Lake

Basler Lake

Upper Carp Lake

Lockhart Lake

Camsell Lake

Kwejinne Lake

442

Beniah Lake

Lac Nez Croche

Wecho River

Wheeler Lake

Gordon Lake

McKinley Lake

McLeod Bay

450

Slemon Lake

Indian Village

Duncan Lake

Winter road

Marian Lake

Russell Lake

Christie Bay

Closed in Summer

Rae

Yellowknife Highway

Edzo

Yellowknife River

François Lake

Beaulieu River

214

Great Slave L.

5   98

Yellowknife

28   4

260

Detah

116°   115°   114°   113°   112°   111°   62°

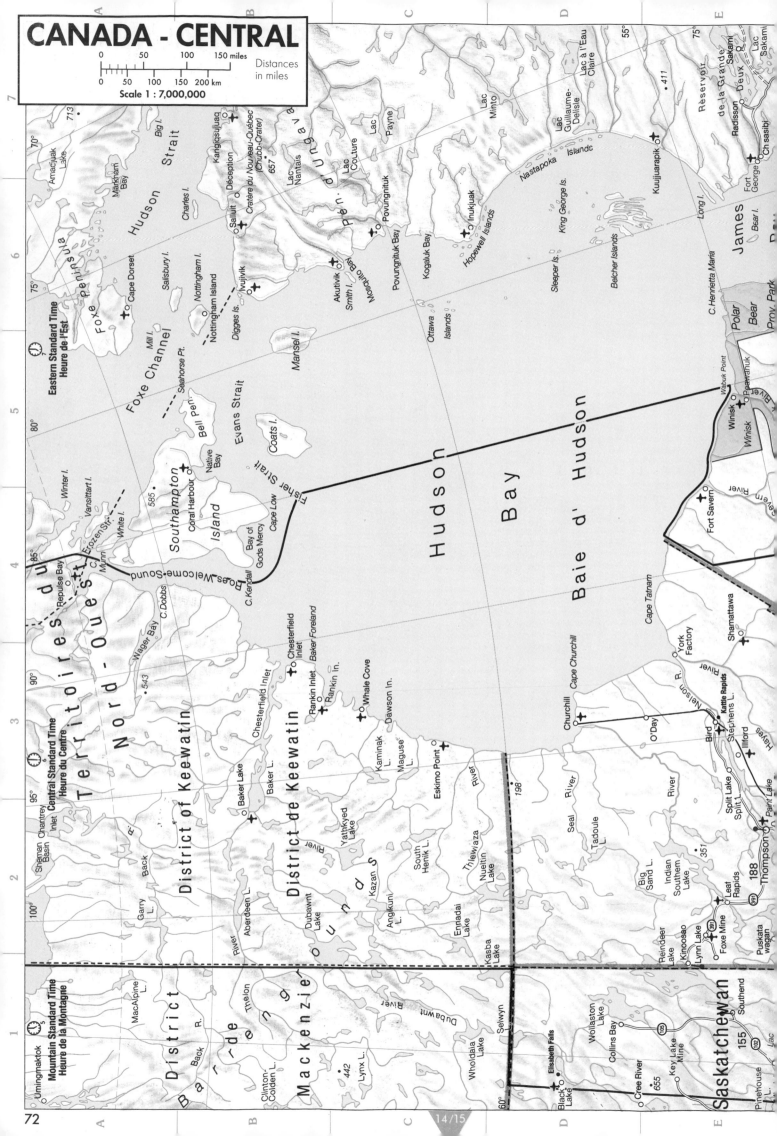

CANADA - CENTRAL

Distances in miles

Scale 1 : 7,000,000

72

14/15

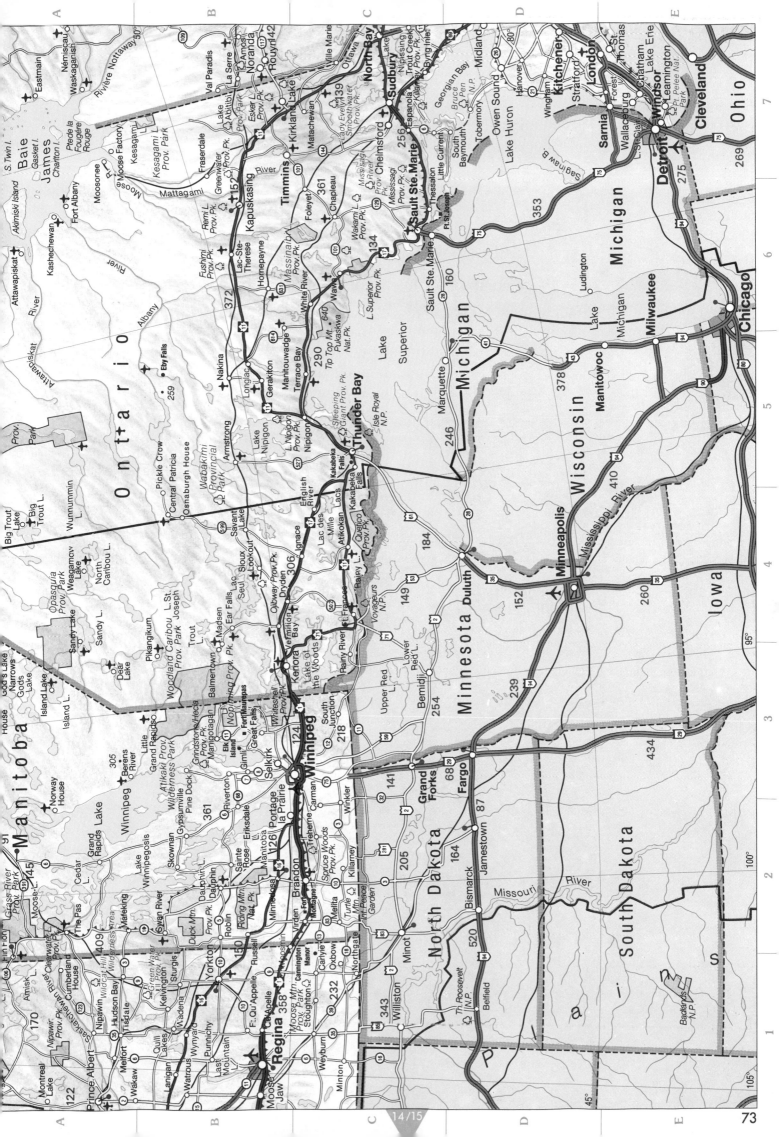

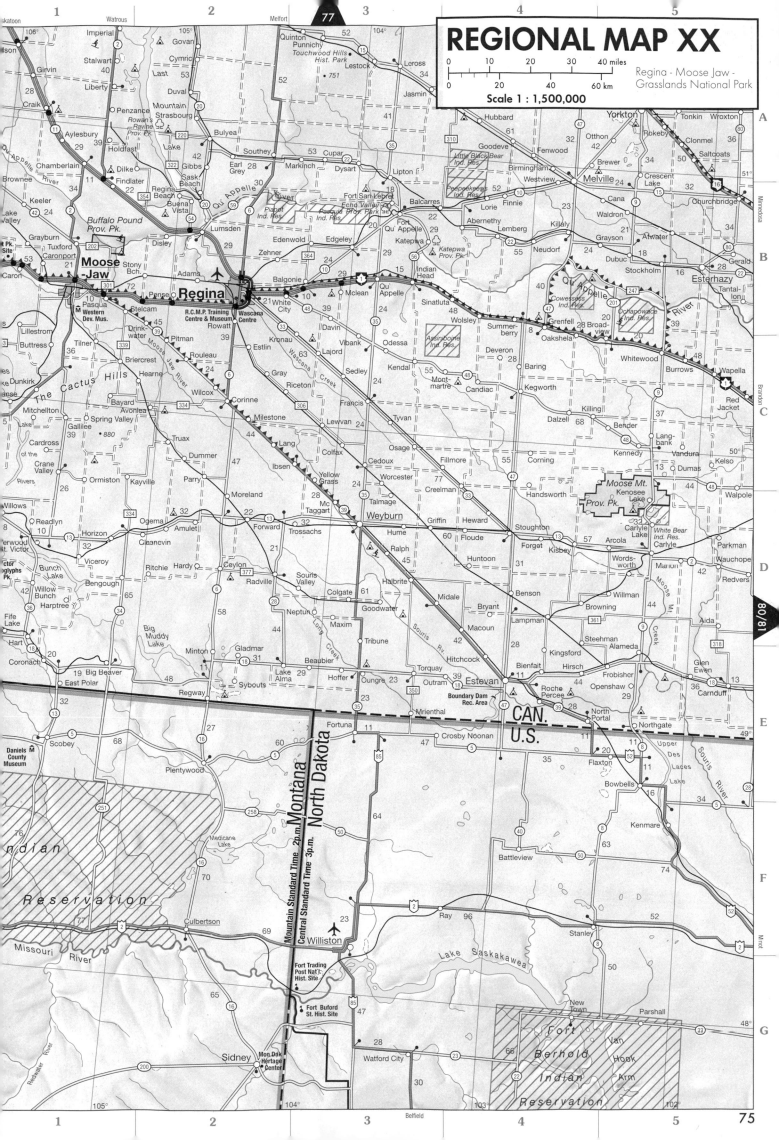

REGIONAL MAP XX

Scale 1 : 1,500,000

Regina - Moose Jaw - Grasslands National Park

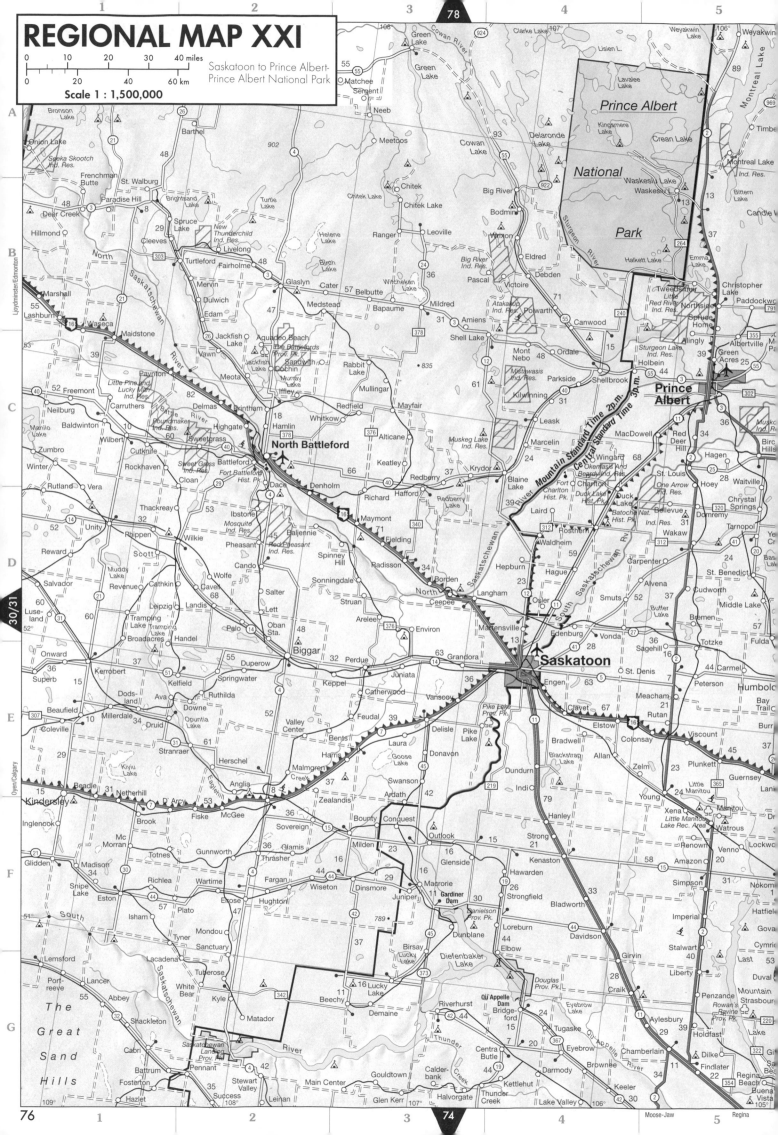

REGIONAL MAP XXI

Scale 1 : 1,500,000

Saskatoon to Prince Albert-
Prince Albert National Park

0 10 20 30 40 miles
0 20 40 60 km

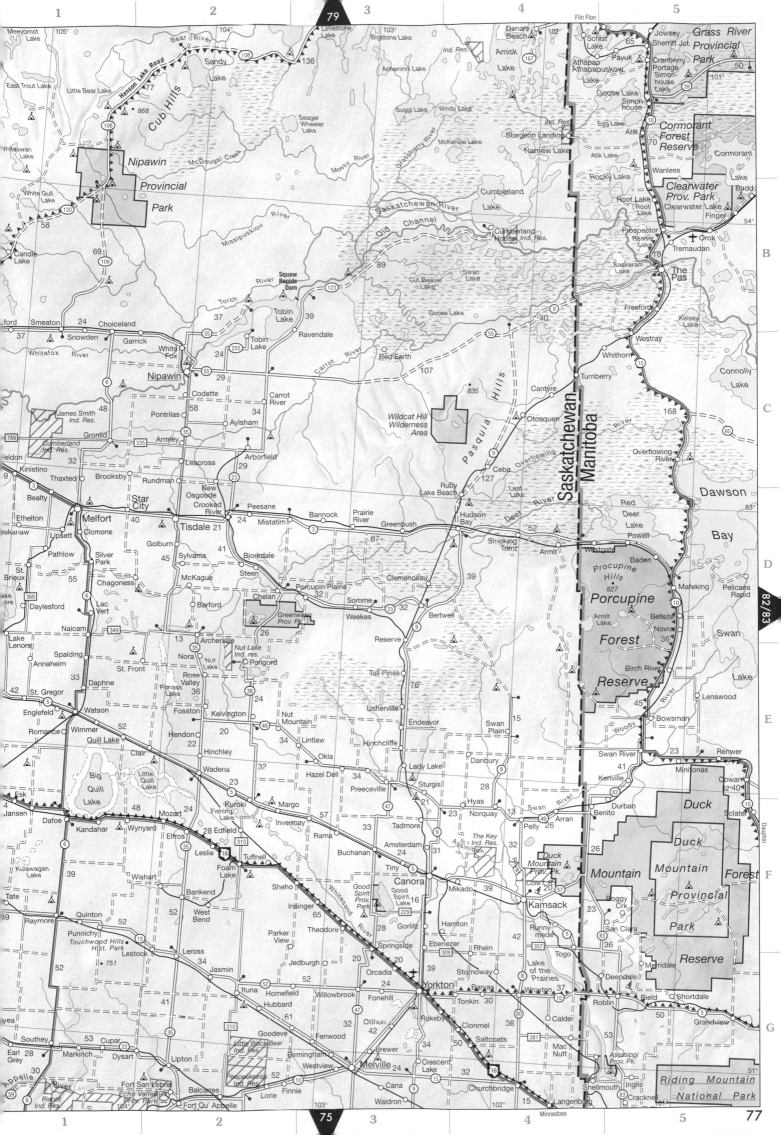

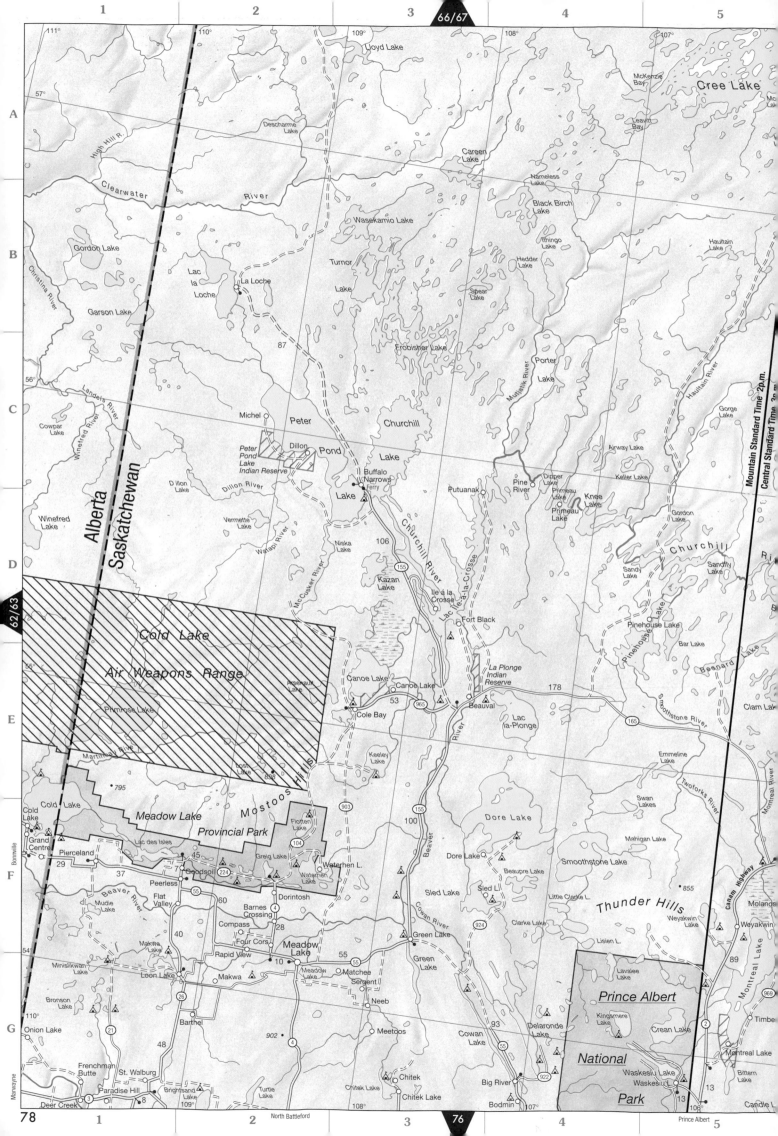

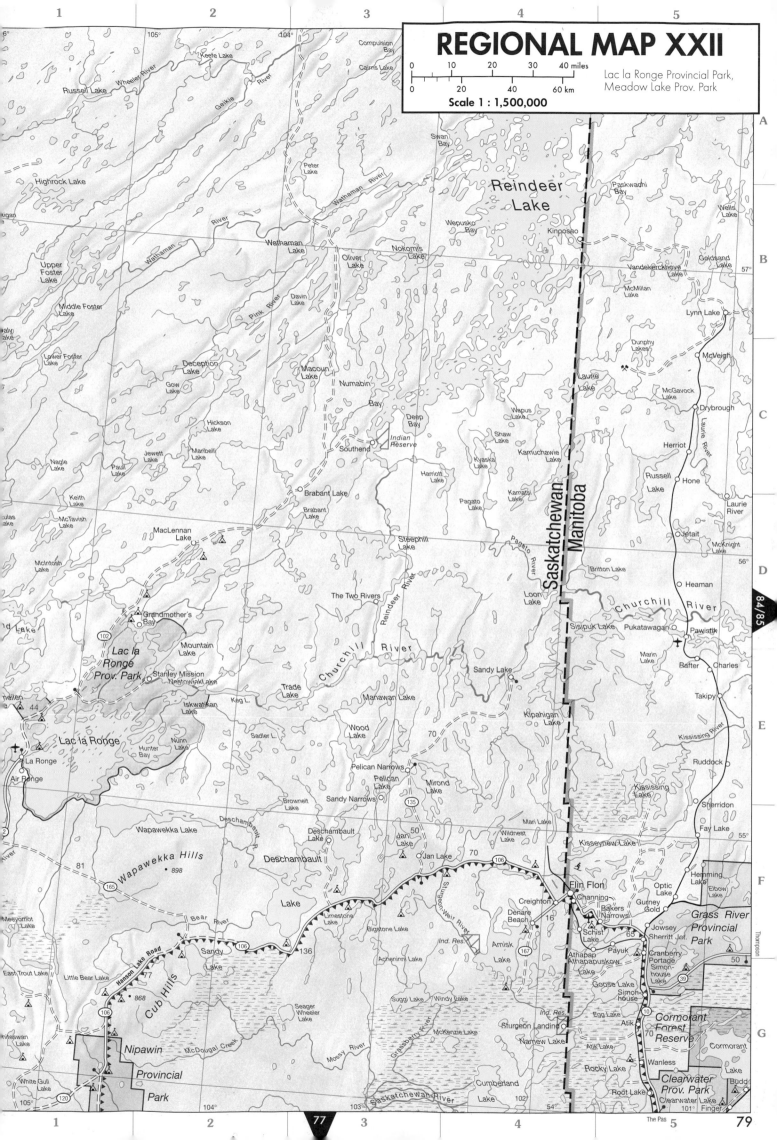

REGIONAL MAP XXII

Lac la Ronge Provincial Park,
Meadow Lake Prov. Park

Scale 1 : 1,500,000

| 0 | 10 | 20 | 30 | 40 miles |

| 0 | 20 | 40 | 60 km |

Russell Lake
Highrock Lake
Upper Foster Lake
Middle Foster Lake
Lower Foster Lake
Nagle Lake
Keith Lake
McTavish Lake
McIntosh Lake

Keefe Lake
Wheeler River
Geikie River
Compulsion Bay
Cairns Lake
Wathaman River
Peter Lake
Swan Bay
Reindeer Lake
Wepusko Bay

Wathaman Lake
Wetaman Lake
Oliver Lake
Nokomis Lake
Kinposao
Paskwachi Bay
Wells Lake

Pink River
Davin Lake
Vandekerckhove Lake
Goldsand Lake
57°
McMillan Lake

Deception Lake
Gow Lake
Macoun Lake
Numabin Bay
Deep Bay
Wapus Lake
Shaw Lake
Lynn Lake
Dunphy Lakes
McVeigh
Laurie Lake
McGavock Lake
Drybrough
Laurie River

Hickson Lake
Jewett Lake
Maribelli Lake
Southend
Indian Reserve
Kyaska Lake
Kamuchawie Lake
Herriot
Harriott Lake
Russell Lake
Hone
Paull Lake
Brabant Lake
Pagato Lake
Kamatsi Lake
Jetait
Laurie River
Brabant Lake
Steephill Lake
McKnight Lake

MacLennan Lake
The Two Rivers
Reindeer River
Loon Lake
Pagato River
Britton Lake
56°
Heaman

Grandmother's Bay
Mountain Lake
Churchill River
Sisipuk Lake
Pukatawagan
Pawistik
Marin Lake
Rafter
Charles

Lac la Ronge Prov. Park
Stanley Mission
Negtowiaki lake
Iskwatikan Lake
Keg L.
Trade Lake
Manawan Lake
Sandy Lake
Takipy

Lac la Ronge
Hunter Bay
Nunn Lake
Sadler L.
Wood Lake
70
Kipahigan Lake
Kississing River

La Ronge
Air Ronge
Pelican Narrows
Mirond Lake
Ruddock

Brownelt Lake
Pelican Lake
Sandy Narrows
Kississing Lake

Wapawekka Lake
Deschambault R.
Deschambault Lake
Mari Lake
Sherridon

Wapawekka Hills
898
Jan Lake
Wildnest Lake
Kisseynew Lake
55°
Fay Lake

81
165
Deschambault
Jan Lake
70
106
Hemming Lake
Elbow Lake
Optic Lake

Bear River
Sturgeon-Weir River
Flin Flon
Grass River Provincial Park

Meeyomot Lake
Limestone Lake
Creighton
Channing
Bakers Narrows
Gurney Gold
Thompson

Little Bear Lake
77
Hanson Lake Road
Sandy Lake
106
136
Bigstone Lake
Denare Beach
16
Schist Lake
Payuk
Jowsey
Sherritt Jct.
65
50
39

East Trout Lake
868
Cub Hills
Achenini Lake
Amisk Lake
167
Athapap
Athapapuskow Lake
Cranberry Portage
Simon-house Simon-house Lake
Goose Lake

Seager Wheeler Lake
Suggi Lake
Windy Lake
Ind. Res.
Egg Lake
Atik
70
Cormorant Forest Reserve

Nipawin Provincial Park
McDougal Creek
Mossy River
Grassberry River
McKenzie Lake
Sturgeon Landing
Namew Lake
Atik Lake
Rocky Lake
Wanless
Clearwater Prov. Park
Cormorant

White Gull Lake
120
Whiteswan Lake
105°
104°
103°
Saskatchewan River
Cumberland Lake
102°
54°
Root Lake
Clearwater Lake
Finger
101°
Budd Lake

Saskatchewan
Manitoba

84/85

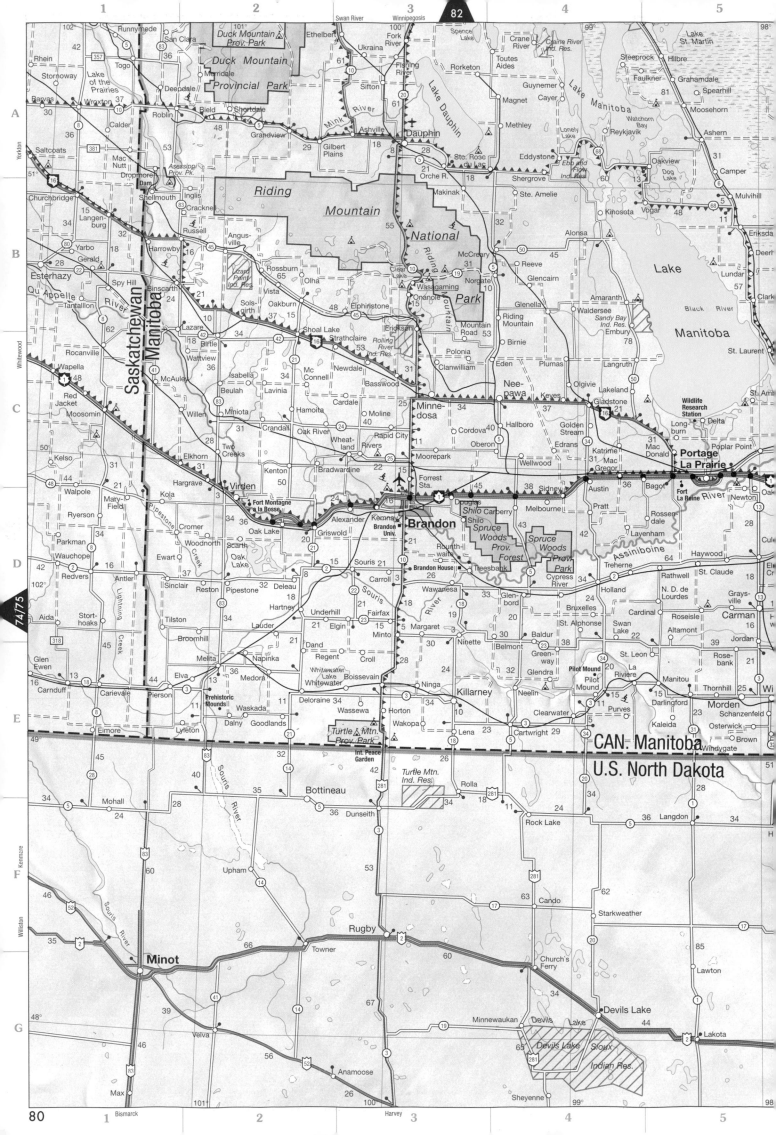

REGIONAL MAP XXIII

Winnipeg – Riding Mountain N.P.

Scale 1 : 1,500,000

WINNIPEG — Pop.: 652,000

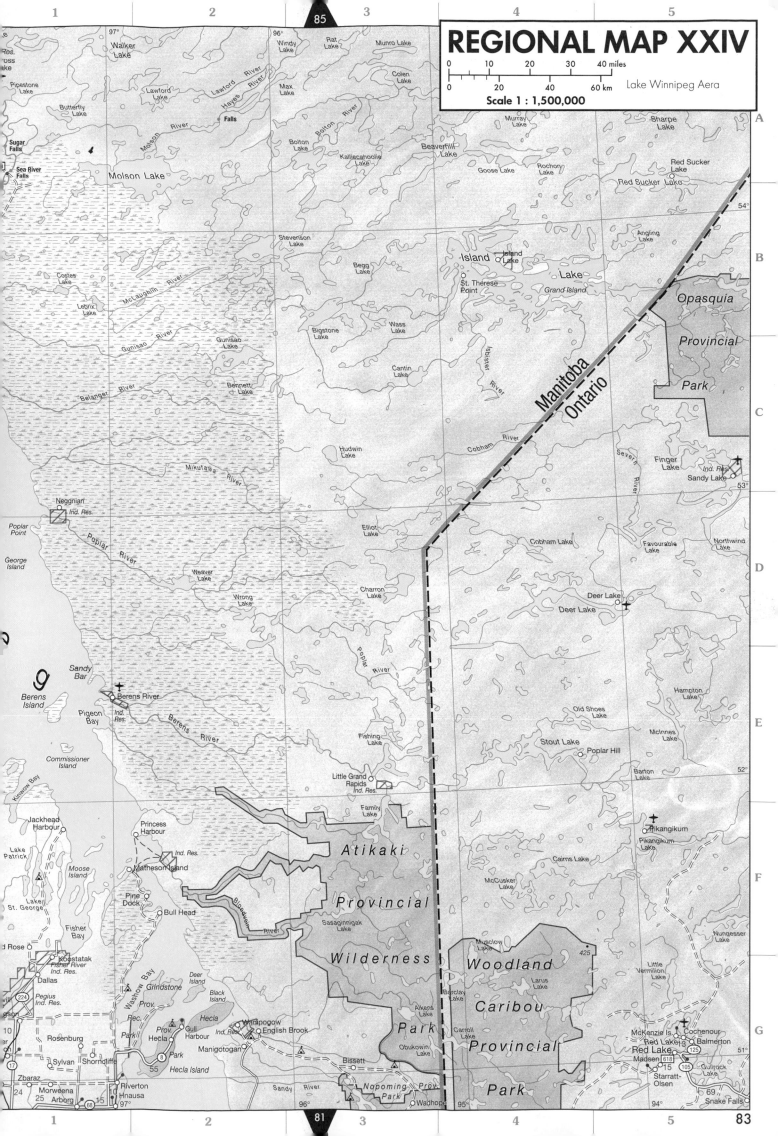

Scale 1 : 1,500,000

Lake Winnipeg Aera

0 10 20 30 40 miles
0 20 40 60 km

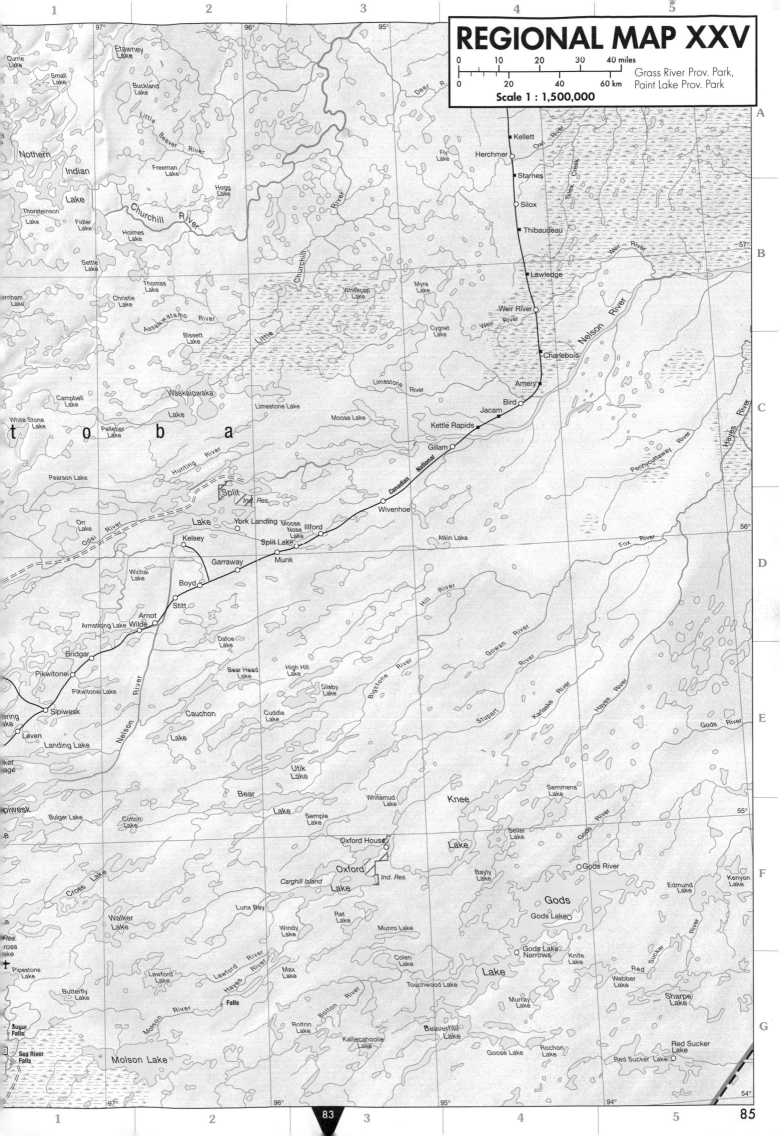

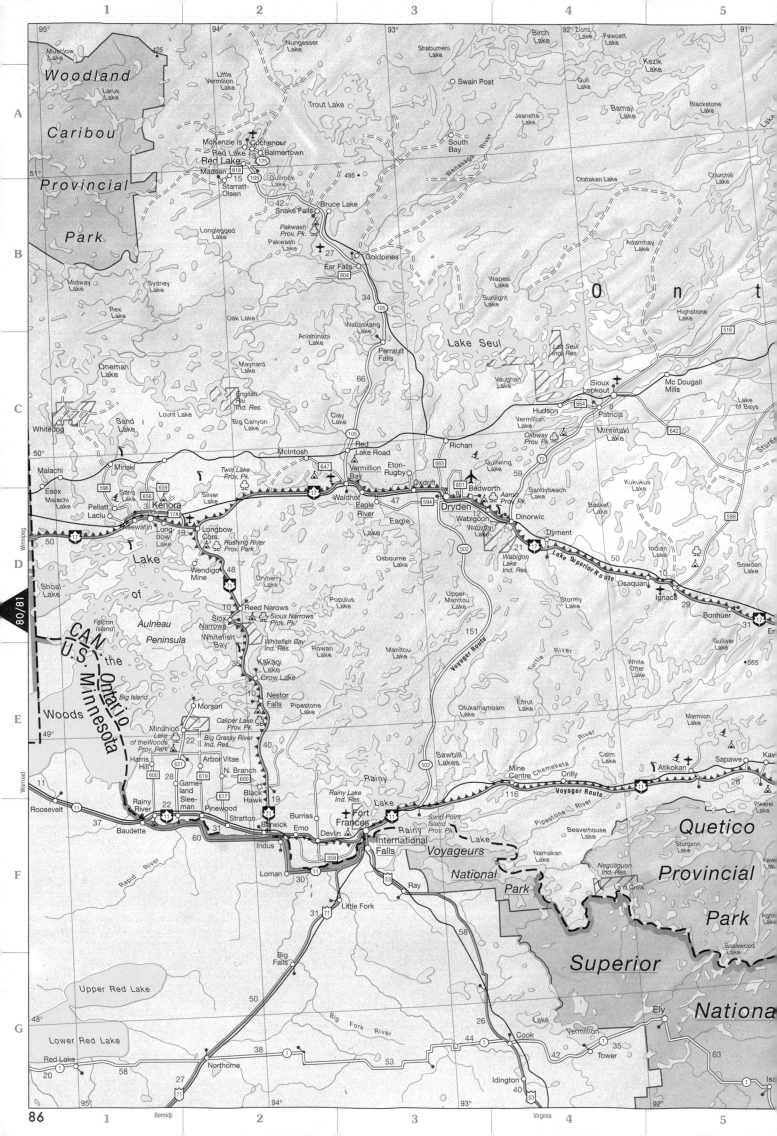

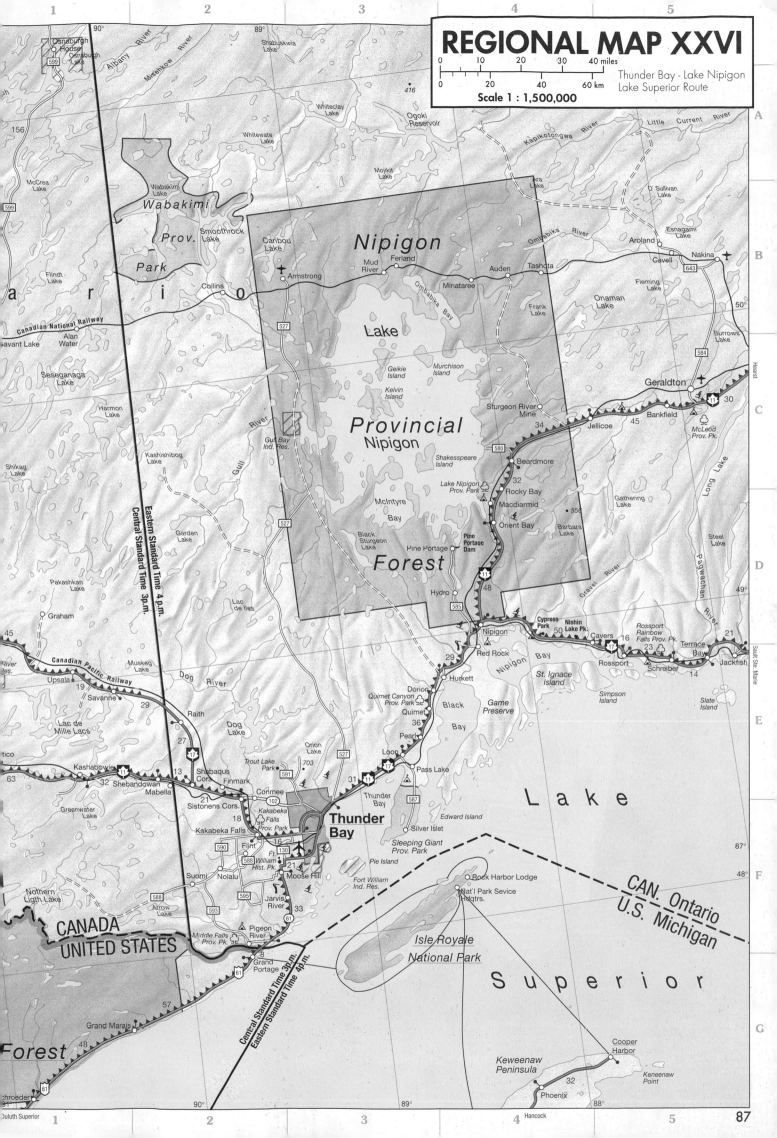

CURRENCY

Canada

The following bank notes and coins are currently in use:
Notes: Dollars 2, 5, 10, 20, 50, 100
Coins: Cents 1 (penny), 5 (nickel), 10 (dime), 25´ (quarter), 100 (loonie)

REISE-INFORMATIONEN

Vorbereitungen

Reisen im Land

Auf den Straßen Kanadas

Wissenswertes

VORBEREITUNGEN

Seit die ehemaligen Sowjetrepubliken Anfang der 90er Jahre selbständig wurden, kann Kanada für sich in Anspruch nehmen, die „größte Nation der Welt" zu sein. Der „wahre Norden, stark und frei" *(true north strong and free)*, wie es in seiner Nationalhymne genannt wird, umfaßt eine Fläche von 9.976.185 qkm. Es erstreckt sich vom Atlantik im Osten bis zum Pazifik im Westen – eine Entfernung von mehr als 7.000 km. Ellesmere Island, der nördlichste Punkt, liegt ein gutes Stück innerhalb des nördlichen Polarkreises; Kanadas südliche Grenze – und gleichzeitig die Grenze zu dem einzigen Nachbarn, den USA – verläuft entlang dem 49. Breitengrad.

Es ist also nicht verwunderlich, daß das Land große Unterschiede in seiner Topographie aufweist. Vom gebirgigen Hochland zu üppigen Wäldern, von ausgedehnten Prärien zu den atemberaubenden Gipfeln der Rockies – Kanada ist berühmt für seine landschaftliche Vielfalt. Sportler, Abenteurer und „Zivilisationsmüde" kommen aus allen Teilen der Welt, um hier die freie Natur in ihrer ursprünglichsten Form zu erleben. Vier Jahreszeiten und regionale Unterschiede bezüglich Temperaturen und Niederschlägen sorgen dafür, daß man irgendwo, irgendwann während des Jahres das richtige Klima für nahezu jede Aktivität im Freien findet.

Weniger bekannt, aber ebenso faszinierend, ist Kanadas kulturelle Vielfalt. Abgesehen von den Engländern und Franzosen, die für die im 17. Jh. einsetzende Immigration bahnbrechend waren, haben sich im Laufe seiner Geschichte zahlreiche Deutsche, Italiener, Osteuropäer, Skandinavier, Chinesen und Ostinder in Kanada niedergelassen. Der Anteil der einheimischen Völker (Indianer, Inuit und Métis) an der Gesamtbevölkerung von 28 Mio. beträgt ungefähr 4 %. Dieses einzigartige ethnische Erbe spiegelt sich wider in Kanadas Kunst, Musik, Literatur, in örtlichen Traditionen und natürlich in der Landesküche.

Dank des ausgedehnten Luft- und Schienennetzes ist es bei sorgfältiger Planung durchaus möglich, während eines Besuches sowohl Ost- als auch Westkanada kennenzulernen. Wer allerdings die kanadische Atmosphäre einfangen möchte, der sollte die großen Entfernungen berücksichtigen und sich genügend Zeit nehmen. Am besten konzentrieren Sie sich auf die Provinz oder Region, die Ihnen am meisten zusagt, um die atemberaubende Landschaft und die legendäre Gastfreundschaft in Ruhe zu genießen.

VISUM

Für die Einreise nach Kanada benötigen Staatsbürger der Bundesrepublik Deutschland, Österreichs und der Schweiz für einen Aufenthalt bis zu drei Monaten kein Visum. Sie müssen über einen Paß, der bis zur Beendigung der Rückreise gültig ist, über ausreichende Geldmittel für den Aufenthalt im Lande und einen Nachweis, daß sie beabsichtigen, Kanada wieder zu verlassen (z. B. Rückflugticket oder Weiterflugticket und alle nötigen Papiere für die Weiterreise), verfügen.

Erwachsene, die mit Kindern unter 18 Jahren reisen, sollten ihre Eltern- bzw. Vormundschaft nachweisen können. Alleinreisende Jugendliche unter 18 Jahren müssen im Besitz eines notariell beglaubigten Briefes der Eltern oder des Vormunds sein, worin ihnen die Erlaubnis, nach Kanada zu reisen, erteilt wird, versehen mit der Adresse oder Telefonnummer, unter der der Unterzeichnende erreicht werden kann.

Kinder bis zu 16 Jahren können entweder im Paß der Eltern eingetragen sein oder einen Kinderausweis mit sich führen. Ab dem 16. Lebensjahr wird ein Reisepaß benötigt. Deutsche, Österreicher und Schweizer, die in Kanada studieren oder arbeiten möchten, müssen sich in ihrem Heimatland beim kanadischen Konsulat um eine entsprechende Erlaubnis bemühen. Nach der Einreise in Kanada wird kein Visum gewährt.

Ausflüge in die USA

Deutsche, österreichische und Schweizer Staatsangehörige, die von Kanada aus direkt in die USA einreisen möchten, benötigen lediglich einen gültigen Reisepaß und den Nachweis (Rück-/Weiterflugticket), daß die Dauer ihres Aufenthalts – inklusive der Zeit, die sie in Kanada verbringen – nicht mehr als 90 Tage beträgt.

GESUNDHEIT

Impfungen

Zur Zeit sind keine Impfungen vorgeschrieben. Reisende, die aus einem Gelbfieber- oder Choleragebiet kommen, müssen einen Immunisierungsnachweis erbringen. Die kanadischen Einwanderungsbehörden behalten sich das Recht vor, den Besucher einer medizinischen Prüfung zu unterziehen, wenn sie es für nötig erachten.

GEFAHREN

Das Reisen in Kanada unterscheidet sich nicht sehr vom Reisen in Mitteleuropa. Da Ferien in Kanada meistens mit Aktivitäten im Freien verbunden sind, können sich die folgenden Hinweise allerdings als hilfreich erweisen:

Camper, Wanderer und diejenigen, die durch spärlich besiedelte Gebiete fahren, sollten auf jeden Fall eine Erste-Hilfe-Ausrüstung mitnehmen. Außer einem Desinfektionsspray für kleinere Verletzungen sollte sie Verbandszeug, Schere, Pinzette, ein Schmerzmittel, Insektenschutz, eine beruhigende Lotion für Insektenstiche und ein Sonnenschutzmittel enthalten.

Eine gute Sonnenbrille benötigen Wanderer, Skifahrer und Autofahrer. Jeder, der im Hochsommer oder im Winter längere Zeit im Freien verbringt, sollte einen Hut tragen. Bei sehr kaltem Wetter sollte man als weitere Vorsichtsmaßnahmen mehrere Kleidungsstücke übereinander tragen, nasse Kleidung so bald wie möglich wechseln und einen Vorrat an leichten Snacks und nichtalkoholischen Getränken mitnehmen.

Moskitos können nach Sonnenuntergang in den Sommermonaten ein echtes Problem darstellen. Mit einem guten Insektenschutz, langärmeligen Hemden und langen Hosen hält man sie sich am besten vom Leibe. Auch der Rauch eines Lagerfeuers tut hier gute Dienste. Bevor man eine Nacht im oder in der Nähe des Waldes verbringt, sollte man die Fliegennetze des Zeltes oder Campmobils auf eventuelle Löcher untersuchen. Da man Insektenstiche nicht völlig vermeiden kann, ist es wichtig, sich mit einem Mittel, das den Juckreiz nimmt, zu behandeln.

Kanadas Bären sind im allgemeinen scheu und stellen keine Gefährdung für den Touristen dar. Dennoch sollte man nicht versuchen, sich ihnen zu nähern oder sie zu füttern. Lebensmittel dürfen auf keinen Fall in Zelten, in denen Menschen schlafen, aufbewahrt werden, und Frauen sollten daran denken, daß einige Parfums anscheinend die Aufmerksamkeit der Bären auf sich ziehen.

VERSICHERUNG

Es wird empfohlen, vor der Abreise ein Versicherungspaket abzuschließen, das die gesamte Dauer Ihres Aufenthaltes in Kanada abdeckt.

ZOLLVORSCHRIFTEN

Zollfreie Artikel
An Bord Ihres Schiffes oder Flugzeugs nach Kanada werden Zollerklärungs-formulare (E-311) verteilt, die vor der Ankunft ausgefüllt werden müssen.

Folgende Waren dürfen zollfrei eingeführt werden:

- persönliche Gegenstände wie Kleidung, Schmuck und Toilettenartikel;

- Sportausrüstungen wie Zelte, Angelruten, Jagdgewehre und bis zu 200 Patronen pro Person;

- Kameras, Filme, Musikinstrumente, Laptops etc. für den persönlichen Gebrauch;

- bis zu 50 Zigarren, 200 Zigaretten und 800 g Pfeifentabak (pro Person ab 16 Jahren);

- 1,1 l Wein oder Spirituosen oder 8,5 l Bier (pro Person ab 18 Jahren in Alberta, Manitoba und Québec; ab 19 Jahren in allen anderen Territories und Provinzen);

- eine begrenzte Menge Lebensmittel für den persönlichen Verzehr (da die Voraussetzungen für die Einfuhr von Lebensmitteln sehr komplex sind, ist es allerdings nicht empfehlenswert;

- Geschenke im Wert von max. Can$ 40 pro Empfänger.

Wertvolle Gegenstände wie Videokameras und Computer müssen bei der Einreise beim Zoll deklariert werden und beim Verlassen des Landes wieder vorgezeigt werden. Gelegentlich wird eine Kaution verlangt, die bei der Ausreise wieder zurückerstattet wird. Es empfiehlt sich, eine Liste wertvoller Gegenstände anzufertigen, mit Fotokopien der Kaufbelege.

Zollbeschränkungen
Die Einfuhr einiger Produkte ist entweder verboten oder wird strengstens kontrolliert:

- frisches Gemüse und Obst;

- Pflanzen, incl. Knollen und Samen (nähere Informationen erhalten Sie von: The Permit Office, Plant Health Division, Agriculture Canada, Ottawa, Ontario, Canada K1A 0C6);

- Fleisch, Fisch und Geflügel (nähere Informationen hierzu bei: Animal Product and By-Product Imports, Agriculture Canada/Animal Health Division, 2255 Carling Avenue, Ottawa, Ontario, Canada K1A 0Y9);

- Schußwaffen zur Selbstverteidigung;

- Narkotika, incl. Marihuana und Haschisch.

Zusätzlich zu den zollfreien Waren dürfen bis zu 9 l alkoholische Getränke gegen Zahlung des Einfuhrzolls und der Getränkesteuern sowie gegen Entrichtung einer Gebühr an die Provinzregierung des Einreiseortes mitgeführt werden.

Haustiere
Unter der Voraussetzung, daß sie gegen Tollwut geimpft sind, können mehr als 3 Monate alte Katzen und Hunde mit nach Kanada gebracht werden. Die Impfung darf höchstens 1 Jahr und muß mindestens 4 Wochen vor der Einreise erfolgt sein. Andernfalls wird das Tier für mindestens einen Monat in Quarantäne genommen.

Andere Tiere sind nur erlaubt, wenn sowohl eine Einfuhrgenehmigung als auch ein tierärztliches Gesundheitsattest vorgelegt werden können (weitere Informationen erteilt: The Chief of Imports, Animal Health Division, Agriculture Canada, Ottawa, Ontario, Canada K1A 0Y9).

Kraftfahrzeuge
Besucher dürfen ein Privatfahrzeug – Auto, Wohnmobil oder Motorrad – einführen, wenn es auf sie zugelassen ist, oder eine Nutzungsbescheinigung des Eigentümers vorliegt.

Bei der Einreise wird eine Zollerlaubnis erteilt und – falls der verantwortliche Zollbeamte es für notwendig erachtet – eine Kaution von Can$ 100 bis Can$ 500 erhoben. Einzelheiten über die Rückzahlung der Kaution sollten bei der Bezahlung geklärt werden.

VORBEREITUNGEN

Um durch die Kontrolle der Plant Health Division zu gelangen, ist es unbedingt erforderlich, daß das Fahrzeug in seinem Ursprungsland gründlich gereinigt wird. Die Gesellschaft, die das Fahrzeug verschifft, sollte in der Lage sein, eine Dampf- oder Hochdruckreinigung zu empfehlen, die bestätigen kann, das die Forderung nach umfassender Reinigung erfüllt wurde.

In allen Provinzen Kanadas ist eine Haftpflichtversicherung obligatorisch; sie sollte sofort nach der Ankunft abgeschlossen werden. Wer eine schriftliche Bestätigung über unfallfreies Fahren während der letzten Jahre vorlegen kann, erhält gewöhnlich einen günstigeren Tarif. Informationen und Tips erhalten Sie bei:

The Insurance Bureau of Canada
181 University Avenue
Toronto, Canada M5H 3M7
Tel. (416) 362-2031

Der nationale Führerschein gilt in Kanada bis zu 3 Monaten; ein internationaler Führerschein in mehreren Sprachen und mit einem Jahr Gültigkeit ist dennoch ratsam.

Die Canadian Automobile Association bietet Mitgliedern angegliederter Automobilclubs, die eine gültige Mitgliedskarte vorweisen, den vollen Mitgliedsservice inklusive Reiseinformationen, Karten, Unterkunftsreservierungen und Hilfe in Notfällen. Weitere Informationen erhalten Sie bei:

Canadian Automobile Association
1775 Courtwood Crescent
Ottawa, Ontario
Canada K2C 3J2
Tel. (613) 226-7631

DEVISEN

Sowohl Ein- als auch Ausfuhr von Landeswährung sowie von Devisen sind unbeschränkt. Die Ausfuhr von Silbermünzen im Wert von mehr als 5 kanadischen Dollar pro Person ist verboten.

Da es schwierig ist, außerhalb der großen Städte ausländische Währungen einzutauschen (ausgenommen amerikanische Dollar), sollte kanadisches Geld bereits vor der Abreise gekauft werden. Die Mitnahme von Travellerschecks in kleinen Stückelungen ist wegen des garantierten Ersatzes im Verlust- oder Diebstahlsfall empfehlenswert.

Eurocheques können in Kanada nicht eingelöst werden. Die bekannten Kreditkarten (Eurocard/Mastercard, Visa, American Express) werden in Kanada fast überall akzeptiert. Die Mitnahme einer dieser Kreditkarten ist auf jeden Fall ratsam, da es ansonsten schwierig werden kann, ein Auto zu mieten oder ein Hotelzimmer zu reservieren.

ANREISE

Mit dem Flugzeug
Die beiden kanadischen Fluggesellschaften Canadian Airlines International und Air Canada fliegen von verschiedenen europäischen Städten aus die wichtigsten Flughäfen in Kanada an.

Weitere Informationen erhalten Sie in Ihrem Reisebüro oder bei:

Air Canada
Friedensstr. 7
60311 Frankfurt
Tel. (069) 27115111

Canadian Airlines International
Eifelstr. 14a
60529 Frankfurt
Tel. (069) 66583089

Canadian Airlines bietet von Frankfurt aus – in Zusammenarbeit mit Lufthansa

– täglich Flüge nach Vancouver und fliegt auch Calgary und Montreal an. In Zusammenarbeit mit Lufthansa wird ebenfalls Toronto täglich direkt angeflogen. Tägliche Nonstopflüge von Frankfurt aus werden zudem von Air Canada angeboten.

Auch von Berlin, Düsseldorf, Zürich und Wien aus fliegt Air Canada nach Toronto.

Außerdem gibt es einen Swissair Nonstop-Flug von Zürich nach Montreal (6mal wöchentlich) und zahlreiche Verbindungen über Amsterdam, London und die wichtigsten amerikanischen Flughäfen. Diverse private Charter-Gesellschaften (Canada 3000, air transat) offerieren während der Sommermonate Direktflüge.

Dank des immer noch andauernden „Preiskrieges" bei Transatlantikflügen sind die Flugpreise für Kanadareisen in den letzten Jahren drastisch gesunken. Dies kömmt zwar dem Touristen zugute, bedeutet aber auch, daß die Flüge in der Hochsaison (Mitte Juni bis Mitte August und über Weihnachten) frühzeitig ausgebucht sind. Wer in der Hoffnung auf weitere Preisnachlässe die Buchung auf die letzte Minute hinausschiebt, wird wahrscheinlich enttäuscht werden.

Auch hier zahlt es sich aus, sorgfältig zu planen und Preisvergleiche anzustellen. Eine Fluggesellschaft bietet dem Einzelreisenden im allgemeinen nur den offiziellen Tarif, ein Rciseveranstalter hingegen, der mit dieser Gesellschaft zusammenarbeitet, verkauft den gleichen Flug oft erheblich billiger. Da das gleiche auch für Hotels und Mietwagenfirmen zutrifft, kann der Preis für ein und dasselbe Reisepaket stark variieren, je nachdem welche Agentur beteiligt ist. Es ist aber fast immer günstiger, ein Gesamtpaket zu kaufen, anstatt einzeln zu buchen. Dazu kommt, daß man bei einer Buchung über einen Reiseveranstalter von den hervorragenden Verbraucherschutzgesetzen Europas profitiert. Es lohnt wirklich nur in äußerst seltenen Fällen die Mühe, einen kanadischen Anbieter direkt zu kontaktieren. Jugendliche und Studenten bis 26 Jahre können Sondertarife in Anspruch nehmen; Kinder bezahlen normalerweise 50-67% des Erwachsenenpreises. Ein Kleinkind pro Erwachsenen reist kostenlos, hat aber keinen Anspruch auf einen Sitzplatz. Ein Wochenendaufschlag kann freitags und samstags bei Flügen in Richtung Westen und samstags und sonntags in Richtung Osten erhoben werden.

In den letzten Jahren war ein Zuwachs bei der Nachfrage nach Luxusreisen zu verzeichnen. Als Antwort darauf haben viele Fluggesellschaften einen Business-Class-Aufschlag für Urlaubsreisende eingeführt. Da der größere Komfort Ihre Freude an den ersten 48 Stunden Ihrer Reise sicher erhöhen wird, lohnt sich die Nachfrage.

Eine Reiserücktrittsversicherung ist nicht teuer und auf jeden Fall zu empfehlen.

Mit dem Schiff
Kanadas wichtigster Hafen im Osten, Montréal, wird regelmäßig von Kreuzfahrtschiffen und Frachtern aus der ganzen Welt angelaufen. Betuchte Reisende, die sich eine zweiwöchige Reise von Europa nach Kanada leisten können, haben mehrere Wahlmöglichkeiten. Jede gute Reiseagentur verfügt über mindestens einen Spezialkatalog für Kreuzfahrten.

Schon etwas komplizierter wird es, wenn Sie einen Platz auf einem Frachtschiff suchen. Fragen Sie bei den Schiffsgesellschaften nach einer Agentur, die solche Überfahrten arrangiert.

Reisezeit
Die meisten Besucher kommen zwischen Juni und September nach Kanada, wenn die Bergpässe schneefrei sind und man draußen im Zelt oder im Wohnmobil übernachten kann. Das ist sicher die beste Zeit, um die Nationalparks zu bereisen; die Tiefsttemperaturen betragen dann zwischen 3° (in Whitehorse) und 14° (in Toronto).

April und Mai sind ebenfalls gute Reisemonate, vor allem an der Westküste, wo der Frühling früher Einzug hält. Im Oktober kann man in vielen Teilen Kanadas den berühmten *Indian summer* erleben. Diese drei Monate sind ideal, um verschiedene Sportarten auszuüben, z. B. Golf und Wandern.

Schlammige Hänge in Europa und garantierte Schneefälle in Kanada haben dem Land zu einer steigenden Anzahl von Wintertouristen verholfen. Die Skisaison dauert im allgemeinen von Ende Dezember bis Mitte April.

REISEGEPÄCK

Die Fluglinien neigen immer mehr dazu, das Gepäck auf internationalen Flügen nach dem „Stückprinzip" zu begrenzen: Jeder Passagier darf 2 Koffer, jeweils bis zu 32 kg, und ein Stück Handgepäck mitnehmen. Das Handgepäck muß unter den Vordersitz passen und darf deshalb nicht größer als 55 x 40 x 20 cm sein. Für sperrige Gegenstände, die nicht eingecheckt werden können, ist zwar ein begrenzter Stauraum vorhanden, man sollte sich aber besser nicht darauf verlassen, diesen auch in Anspruch nehmen zu können. Zusätzlich zum Gepäck können eine Kamera und eine Handtasche mitgenommen werden. Mütter mit Babys dürfen eine Windeltasche mit an Bord nehmen, obwohl viele Fluggesellschaften auf Nachfrage sowohl Windeln als auch Babykost zur Verfügung stellen.

Sie sollten eine komplette Liste der Dinge, die Sie einpacken (unabhängig von ihrem Wert), erstellen, für den Fall, daß das Gepäck verloren geht. Aus dem gleichen Grund ist es ratsam, das Notwendigste für eine Übernachtung im Handgepäck zu verstauen.

Für die meisten Gelegenheiten reicht in Kanada legere Kleidung aus. Hosen, Pullover, Baumwollhemden und -blusen sind praktische Kleidungsstücke, mit denen man sich fast überall sehen

lassen kann. Wenn Sie in einem vornehmen Restaurant essen, ein Kasino besuchen oder ähnliches unternehmen möchten, dann genügt für Frauen ein einfaches Kleid und für Männer ein Sportjackett mit Schlips. Wertvollen Schmuck sollte man generell nicht mit auf Reisen nehmen. Wichtig sind gutes Schuhwerk und ein leichter Mantel, denn auch im Hochsommer kann es kühl und feucht sein.

Eine Sonnenbrille ist das ganze Jahr über empfehlenswert, und wer Kontaktlinsen oder eine Brille trägt, sollte eine Kopie der Verschreibung mitnehmen. Wenn Sie regelmäßig Medikamente einnehmen müssen, dann denken Sie an die Originalverpackung, evtl. mit einer Kopie des Rezeptes. Das wird dem Apotheker eine Hilfe sein, falls Sie in Kanada etwas ähnliches benötigen. Die Mitnahme eines Französisch- und/oder Englisch-Taschenwörterbuchs wird sich vielleicht als nützlich erweisen.

Für Ihre Wertsachen (Paß, Ticket, Travellerschecks, Kreditkarte, Bargeld) empfiehlt sich ein Beutel, der versteckt in die Kleidung eingearbeitet ist.

Checkliste
Paß, Visum .... ☐
Tickets .... ☐
Flugbestätigung 48 Stunden vor Abflug .... ☐
Travellerschecks, kanadische Dollar ☐
Kreditkarte .... ☐
Führerschein, national und international .... ☐
Versicherungspaket (Reiserücktritt, Krankheit, Gepäck) .... ☐
Medikamente und Rezepte .... ☐
Verschreibungen für Brille und Kontaktlinsen .... ☐
Sonnenbrille .... ☐
Kamera und Filme .... ☐
Robustes Schuhwerk .... ☐
Leichter Mantel .... ☐
Hut .... ☐
Versteckter Beutel für Wertsachen ☐
Liste aller Wertgegenstände, Kopien der Kaufbelege .... ☐
Komplette Liste des Kofferinhalts ☐

REISEN IM LAND

Kanadas Infrastruktur ist hochentwickelt, und Besucher haben keinerlei Probleme, ihr Reiseziel zu erreichen. Überlandbusse und Züge ergänzen das ausgedehnte Inlandsflugnetz, und die Landstraßen laden geradezu ein, das Land per Auto zu entdecken. Im Gegensatz zu dem hektischen Betrieb auf europäischen Straßen, sind die kanadischen Highways nicht überfüllt und in gutem Zustand.

ANKUNFT

Gepäcktransport

Auch die großen Flughäfen Kanadas sind relativ klein und übersichtlich. Ausschilderungen sind in englischer Sprache (oder Englisch und Französisch), und ein Großteil des Personals der beiden nationalen Fluggesellschaften spricht deutsch. Reisende, die bei ihrer Ankunft auf Hilfe angewiesen sind (Gehbehinderte, Mütter mit kleinen Kindern etc.) sollten diese bereits bei der Buchung des Fluges mit anfordern.

Gepäckkarren sind überall verfügbar, allerdings benötigt man meistens Kleingeld, um sie zu leihen. Da es am Flughafen keine Geldwechselmöglichkeiten gibt, ist es ratsam, ungefähr zwei Dollars in Quarters (25-Centstücke) dabei zu haben. Da die Banken aber ungern Münzen in Fremdwährung vorrätig haben, braucht man Geduld und Glück.

Zoll

Die kanadischen Zollbeamten haben den Ruf, freundlicher als ihre Kollegen anderswo zu sein, wenn auch nicht unbedingt weniger bürokratisch. Es gibt zwei Standardfragen: *„What is the purpose of your visit?"* (Was ist der Zweck Ihres Besuches?) und *„How long do you intend to stay?"* (Wie lange werden Sie bleiben?). Die Abfertigungszeiten sind auf den großen kanadischen Flughäfen recht kurz, und man kann gewöhnlich damit rechnen, eine Stunde nach der Landung alle Formalitäten erledigt zu haben.

Erste Übernachtung

Die meisten kanadischen Flughäfen verfügen nicht über einen Informationsschalter für Touristen, der bei der Beschaffung einer Unterkunft behilflich sein könnte. Eine Anzeigetafel mit der Beschreibung einiger größerer Hotels und ein Freitelefon sind zwar meist vorhanden, doch das wird Ihnen wenig nützen, wenn Sie ausgerechnet während einer Ärztekonferenz ankommen! Wenn Sie nicht gerade ein extrem flexibler und erfahrener Reisender sind, ist es also ratsam, für die erste Nacht ein Hotel im voraus zu buchen.

Transfer vom Flughafen

Bequeme und günstige öffentliche Transportmittel vom Flughafen ins Stadtzentrum sind leider selten (Winnipeg bildet hier eine bemerkenswerte Ausnahme). Pendelbusse bieten für jedermann eine Alternative; wer es sich leisten kann wählt Taxi oder Limousine.

Im folgenden die ungefähren Entfernungen, Fahrzeiten und Transferkosten auf Kanadas wichtigsten Flughäfen:

Vancouver (15 km – 20 Min)
                Can$ 9 Bus   Can$ 30 Taxi
Calgary   (19 km – 30 Min)
                Can$ 8 Bus   Can$ 20 Taxi
Edmonton (28 km – 45 Min)
                Can$ 11 Bus Can$ 34 Taxi
Toronto   (28 km – 20 Min)
                Can$ 11 Bus Can$ 28 Taxi
Montréal   (21 km – 25 Min)
                Can$ 11 Bus Can$ 58 Taxi

Die meisten Busse fahren ungefähr jede halbe Stunde und halten an mehreren größeren Hotels der Stadt. Der Fahrer kann Ihnen Auskunft erteilen, wie weit es von der Haltestelle zu Ihrer Unterkunft ist: Fragen Sie, bevor Sie ein Tikket kaufen, denn Sie werden nicht viel sparen, wenn Sie nach der Busfahrt doch noch mit dem Taxi weiterfahren müssen.

MIT DEM FLUGZEUG

In einem Land mit den Ausmaßen Kanadas ist das Reisen per Flugzeug fast eine Selbstverständlichkeit. Viele Orte, in denen man nicht einmal einen Busbahnhof erwarten würde, verfügen über einen bescheidenen Flughafen, und ihre Bewohner benutzen genauso bereitwillig ein Flugzeug wie ihr eigenes Auto. Einige dieser Außenposten werden von den internationalen Fluggesellschaften und ihren Partnern im Pendelverkehr angeflogen; die meisten gehören zu dem Netz regionaler Fluggesellschaften mit einer sehr kleinen Anzahl an Flugzeugen und exotischen Namen wie „Aklak Air" oder „Antler Aviation".

Der durchschnittliche Tourist wird wahrscheinlich mit Canadian Airlines und Air Canada gut beraten sein. Vor allem auf Routen, die von beiden bedient werden und wo oft systematisch reduzierte Tickets zu bekommen sind, ist das Fliegen häufig eine attraktive Alternative zu den langen Stunden im Bus oder im Zug. Beide Gesellschaften bieten außerdem für Touristen Ermäßigungen auf normale Einfachtikkets, wenn sie diese bereits vor der Abreise zu Hause kaufen. Diese VUSA („Visit USA")-Tarife sind vor allem bei Reisenden beliebt, die nur ein oder zwei Flüge benötigen, da es kaum Einschränkungen gibt: Bei Rücktritt wird der Preis zu 100% zurückerstattet, man kann ohne Aufpreis umbuchen, und sie gelten die ganze Woche über.

Coupon Air Passes

Ausländische Besucher können auch die vorteilhaften „Air Passes" in Anspruch nehmen. Es gibt sie in verschiedenen Ausführungen, aber die grundlegenden Regeln sind immer die gleichen:

1. Sie müssen im Besitz eines internationalen Rückflugtickets sein;
2. pro Inlandsflug wird ein Coupon benötigt;
3. Sie müssen eine Mindestzahl an Coupons (3) kaufen;
4. die Anzahl der Coupons (8) ist begrenzt;

5. die Pässe gelten 60 Tage lang;
6. Sie müssen die komplette Route auswählen, bevor das Ticket ausgegeben wird, und der erste Flug muß vor der Abreise gebucht werden.

Mit solchen Sondertarifen können Sie viel Geld sparen. Der normale Economy-Tarif von Toronto nach Vancouver z. B. beträgt Can$ 793, der VUSA-Tarif Can$ 571. Einen 3-Coupons-Air-Pass (d. h. einmal Toronto-Vancouver plus 2 weitere Flüge) bekommt man schon für Can$ 570. Während der Hochsaison (1.7.-31.8.) kostet der 3-Coupons-Pass zusätzlich Can$ 45. Reisende, die keinen Transatlantik-Flug bei Air Canada oder Canadian gebucht haben, zahlen ebenfalls mehr: drei Inlandsflüge mit Canadian kosten dann z.B. Can$ 600 – immer noch ein gutes Geschäft! Die Preise bei Air Canada sind ähnlich.

BUSREISEN

Busse stellen die kanadische Alternative zu Europas hochentwickeltem Eisenbahnnetz dar. Sie sind sauber, sicher und bieten relativ preisgünstige und gute Verbindungen zu fast jedem Ort. Vorausbuchungen sind selten erforderlich; Sie brauchen lediglich am Busbahnhof ein Ticket zu kaufen und einzusteigen. Wenn mehrere Buslinien in einem Gebiet fahren, dann teilen sie sich ein zentrales Busterminal. Die Adresse findet man in der Regel im Telefonbuch unter „Greyhound Bus Lines" im westlichen Kanada oder „Voyageur Colonial" im Osten.

Zusätzlich zu speziellen Studenten- und Ausflugtarifen bieten mehrere Linien attraktive „Passes" an. Greyhound bietet zwei „Passes" an, die gut für unbegrenztes Reisen in Kanada sind. Der „International Canada Coach Pass" gilt für alle Strecken zwischen British Columbia und Ontario mit Verbindungen nach Quebec und verschiedenen amerikanischen Grenzstädten. Preise : 7 Tage/Can$ 213, 15 Tage/Can$ 278, 30 Tage/Can$ 374, 60 Tage/Can$ 481.

Der „International Canada Coach Pass Plus" beinhaltet zusätzlich diverse Routen der Atlantik-Provinzen. Preise: 15 Tage/Can$ 348, 30 Tage/ Can$ 444, 60 Tage/Can$ 551.

Service und Ausstattung

Busreisen sind eine recht lockere Angelegenheit. Plätze können nicht im voraus reserviert werden, und Sie müssen Ihr Gepäck selbst zum Bus tragen bzw. es dort wieder in Empfang nehmen, was allein schon ein Anreiz ist, die Gepäckbegrenzung von 2 Gepäckstücken und 45 kg Gewicht einzuhalten.

Nur in den seltensten Fällen bietet man Mahlzeiten an: Im allgemeinen müssen Sie mit dem vorliebnehmen, was in den Cafeterias der Busbahnhöfe angeboten wird. Auf längeren Routen legt der Busfahrer etwa alle drei Stunden eine Pause ein.

Die meisten Busse sind mit Panoramafenstern, verstellbaren Sitzen mit Fußstützen, Klimaanlage und Toiletten ausgestattet. Obwohl es keine richtigen Schlafmöglichkeiten gibt, werden Sie sicherlich nicht der einzige sein, der sich zusammenrollt, die Augen schließt und eine Nachtfahrt ausnutzt, um Hotelkosten zu sparen. Wenn Sie dies beabsichtigen, sollten Sie versuchen, mit einem Express-Bus zu fahren. Leselampen gehören zur Standardeinrichtung, Rauchen ist nur auf den hinteren Sitzen gestattet, und der Konsum von alkoholischen Getränken wird nicht gerne gesehen.

Weitere Informationen erhalten Sie bei:

Greyhound Bus Lines
877 16th Street S.W.
Calgary
Canada T3C 3V8
Tel. (403) 260-0877

ZUGREISEN

Das transkontinentale Eisenbahnsystem, das für Kanadas Entwicklung so wesentlich war, spielt heute nur noch eine geringe Rolle im Personenverkehr. Beschneidungen der öffentlichen Mittel während der letzten Jahre haben zu relativ hohen Tarifen und eingeschränktem Service geführt. Das Reisen mit dem Zug sollte eher als eine eigene Erfahrung denn als Alternative zu Flug- oder Busreisen angesehen werden. Für denjenigen, der – was Zeit und Geld betrifft – genügend Spielraum hat, ist es bestimmt eine der angenehmsten und nostalgischsten Möglichkeiten, das Land kennenzulernen. Es gibt verschiedene Unterkünfte (inklusive einiger Räume mit Privattoiletten), der Speisewagen wird im allgemeinen durch einen Barwagen und ein Angebot an Snacks ergänzt, rundumverglaste Waggons bieten einige phantastische Aussichten, und die Atmosphäre ist einzigartig.

Die meisten Personenzüge werden von der staatlichen VIA Rail unterhalten. Ausländische Besucher können deren „Canrailpass" in Anspruch nehmen. Ein 12 Tage gültiger, innerhalb von 30 Tagen einzulösender Pass kostet in der „coach class" (Sitzplätze) Can$ 540 vom 1. Juni bis zum 15. Oktober, außerhalb dieser Zeit Can$ 369. Senioren (60 Jahre und älter) und Jugendliche (bis zu 24 Jahren) bezahlen etwas weniger: Can$ 486 in der Hochsaison, Can$ 332 vom 15. Januar bis zum 30. Mai und vom 16. Oktober bis zum 14. Dezember.

Ähnlich verhält es sich mit dem „Rail&Drive Pass", der zusätzlich einen Hertz-Mittelklasse-Mietwagen für 3 Tage beinhaltet. Er kostet während der Hochsaison Can$ 655 für Jugendliche und Senioren, Can$ 710 regulär. Die Nebensaisonpreise betragen Can$ 475 bzw. Can$ 510.

Der bekannteste VIA-Rail-Zug ist der „Canadian", der dreimal wöchentlich von Toronto nach Vancouver fährt.

Ein weiterer beliebter Zug, der „Rocky Mountaineer", fährt von Vancouver nach Calgary durch die Urlaubsorte Jasper und Banff. Die Fahrpreise beinhalten sowohl Mahlzeiten und nichtalkoholische Erfrischungen als auch eine Nacht in einem Hotel in Kamloops. Während der Hochsaison beträgt der einfache Tarif zur Zeit Can$ 675 (Doppelzimmer).

Berühmt ist auch die „Hudson Bay Railway" von Winnipeg, Manitoba nach Churchill, und wer einen Besuch im hohen Norden plant, sollte ihre Benutzung durchaus in Betracht ziehen.

Informationen sind erhältlich bei:

in Deutschland:
VIA RAIL
Canada Reise Dienst
Rathausplatz 2
22926 Ahrensburg
Tel. (04102) 8877-0

in der Schweiz:
VIA RAIL
Touring Club Suisse
Pierre-Fatio-Straße 9
1211 Geneva 3
Tel. (022) 7371212

in Österreich:
VIA RAIL
Gateway Holidays
Buchberggasse 34
3400 Klosterneuburg
Tel. (02243) 255700

in Kanada:
VIA RAIL
2 Place Ville Marie
Montreal, Quebec
Canada H3B 2C9
Tel. (514) 871-1331

MIT DEM AUTO

Umweltbewußte Europäer tendieren zu der Vorstellung, daß die Kanadier, wie ihre südlichen Nachbarn, ziemlich „autoversessen" sind. Tatsache ist, daß die öffentlichen Verkehrsmittel einfach nicht auf einem Entwicklungsstand angelangt sind, der den Durchschnittskanadier dazu veranlassen würde, sein wichtigstes Fortbewegungsmittel in

Frage zu stellen. Auf jeden Fall stellen die eigenen vier Räder die typisch kanadische Art dar, das Land zu bereisen, und Touristen, die sich für diese Methode des Reisens entscheiden, werden ihre Reize sehr bald entdecken. Gute Nebenstraßen, zahlreiche Tankstellen, Picknick- und Zeltplätze an idyllischen Stellen und viele „drive-in"-Unterkünfte erlauben es dem Urlauber, seine Ferien individuell zu gestalten und sein eigenes Tempo vorzulegen.

Obwohl es nicht schwierig ist, das eigene Auto mit ins Land zu bringen, handelt es sich um ein kostspieliges Unterfangen, das sich für die meisten Touristen nicht rentiert. So kostet z. B. der Transport eines Autos von Europa nach Halifax ungefähr Can$ 1500,-.

Ein Auto zu kaufen und vor der Abreise wieder zu verkaufen, kann ebenfalls nicht empfohlen werden, es sei denn, man beabsichtigt einen mindestens 6monatigen Aufenthalt in Nordamerika.

Mietwagen sind preisgünstiger, als man vielleicht erwartet, und in allen Varianten und Größen erhältlich. Im folgenden die häufigsten Kategorien und ungefähren Mietpreise während der Hochsaison:

Economy models mit 2 Türen und einer Heckklappe sind für längere Fahrten mit zwei Erwachsenen oder für Stadtfahrten mit vier Erwachsenen geeignet. Ihr einziger Nachteil besteht darin, daß sie nicht über einen getrennt abschließbaren Kofferraum verfügen. Die Preise von April bis Oktober liegen bei Can$ 350 pro Woche aufwärts.

Compacts haben 4 Türen und bieten auch bei längeren Fahrten für zwei Erwachsene und ein oder zwei Kinder genügend Fahrkomfort. Der Kofferraum ist zwar separat, aber ziemlich klein. Preise: ab Can$ 375 pro Woche.

Midsize cars haben 4 Türen und einen relativ großen Kofferraum. Zwei Erwachsene und zwei Kinder können

bequem in einem Auto dieser Klasse reisen. Preise: ab Can$ 400 pro Woche.

Fullsize cars verfügen ebenfalls über 4 Türen und geräumigen Kofferraum. Sie können gut vier Erwachsene oder auch eine fünfköpfige Familie befördern. Preise: ab Can$ 445 pro Woche.

Minivans haben vier Türen und eine Heckklappe und eignen sich für ausgedehnte Campingtouren. Es gibt sieben Sitzplätze, so daß auch eine große Familie genug Platz für ihre Sachen vorfindet. Preise: ab Can$ 570 pro Woche.

In den genannten Preisen sind Haftpflichtversicherung, Vollkasko und unbegrenzte Kilometerleistung inklusive. Benzin, Steuern und Gebühren, die erhoben werden, wenn die Rückgabe an einem anderen Ort erfolgt, gehen extra. Die Hinterlegung einer Kaution von Can$ 250 ist obligatorisch, und die Mietwagenfirma kann bis zu eineinhalbmal soviel in bar verlangen, wenn der Mieter nicht im Besitz einer gültigen Kreditkarte ist. Der Fahrer muß mindestens 21 Jahre alt sein. Manche Mietwagenfirmen erheben zusätzliche Gebühren bei einem zweiten Autofahrer (in etwa Can$ 10 pro Tag). Kindersitze sind für Kinder unter 3 Jahren vorgeschrieben: Sie werden kostenlos zur Verfügung gestellt, wenn man sie bei der Buchung bereits anfordert.

Die Mindestmietdauern variieren je nach Verleiher (oft 4/5 Tage). Autos, die in den USA angemietet wurden, dürfen nur dann mit nach Kanada gebracht werden, wenn dies im Mietvertrag ausdrücklich vereinbart ist. Die Fahrzeuge sind im allgemeinen mit Servolenkung und -bremsen, Automatikgetriebe, Klimaanlage und Radio ausgestattet.

Der weitaus einfachste – und gewöhnlich auch preisgünstigste – Weg, ein Auto zu mieten, ist die Vorausbuchung durch ein Reisebüro. In diesem Fall treffen Sie in Kanada ein mit einer Reservierungsbestätigung, einem Zahlungsbeleg und dem vollen Schutz Ihrer heimischen Verbrauchergesetze.

Urlauber, die an europäische Verkehrsverhältnisse gewöhnt sind, sollten sich von der Vorstellung, in Kanada zu fahren, nicht einschüchtern lassen. Dank einer strikt einzuhaltenden Geschwindigkeitsbeschränkung ist das haarsträubende Tempo, das auf Europas Autobahnen gefahren wird, hier unbekannt. Verkehrsregeln sind fast überall auf der Welt die gleichen und die kanadischen Schilder leicht verständlich. Ein RV wird erst übergeben, nachdem dem Fahrer alle Besonderheiten erklärt worden sind und er die Gelegenheit gehabt hat, Fragen zu stellen. Das gleiche gilt für Motorräder. Die Rush-hour in Kanadas Städten kann zugegebenermaßen nervtötend sein, obwohl die Bewohner es mit Gelassenheit nehmen. Besucher, die in einen Stau geraten sind, sollten die Klimaanlage einschalten, das Radio anstellen und von der offenen Straße träumen. Egal, wo sie sich in Kanada befinden, sie wird nicht weit weg sein.

ÖFFENTLICHE TRANSPORTMITTEL

Die öffentlichen Transportmittel der großen Städte befinden sich auf europäischem Niveau. Der wichtigste Unterschied, den der Reisende wahrnimmt, ist die Dominanz von Dieselbussen gegenüber U- und Straßenbahnen. Man sollte beachten, daß die Fahrgäste im allgemeinen beim Einsteigen bezahlen und die Fahrer kein Wechselgeld zurückgeben. Ein Einfachfahrschein, der für Fahrten in eine Richtung innerhalb eines vernünftigen Zeitrahmens (ca. 90 Min.) gilt, kostet zwischen Can$ 1,50 und Can$ 4, je nach Fahrunternehmen und zurückzulegender Entfernung. Umsteigen auf Anschlußlinien ist gewöhnlich erlaubt, man sollte aber bei Fahrtantritt nachfragen. Tageskarten für unbegrenztes Fahren kosten ca. Can$ 6 und sind in den meisten Städten, wie z. B. Vancouver, Calgary und Toronto, erhältlich. In einigen Orten, wie Winnipeg, verkehren kostenlose Pendelbusse im Stadtzentrum.

SIGHTSEEING

Zusätzlich zu der bekannten Gray Line bieten Dutzende von regionalen und örtlichen Busgesellschaften Sightseeing-Touren an. Alle Touristeninformationsbüros haben eine große Auswahl an Broschüren vorrätig; im allgemeinen werden hier auch Buchungen entgegengenommen. Das gleiche gilt für Reisebüros und größere Hotels. Städte-Touren und Tagesreisen müssen oft nicht im voraus gebucht werden: Warten Sie an den entsprechenden Haltestellen und bezahlen Sie beim Fahrer.

Als Sightseeing-Touren getarnte Verkaufsfahrten sind in Kanada nicht üblich. Nichtsdestoweniger ist es ratsam, sich vorher zu erkundigen, wofür man zahlt. Sind Mahlzeiten inklusive oder muß man extra zahlen? Wird die Tour in einer Sprache, die Sie verstehen, geführt, auch wenn nur wenige Leute nachfragen? Wie viele andere Sprachen wird der Reiseführer benutzen? Wenn es mehr als eine Sprache ist, dann erhalten Sie die Erklärung zu einer Sehenswürdigkeit vielleicht erst lange, nachdem diese schon wieder außer Sicht ist! Als Regel gilt, Touren, die eine große Ausgabe darstellen, über das Reisebüro zu Hause zu buchen. Das Reiseverkehrsrecht Ihres Heimatlandes wird dann angewendet, wenn etwas schiefgeht.

VERKEHRSREGELN

Der Canadian Automobile Association angegliederte Automobilclubs können ihre Mitglieder mit ausführlichen Informationen über das Autofahren in Kanada versorgen. Hierzu gehören: ADAC, AvD, DTC, DCC, DMYV und DSV in Deutschland; OAMTC und OCC in Österreich; TCS, CCS, SRB, ZKZ und ONST in der Schweiz.

Als ausländischer Fahrer sollten Sie sich folgende Tatsachen vergegenwärtigen:

– Das Tempolimit in Kanada muß genau eingehalten werden. Wenn nichts anderes ausgeschildert ist, gilt 100 km/h auf Highways (Fernstraßen), 80 km/h auf sonstigen Landstraßen und 50 km/h in Ortschaften.

– In der Umgebung von Schulen und Spielplätzen dürfen Sie nur 30 km/h fahren: Achten Sie auf Schilder, die Kinder zeigen, oder auf denen *School* zu lesen ist. Es ist sowohl verboten als auch gefährlich, einen Schulbus in beiden Richtungen zu überholen, während er anhält und blinkt. Die ein- oder aussteigenden Kinder erwarten, daß der Verkehr in beiden Richtungen zum Stehen kommt, so daß sie die Straße überqueren können.

– Radarwarngeräte sind in einigen Provinzen illegal und können auch wenn sie nicht in Gebrauch sind, konfisziert werden. Klären Sie dies mit der CAA ab, bevor Sie ein solches Gerät kaufen.

– Wenn ein Polizeiauto mit eingeschalteter Sirene oder Blaulicht hinter

Stop	Linksabbiegen verboten	Schienenkreuzung (Vorwarnung)
Enge Durchfahrt	Rechts vorbeifahren	Spielplatz
Schule	90 Grad Rechtskurve	Kurvenreiche Strecke
Vorfahrt achten	Einfache Rechtskurve	Scharfe Kurve
Einbahnstraße	100 km/h Haupt/ Landstraßen	80 km/h Landstraßen	50 km/h Ortschaften

Ihnen fährt, halten Sie – sobald es gefahrlos möglich ist – an und stellen den Motor ab. Bleiben Sie sitzen, öffnen Sie die Wagenfenster, und halten Sie Ihre Hände so, daß sie deutlich erkennbar sind.

- An Kreuzungen, in Kurven oder vor einer Bergkuppe herrscht, wie auch in Europa, Überholverbot.
- In den meisten Provinzen besteht Gurtanlegepflicht.
- Für Motorradfahrer und Beifahrer ist es erforderlich, daß sie einen Helm tragen. In einigen Provinzen müssen Motorräder auch tagsüber mit eingeschaltetem Licht fahren.
- Bahnübergänge haben häufig keine Schranken, sondern nur ein rundes Schild mit einem diagonalen Kreuz und der Aufschrift „RR". Stoppen Sie, und schauen Sie in beide Richtungen, bevor Sie weiterfahren.
- Die Verkehrsampeln schalten in folgender Reihenfolge: rot, gelb, grün, rot. Ein gelb blitzendes Licht bedeutet: vorsichtig weiterfahren; ein rot blitzendes Licht bedeutet: halt und dann vorsichtig weiterfahren.
- Außer in Québec dürfen Sie an einer roten Ampel rechts abbiegen, nachdem Sie zum Stehen gekommen sind und den Verkehr von links beachtet haben.
- An einigen Kreuzungen steht an jeder Ecke ein Stopschild, und wer zuerst kommt, fährt zuerst.
- Das Parken in städtischen Gebieten ist streng reglementiert; einfach auf dem Gehsteig zu parken, ist nicht erlaubt. Öffentliche Parkplätze sind billig, es kann aber schwierig sein, einen freien Platz an einer Parkuhr zu finden. Mit einer Geldbuße und kräftigen Abschleppgebühren müssen Sie rechnen, wenn Sie Ihr Auto in einer *No Parking*-Zone, zu nahe an einer Kreuzung, oder in der Zufahrt zu einem Feuerhydranten abstellen. Private Parkflächen gibt es reichlich, aber die Gebühren sind außerordentlich hoch. Normalerweise ist das beste, was Sie in großen Städten tun können, Ihr Fahrzeug in der Hotelgarage stehenzulassen und öffentliche Verkehrsmittel zu benutzen.

UNTERKUNFT

Hotels

Mit kanadischen Hotels verhält es sich ähnlich wie überall auf der Welt. Die meisten internationalen Hotelketten haben hier Niederlassungen, und es gibt jede Kategorie – von der 2stöckigen Präsidentensuite bis zum einfachen Zimmer ohne jeglichen Komfort. Touristenhotels in der mittleren Preisklasse sind häufig komfortabel möbliert.

Die Räume sind, gemessen an europäischem Standard, recht groß und verfügen oft über zwei Doppelbetten. Private Badezimmer sind die Norm; Handtücher, Seife und Shampoo werden gestellt. Abgesehen von wenigen Ausnahmen sind die Zimmer mit Telefon, Radio, Farbfernseher und Klimaanlage ausgestattet. Mini-Bars sind üblich, aber der Schlüssel dazu wird im allgemeinen nur gegen Vorlage einer gültigen Kreditkarte ausgehändigt. Zur Herstellung der in Nordamerika unentbehrlichen Eiswürfel gibt es im Flur eine *ice machine*. Wenn gewünscht, wird gewöhnlich kostenlos ein Kinderbett zur Verfügung gestellt.

In den meisten Hotels gibt es einen Coffee-shop und einen *beer parlour* (Bierstube) oder einen *beer lounge* (Biersalon). Bierstuben servieren üblicherweise nur Bier. Auf ihre charakteristische Atmosphäre weist schon die Tatsache hin, daß sie traditionell zwei Eingänge haben – einen für *Ladies and Escorts* (Damen mit Begleitung) und einen für *Gents* (Herren). Da jeder im gleichen Raum landet, bleibt der beabsichtigte Effekt dieser Trennung letztlich im dunkeln. Ein guter Biersalon besitzt mindestens einen Billardtisch und einige andere Spiele.

Biersalons sind dezent beleuchtet und servieren sowohl Bier als auch Cocktails. Es können auch Snacks, wie Erdnüsse und *nachos* (Tortilla-Chips), bestellt werden. Außerdem scheinen heutzutage eine oder mehrere Breitwand-TVs, die Musikvideos oder Sport-

sendungen übertragen, unerläßlich zu sein. Biersalons in Hotels können eine recht angenehme Angelegenheit sein, und während der *happy hour*, wenn zwei Drinks zum Preis von einem serviert werden, sind sie auch ziemlich günstig.

Zusätzlich zu Lounge und Coffee-shop haben die größeren Hotels normalerweise mindestens ein Restaurant und eine Disco. Swimmingpools, schon lange eine Selbstverständlichkeit, wurden durch Sauna und andere Fitneßeinrichtungen ergänzt. Zur weiteren üblichen Ausstattung gehören u.a. Souvenirshop, Schönheitssalon und Zeitungsstand, der auch noch „das Nötigste" wie Zahnpasta und Papiertaschentücher verkauft.

Reservierungen werden bis 18 Uhr aufrecht erhalten; wenn Sie später eintreffen möchten, unterrichten Sie unbedingt vorher Ihr Hotel.

Motels

Die Erfindung des Motels ist auf die legendäre Liebe der Nordamerikaner zu ihrem Auto zurückzuführen. Dank ihrer weiten Verbreitung können Sie – außer im hohen Norden – überall ins Blaue hineinfahren, ohne einen Gedanken an Ihre Übernachtung zu verschwenden.

Sogar die kleinste Stadt kann ein *motor hotel* vorweisen. Wenn es sich wegen zu geringem Durchgangsverkehr nicht rentiert, dann wird es entweder mit einem Wohnwagen-Park kombiniert, oder man betreibt eine Drive-in-Hamburger-Bude, oder öffnet den Swimmingpool im Sommer für die Allgemeinheit. Die Unterhaltskosten sind minimal: Die meisten Motels sind Familienbetriebe, die nur einen Rezeptionisten und eine Putzfrau (häufig die Besitzer selbst) benötigen.

Die Motels sind deutlich sichtbar am Straßenrand gelegen. Große Schilder ermöglichen Ihnen, auf einen Blick die angebotenen Einrichtungen zu erfassen (Kabel-TV, Coffee-shop, beheizter

Swimmingpool etc.) und festzustellen, ob noch Zimmer verfügbar sind (*vacancies* = „frei"; *no vacancies* = „besetzt"). Nach der Anmeldung an der Rezeption ist es üblicherweise möglich, direkt vor die Tür Ihrer Wohneinheit zu fahren und dort zu parken. Eingangshallen und gemeinsame Korridore sind selten. Jede Einheit verfügt über ein Badezimmer (inkl. Handtücher und Seife) und, normalerweise, eine Kochnische. Zur Standardausstattung gehören Telefon, Teppich und Klimaanlage.

Manchmal bezeichnet *motel* einfach ein preisgünstiges, familienorientiertes Hotel mit geringem Komfort. Zimmer- und Wäscheservice werden z. B. nicht angeboten, aber Möglichkeiten zum Kaffeekochen und Münzwaschmaschinen sind vielleicht vorhanden. Solche Häuser werden auch *motor inns* genannt.

Mehrere namhafte Motor-inn-Ketten sind an einem „Canada Hotel Pass"-Programm beteiligt, das von Guest International, Inc. vertrieben wird. Die Preise sind zivil (Can$ 60-90 pro Zimmer, inkl. Steuer), und für unbenutzte Gutscheine wird eventuell ein Teil des Geldes zurückerstattet.

Weitere Informationen erhalten Sie bei Guest International in Deutschland, Tel. (06172) 26023.

Gästehäuser

Guesthouse (Gästehaus) bezieht sich auf verschiedene Arten von Unterkünften für Reisende mit begrenztem Budget. Es kann sich hierbei um eine Privatwohnung handeln, in der ein oder mehrere Räume für die Nacht vermietet werden, ein kleines bescheidenes Hotel oder ein Häuschen, das wochen- oder monatsweise vermietet wird. Vor allem im Osten sind viele prächtige alte Häuser in *tourist homes* umgewandelt worden. Das sind die Gegenstücke zu den europäischen Pensionen: Bad und Toilette werden meist gemeinsam benutzt, die Zimmer sind einfach, und das Frühstück ist manchmal im Preis inbegriffen.

Bed and Breakfast

Während der letzten Jahre sind B&B (Bett und Frühstück)-Verbände im ganzen Land nur so aus dem Boden geschossen. Ihre Mitglieder vermieten Räume in ihrem eigenen Haus und servieren den Gästen ein komplettes Frühstück. Badezimmer können sowohl separat sein als auch gemeinsam benutzt werden. Die diversen Verbände überwachen den Standard und vermitteln künftigen Gästen die für sie passende Unterkunft. B&B-Unterkünfte sind im allgemeinen von den örtlichen Behörden anerkannt und genehmigt. Abgesehen vom Kostenfaktor sind sie für viele Reisende aufgrund ihrer Lage in Wohngebieten und ihrer ungezwungenen Atmosphäre attraktiv.

YMCA/YWCA

Die Young Men's/Women's Christian Association, eine internationale Service-Organisation, ist auf Studenten und junge Reisende ausgerichtet. *The Y* unterhält nicht nur eine Anzahl von Erholungs- und Freizeitmöglichkeiten (wie Swimmingpools und Turnhallen), sondern vermietet auch billige, zentral gelegene Unterkünfte in vielen Städten. In der Regel stehen neben dem Schlafsaal sowohl Einzel- als auch Doppelzimmer zur Verfügung; die Badezimmer werden gemeinsam benutzt. Eine preiswerte Cafeteria stellt häufig einen zusätzlichen Vorteil dar.

The Y verfügt über Niederlassungen in Victoria, Vancouver, Yellowknife, Banff, Calgary, Edmonton, Toronto, Ottawa, Québec City, Montréal, St. John und Halifax. Die Preise rangieren von Can$ 25 pro Nacht im Schlafsaal bis Can$ 60 pro Nacht im Doppelzimmer. Da einige nur Frauen und Paare, andere nur Männer annehmen, ist es sinnvoll, sich im voraus zu erkundigen und zu buchen.

Weitere Informationen erteilt:

YMCA of Greater Toronto
15, Breadalbane Street
Toronto, Ontario
Canada M4Y 1C2
Tel. (416) 324-4221

Jugendherbergen

Jugendherbergen in ganz Kanada bieten Schlafmöglichkeiten schon ab Can$ 12 pro Nacht. Zum Standard gehören Selbstbedienungsküchen und Wäschereieinrichtungen; viele erfreuen sich auch einer günstigen, zentralen Lage. Die meisten werden von der Canadian Hostelling Association (CHA) unterhalten. Die privaten Jugendherbergen bieten ähnliche Einrichtungen zu ungefähr dem gleichen Preis.

Die CHA gehört zu der Internationalen Jugenderherbergsorganisation (International Youth Hostelling Federation, IYHF). Mitglieder der IYHF haben Anspruch auf Vorzugspreise in den angegliederten Jugendherbergen überall auf der Welt.

Der Einjahresbeitrag kostet ca. Can$ 30 und kann sowohl in Kanada als auch in Ihrem Heimatland, was zu empfehlen ist, entrichtet werden. Da einige kanadische Herbergen nicht das ganze Jahr über geöffnet und andere während der Hochsaison häufig belegt sind, ist es ratsam, das IYHF-Verzeichnis zu studieren und mit den Jugendherbergen, die in Frage kommen, bereits vor der Abreise Kontakt aufzunehmen.

Weitere Informationen erteilt:

Deutsches Jugendherbergswerk e.V.
Bismarckstraße 8
32756 Detmold
Tel. (05231) 74010

Hostelling International – Canada
205 Catherine Street, Suite 400
Ottawa, Ontario, Canada K2P 1C3
Tel. (613) 237-7884
Fax (613) 237-7868

Universitätswohnheime

Während der Sommerferien – von ca. Mitte Mai bis Ende August – öffnen viele kanadische Universitäten ihre Studentenwohnheime zu einem günstigen Preis für Besucher. Die Unterkunft ist einfach, aber sicherlich ausreichend. Die

AUF DEN STRASSEN KANADAS

Zimmer sind klein, haben Einzelbetten, Schreibtische und genügend Platz in den Schränken. Sie sind natürlich sauber und warm. Teppiche, Fernseher und Radios sollten Sie nicht erwarten.

Im allgemeinen gibt es auf jeder Etage öffentliche Münzfernsprecher. Gäste können häufig die Universitätscafeteria und die Sporteinrichtungen benutzen.

Um weitere Informationen zu erhalten, nehmen Sie am besten Kontakt auf mit dem Touristenbüro der Stadt, die Sie besuchen möchten, oder schauen Sie in das Telefonbuch.

Farmen und Ranches

Die Farmen und Ranches sind die Hauptstützen der kanadischen Wirtschaft seit der Gründung des Landes 1867 gewesen. Trotz der ökonomischen Änderungen der letzten Jahrzehnte spielen sie weiterhin eine wichtige Rolle. Farmer und Cowboy stellen auch in der kanadischen Mythologie wichtige Figuren dar. Obwohl sie im Ausland weniger berühmt sind als ihre amerikanischen Kollegen (da sie seltener im Fernsehen aufgetreten sind), bilden sie nichtsdestoweniger einen wesentlichen Teil von Kanadas Selbstverständnis.

In vielen Teilen des Landes haben Ranches und Farmen inzwischen ihre Tore für Besucher geöffnet. Hier können Gäste nicht nur eine einmalige Lebensweise erfahren, sondern außerdem eine entspannte Atmosphäre, selbstgekochte Mahlzeiten und eine Vielzahl von Aktivitäten im Freien genießen. Je nachdem, wo das Anwesen gelegen ist, kann es sich dabei um Schwimmen, Angeln, Wandern, Radfahren, Schlittschuhfahren und Skilanglauf handeln. Organisierte Aktivitäten wie Ausflüge mit dem Heuwagen (*hay rides*), Schlittenfahrten, Grill- und Tanzveranstaltungen sind ebenfalls üblich.

Die Art der Unterkunft reicht von Zimmern im Haus des Gastgebers über Hütten bis zu Zelt- oder Wohnwagenplätzen.

Guest ranches sind speziell auf die Bedürfnisse ihrer Gäste ausgerichtet. Sie bieten zu den üblichen Sportarten häufig noch etwas spektakulärere, wie z. B. *heli-hiking* (Helikopter-Wandern), Snowmobil-Fahren und Golf. Kuhmelken und Rindertreiben kommen nicht in Frage: Als Ausgleich offerieren die Ranches Eßräume mit Schankerlaubnis, *hot tubs* und luxuriöse Unterkünfte.

Einige Ranches leiten spezielle Kurse in Überlebenstraining und Umweltbewußtsein. Andere organisieren Workshops (z. B. Literatur oder Photographie) oder *murder mystery weekends* (Krimi-Wochenenden).

Farmen und Ranches, die Gäste aufnehmen, müssen den Anforderungen der Touristenbehörde der Provinz oder der Hotelvereinigung genügen.

Camping

Manche Touristen kommen mit einem recht verzerrten Bild von dem Land, das sie besuchen, in Kanada an. Wenn sie an die breite Masse der Bevölkerung denken, sehen sie ein freundliches, einfaches Volk vor sich, das in zwei Gruppen geteilt ist: Die eine Gruppe drängt sich um den 49. Breitengrad und erinnert stark an die Einheimischen, die man in New York, Kalifornien oder Florida vielleicht einmal kennengelernt hat. Das dunklere Antlitz der zweiten Gruppe wird durch den Pelz ihrer Parkas versteckt. Zwischen diesen beiden Polen sehen solche Touristen eine riesige, spektakuläre Wildnis, in der sie völlig alleine sind. Sie sehen sich selbst lebhaft im Geiste, wie sie an dem Ufer eines unberührten Sees entlanglaufen, am verglimmenden Lagerfeuer in den Sternenhimmel blicken und im klaren Licht der Morgendämmerung beim traurigen Schrei eines Seetauchers erwachen. Solche Touristen betrachten Camping nicht als eine billige Art und Weise, das Land kennenzulernen; für sie ist Camping das wahre Wesen Kanadas. Solche Touristen haben Glück!

Kanada verfügt im wahrsten Sinne des Wortes über Hunderte von Camping-plätzen, viele davon in atemberaubenden Naturlandschaften gelegen. In den meisten National- und Provinzparks ist Camping erlaubt, und es stehen einige entsprechende Einrichtungen zur Verfügung. Zur Grundausstattung gehören hölzerne Picknicktische, Grillstellen und Toiletten. Je nach Beliebtheit und Eignung des Platzes, können noch Unterstände, Umkleidehäuser, Duschen, Stromanschlüsse, Wasserentsorgung, öffentliche Fernsprecher usw. dazukommen. Viele Parks verfügen über Bootsstege und gespurte Langlaufloipen. Programme mit landeskundlichen Erläuterungen der Umgebung einschließlich Vorträgen und geführten Wanderungen werden ebenfalls häufig angeboten.

Die staatlichen Campingplätze arbeiten – mit wenigen Ausnahmen – nach dem „Wer-zuerst-kommt-mahlt-zuerst-Prinzip", so daß es ratsam ist, bereits am frühen Nachmittag einzutreffen. Wenn es am Eingang kein Besucherzentrum gibt, können Sie sich Ihren Platz selbst aussuchen. Ein *Ranger* (Aufseher) geht normalerweise herum und sammelt die Gebühr ein (zwischen Can$ 5 und Can$ 20 pro Nacht). In der Nebensaison kann es auch vorkommen, daß sich niemand sehen läßt. Mehrere Parks schließen Mitte September oder können von Oktober bis Mai nur tagsüber benutzt werden.

Private Campingplätze sind etwas teurer (Can$ 15 bis Can$ 25 pro Nacht für 2 Personen, plus Can$ 2 pro weitere Person), haben aber fast immer den Luxus von Elektrizität oder heißen Duschen zu bieten. Da sie meist auch über Abfallentsorgung verfügen, werden sie von *recreational vehicles* (RVs) bevorzugt. Einige sind sogar als *RV Parks* ausgewiesen. Die Vermieterfirmen stellen meistens einen Campingführer zur Verfügung.

Wenn der Campingplatz, den Sie ausgesucht haben, belegt ist, bedenken Sie, daß der nächste wahrscheinlich weniger als 100 km entfernt liegt. Am Straßenrand zu campieren, wird auf jeden Fall nicht gern gesehen.

Den meisten Kanada-Reisenden wird der kanadische *way of life* nicht unbekannt sein. Da die Kanadier herzliche und gastfreundliche Zeitgenossen sind, werden ausländische Besucher während ihres Aufenthaltes dort kaum Probleme haben. Dennoch gibt es einige Besonderheiten, mit denen die nachfolgenden Informationen Sie vertraut machen wollen.

WÄHRUNG

Gesetzliches Zahlungsmittel in ganz Kanada ist der kanadische Dollar (Can$, unterteilt in 100 Cents). Scheinen zu 5, 10, 20 und 50 Dollar begegnet man am häufigsten. Ein 1-Dollar-Schein existiert zwar, wird aber durch eine goldfarbene 1-Dollar-Münze ersetzt und ist daher selten geworden. Höhere Nennwerte ($100 und $1000) werden wegen des Falschgeldrisikos ungern gewechselt, und man sieht sie folglich selten. Im Gegensatz zu ihren amerikanischen Pendants sind kanadische Geldscheine von unterschiedlicher Farbe. Von manchen Scheinen sind auch noch ältere Versionen im Umlauf, was zu einer kunterbunten Sammlung in der Brieftasche führt.

Pennies (1 Cent), *nickels* (5 Cents), *dimes* (10 Cents), *quarters* (25 Cents) und *loonies* (1 Dollar) sind die geläufigen Münzen. Die Dollarmünze wird nach dem darauf abgebildeten Eistaucher (*common loon*) genannt, einem Wasservogel, dessen charakteristischer Schrei in der kanadischen Wildnis zu hören ist. Daß diese Münze kurz nach ihrer Erscheinung *loonie* getauft wurde (Verrückte werden salopp *loonies* genannt), ist bezeichnend für den Humor der Kanadier. Quarters bezeichnet man oft als *two bits*.

Touristen wird empfohlen, den Großteil ihrer Geldmittel in Form von Kanadische-Dollar-Travellerschecks in kleinen Stückelungen mitzunehmen. Diese können in Banken und Hotels eingelöst werden, und die meisten Restaurants, Tankstellen und Geschäfte nehmen sie als Zahlungsmittel an. Geschäftszeiten der Banken sind normalerweise von 9.00 bis 16.00 Uhr.

Die üblichen Kreditkarten, einschließlich VISA, Mastercard (Eurocard), Diner's Club und American Express, sind in Kanada gut bekannt.

STEUERN

In Kanada ist die eine oder andere Steuer im Preis der meisten verkauften Waren und erbrachten Dienstleistungen enthalten. Eine von den einzelnen Provinzen erhobene Umsatzsteuer ist durchaus üblich, obwohl Höhe und Anwendung unterschiedlich sind. In manchen Fällen können Auswärtige eine Teilerstattung beantragen, doch in der Regel ist es die Mühe nicht wert, es sei denn, es handelt sich um eine größere Anschaffung. Mehrere Provinzen erheben keine Umsatzsteuer, wenn die Ware direkt vom Geschäft an die Heimatadresse des Besuchers versandt wird.

Die 7%-Steuer für Güter und Dienstleistungen (Goods and Service Tax, GST) ist allgemein üblich. Obwohl diese unbeliebte Steuer zweifellos zum Sturz der letzten konservativen Regierung beigetragen hat, ist es unwahrscheinlich, daß sie nun wieder aufgehoben wird. Touristen werden darin unterstützt, für kurzen Aufenthalt (weniger als ein Monat) und für Waren, die im Ausland verwendet werden, eine Erstattung zu beantragen. Bei den folgenden Waren und Diensten wird die GST nicht erstattet: Mahlzeiten, alkoholische Getränke, Tabakwaren, Dienstleistungen (z. B. Reinigung), Automobiltreibstoffe und -mietbeträge. Der Antrag auf Erstattung kann innerhalb eines Jahres nach dem Kauf den Behörden (*Revenue Canada*) per Post eingereicht oder bei einem der an diesem Programm teilnehmenden Duty-free-Shops abgegeben werden. Dem Antrag müssen Originalquittungen beigelegt werden; Kreditkartenbelege und/oder Fotokopien reichen nicht aus. Ein von der Regierung in Englisch und Französisch herausgegebenes Merkblatt enthält ein Antragsformular (*Visitors Application for Rebate*) und alle nötigen Informationen. Erhältlich bei Revenue Canada, Customs and Excise, Visitors' Rebate Program, Ottawa, Canada K1A 1J5.

Innerhalb Kanadas werden Informationen gebührenfrei unter der Telefonnummer 1-800-668-4748 erteilt.

TRINKGELD

Das Dienstleistungspersonal wird in Kanada nicht so gut bezahlt wie in Europa. Deshalb stellen Trinkgelder einen beträchtlichen Teil seines Einkommens dar. In Restaurants ist es üblich, 10-15 % des Rechnungsbetrages (ausschließlich Steuer) für die Bedienung auf dem Tisch liegenzulassen.

Obwohl freiwillig, ist dieser Brauch so zur Regel geworden, daß es deutlich Unzufriedenheit zum Ausdruck bringt, wenn man kein Trinkgeld gibt.

Taxifahrer erwarten circa 10-15 % des Fahrpreises, und Hotelpagen bekommen mindestens einen Dollar pro Gepäckstück. In Motels ist Trinkgeld nicht erforderlich, aber ein kleiner Betrag für das Zimmermädchen im Hotel ist angebracht. Sonderleistungen wie Wäscherei oder Zimmerservice sollten belohnt werden. In der Regel bekommt der Friseur 1-2 Dollar, der Fahrer und/oder Führer einer organisierten Busrundfahrt ebenso.

STROMVERSORGUNG

Die Stromspannung in Kanada beträgt 110 V, 60 Hz Wechselstrom. Da Transformatoren zu schwer sind, um sie mit sich herumzutragen, sollten nur Geräte mitgenommen werden, die mit dieser Spannung funktionieren. Kaufhäuser haben normalerweise Adapter (Amerika-Stecker) vorrätig: Erkundigen Sie sich in der Elektro- oder Haushaltsabteilung.

WISSENSWERTES

TELEFON

Kanada besitzt ein ausgedehntes Telefonsystem, das leicht zu benutzen ist. Münzfernsprecher findet man in Hotelfoyers, Restaurants, Bars, Einkaufszentren, Kaufhäusern und an Tankstellen. Telefonzellen stehen an belebten Straßenkreuzungen und in regelmäßigen Abständen entlang der Hauptverkehrsadern. Der einzige Ort, an dem man nicht suchen sollte, ist die Post: Die Kanadische Bundespost (Canada Post) hat nichts mit den privaten Fernmeldegesellschaften zu tun.

Ortsgespräche kosten in öffentlichen Telefonzellen 25 Cents, die Gebühren für Ferngespräche variieren, je nachdem um welche Art von Gespräch es sich handelt. Vorausgesetzt man kennt die Vorwahl für das Land und die Stadt, kann man praktisch überall in der Welt eine Nummer direkt anwählen. Vermittelte Ferngespräche kosten zwar mehr, bieten aber die Möglichkeit eines R-Gesprächs (nach Rückfrage werden die Gebühren vom Angerufenen übernommen) oder eines *person-to-person*-Gesprächs (falls der gewünschte Teilnehmer nicht erreicht werden kann, werden keine Gebühren erhoben). Benutzungsanweisungen, die Nummer der Vermittlung sowie verschiedene Notfallnummern finden Sie bei jeder öffentlichen Fernsprechanlage.

Ferngespräche sind nachts und an Wochenenden viel günstiger. Weitere Informationen und genaue Uhrzeiten finden Sie im vorderen Teil des Telefonbuches.

Telefonkarten sind in Kanada noch nicht so verbreitet wie in Mitteleuropa. Immer mehr öffentliche Fernsprecher – z. B. in Flughäfen – können mit Kreditkarten bedient werden.

Viele Geschäfte und Regierungsämter arbeiten mit gebührenfreien Telefonnummern. Jede mit „1-800" beginnende Nummer wird als Ortsgespräch berechnet.

POSTDIENST

Die kanadische Post ist zuverlässig und ihre Gebühren sind gemäßigt. Briefmarken kann man an der Rezeption jedes größeren Hotels, an Automaten oder bei den vielen, meist in Drugstores befindlichen Mini-Postämtern kaufen.

Briefe und Postkarten bis 30 g kosten innerhalb Kanadas 45 Cents, nach U.S.A. 52 Cents und als internationale Luftpost 90 Cents. Für ein Einschreiben bezahlt man zusätzlich Can$ 5,15. Die Expreßgebühr (Eilzustellung) beträgt Can$ 7. Für Drucksachen gelten ermäßigte Gebühren. Päckchen dürfen auch *first class* (per Briefpost) geschickt werden: Bis 500 g gelten sie noch als *petits paquets*, darüber gehören sie zur Paketpost. Für Can$ 6,80 wird ein 1-kg-Paket auf dem Land- und Seeweg nach Europa befördert. Das gleiche Paket kostet per Luftpost Can$ 15,20.

Besucher, die noch keine Adresse in Kanada haben, können ihre Post im Hauptpostamt der jeweiligen Stadt zur Abholung bereitlegen lassen. In diesem Falle sollte die Post an die folgende Adresse in der Stadt, wo Sie sie abholen möchten, gerichtet sein: c/o General Delivery, Main Post Office

TELEGRAMME

Der Telegrammdienst wird in Kanada von mehreren privaten Gesellschaften betrieben und nicht von der Post. Örtliche Anlaufstellen findet man in den Gelben Seiten. Unitel verfügt über ein internationales Netzwerk und kann von überall in Kanada unter der folgenden Freinummer erreicht werden: 1-800-361-1872.

WÄSCHESERVICE

Die meisten Hotels bieten einen Wäschedienst an, der gebügelte Wäsche binnen 24 Stunden (oder weniger) liefert. Zahlreiche *laundromats* (Waschsalons) stellen eine kostengünstige Alternative dar. Die Bedienung der Maschinen ist einfach, aber zeitraubend: Man sollte ungefähr 2 Stunden Zeit und eine Menge Quarters mitbringen.

Private Campingplätze stellen ihren Gästen meistens einige Waschmaschinen und Trockner zur Verfügung. Zumindest wird ein großes Waschbekken vorhanden sein. Eine Leine, zwischen zwei Bäume gespannt, und einige Wäscheklammern werden sich als sehr nützlich erweisen.

FEIERTAGE

An den folgenden Nationalfeiertagen bleiben Banken, Ämter und die meisten Geschäfte geschlossen:

New Year's Day (1. Januar), *Good Friday* (Karfreitag), *Easter Monday* (Ostermontag), *Victoria Day* (23. Mai 1994), *Canada Day* (1. Juli), *Labour Day* (5. September), *Thanksgiving* (10. Oktober 1994), *Remembrance Day* (11. November), *Christmas* (Weihnachten).

Zusätzlich wird an einem *provincial heritage day* (im August) in British Columbia, Alberta, Saskatchewan, Manitoba, Ontario, New Brunswick, Yukon und den Northwest Territories das Erbe dieser Provinzen zelebriert. Der 24 Juni, der Festtag des hl. Johannes (*Saint-Jean Baptiste*), ist ein Feiertag in Québec (*Québec National Holiday*). Neufundland feiert *St. Patrick's Day* (Mitte März), *St. George's Day* (Ende April), *Discovery Day* (Tag der Entdeckung, Ende Juni), *Memorial Day* (Gedenktag, Anfang Juli) und *Orangeman's Day* (Mitte Juli).

ZEITZONEN

Wer Kanada durchquert, erlebt sechs verschiedene Zeitzonen. Um 12 Uhr mittags in Vancouver (*Pacific Standard Time*) ist es in Calgary (*Mountain Standard Time*) 13 Uhr, in Winnipeg (*Central Standard Time*) 14 Uhr, in Ottawa (*Eastern Standard Time*) 15 Uhr, in Halifax (*Atlantic Standard Time*) 16 Uhr und in Neufundland (*Newfoundland Standard Time*) 16.30 Uhr. Kanada liegt „hinter" Europa: Auf dem Hinflug müssen die Uhren zurück- und auf dem Heimflug vorgestellt werden. Zwischen dem ersten Sonntag im April und dem letzten Sonntag in Oktober gilt die Sommerzeit.

Die 24-Stunden-Skala der Uhr ist in Kanada (außer beim Militär) nicht gebräuchlich. Von 00.01 bis 12.00 Uhr wird die Zeit mit *a.m.* (ante meridiem, vormittags) bezeichnet, von 12.01 bis Mitternacht mit *p.m.* (post meridiem, nachmittags).

KLIMA

Selbstverständlich kann ein so großes Land wie Kanada kein einheitliches Klima vorweisen. Alle Regionen erleben zwar vier ausgeprägte Jahreszeiten, deren Härte und Dauer sind jedoch sehr unterschiedlich.

Juni, Juli und August sind fast überall warm und trocken mit Tageshöchsttemperaturen zwischen 17° und 27°C. Der September ist in vielen Landesteilen warm, aber im Norden liegen die Höchsttemperaturen am Tag bei lediglich 11°C. Im Oktober kann man in den Wäldern Ontarios und Québecs die Farbenpracht der Herbstblätter bewundern. Zur gleichen Zeit beginnt die Hudson Bay zuzufrieren. Von November bis Februar herrscht Winter: Die höchsten Temperaturen des Tages liegen zwischen -25° und 9°C, die tiefsten zwischen -33° und 3°C. An der Westküste wird es im Februar Frühling. Narzissen und Golfspieler zeigen sich nach ihrem Winterschlaf. Und wenn das milde Wetter allmählich das Landesinnere erwärmt, hat an der Pazifikküste der Sommer schon begonnen.

ESSEN UND TRINKEN

Kanada hat nicht nur eine, sondern mehrere Küchen aufzuweisen. Authentisches kanadisches Essen spiegelt sowohl die ethnische Vielfalt der Bevölkerung als auch die natürlichen Reichtümer des Landes wider. Von den wirklich einzigartigen Gerichten, wie z. B. *reindeer stroganoff* (Rentierfleisch à la Stroganoff) und *fried saskatoons* (saftige, purpurrote Beeren, die gebraten werden) sind leider nur sehr wenige in der kommerziellen Gastronomie erhältlich. Das heißt nicht, daß es einen Mangel an guten, bezahlbaren Gerichten in Restaurants gibt, sondern lediglich, daß Besucher manchmal ein falsches Bild von der kanadischen Küche haben.

Die breite Palette der Gaststätten reicht von Fast-food-Ketten bis zu exklusiven Restaurants. Die meisten Schnellgaststätten werden Ihnen bekannt sein, aber lassen Sie sich auch mal überraschen: Fast food in Kanada bedeutet auch *scallop burger* (Klöße aus Jakobsmuscheln), *Caesar salads* und *Sushi* zum Mitnehmen.

Coffee-shops sind weit verbreitet und relativ günstig. Frühstück gibt es bis ca. 11 Uhr: *Bacon*, gebratene Würstchen, Eier und Toast sind die üblichen Bestandteile des Frühstücks, aber *muffins* (kleine Kuchen), *cereal* (Getreideprodukte, wie z. B. Cornflakes) und Pfannkuchen sind auch beliebt. Manche Coffee-shops in Hotels servieren *Continental breakfast* (Kaffee und Brötchen) sowie anspruchsvollere Gerichte wie *eggs Benedict* (Toast mit einer Scheibe Schinken, pochiertem Ei und Sauce hollandaise) oder Omelett mit Räucherlachs. Zum *lunch* (Mittagessen) werden meistens Suppen (oft hausgemacht), Salate und eine Auswahl an Sandwiches angeboten. Das kanadische Brot findet unter Europäern wenig Beifall, aber die meisten Leute sind sich einig, daß Sandwiches aus Vollkorntoast eine wesentliche Verbesserung darstellen. Burger, *fish and chips*, Gulasch und ähnliche Gerichte sind in einem traditionellen Coffee-shop den ganzen Tag über erhältlich.

Cafés und Bistros sind modernere, vornehmere Versionen des Coffee-shops. Ihre Speisekarten weisen modische Gerichte wie Linguini mit Muscheln oder Vollwertcurry auf. Wichtiger noch ist die Tatsache, daß man hier Espresso, Cappuccino und andere italienische Kaffees trinken kann.

Chinesische, vietnamesische, griechische und italienische Restaurants sind fast überall zu finden und haben vernünftige Preise. Verglichen mit europäischen Maßstäben ist indisches Essen in Kanada recht billig, jedoch außerhalb der Großstädte schwer zu bekommen. Dies gilt auch für mexikanische Speisen. Japanische Restaurants sind reichlich vorhanden, meistens hervorragend, dann aber auch nicht gerade billig.

Eine weltberühmte kanadische Spezialität ist das *Alberta grain-fed beef*, das Fleisch der mit Korn gefütterten Rinder Albertas. Steakhäuser gibt es überall; Kenner wählen immer *prime rib*. Das durchwachsene kanadische Rindfleisch ist auch vom Grill vorzüglich.

An der Küste stehen natürlich Meeresfrüchte an erster Stelle auf der Speisekarte. Viele pazifische Lachsarten – einschließlich des schmackhaften roten oder *sockeye* Lachses – sind in Europa nicht bekannt und sollten unbedingt gekostet werden. Für Camper ist es ein unvergeßliches kulinarisches Erlebnis, wenn sie einen ganzen Lachs in Folie einwickeln und über dem offenen Feuer backen. In den Maritimprovinzen des Ostens sind Schalentiere köstlich und erschwinglich. Gedünsteter, in zerlassene Butter getunkter und mit frischen Brötchen servierter Hummer ist wahrlich eine Gaumenfreude. Viele vor allem von Touristen besuchte Restaurants haben oft Platzdeckchen mit Schaubildern, die erläutern, wie man einen gekochten Hummer ißt.

Obst und Beeren spielen eine wichtige Rolle in der kanadischen Küche, vor allem was Desserts betrifft. Vielerlei Sorten hausgemachter *pies* (gedeckte Obstkuchen), *strawberry shortcake* (Erdbeer-Mürbeteigkuchen) und Käsekuchen mit Obstbelag sind nur einige

Beispiele. Typisch kanadisch und schwer zu übertreffen sind heiße, mit Butter servierte *blueberry muffins* (Blaubeerküchlein) zum Frühstück.

In vielen Gebieten stellen die Bauern während des Sommers Straßenstände auf, um ihre Produkte zu verkaufen. Reisende können sich dort mit einem Glas *apple cider* (eine Art Apfelwein) erfrischen und dabei die Auswahl an sonnengereiftem Obst bewundern.

Unter den kanadischen Käsesorten sind einige – vor allem Cheddar und Oka – mit Recht weltweit bekannt. Oka wurde nach der Region in Québec genannt, wo er ursprünglich von Trappisten hergestellt wurde.

Der Einfluß der französischen Küche ist natürlich in Québec am größten. Besucher der *belle province* sollten unbedingt einige der mehr als 100 dort hergestellten Käsesorten, die *green pea soup* (Grüne-Erbsen-Suppe), *tourtière* (Schweinefleisch-Pastete), *johnny cake* (in Öl ausgebackene Mehlpfannkuchen), *Bouillabaisse* und alles, was mit Ahornsirup gemacht wird, probieren.

Während der letzten Jahre hat man ein wachsendes Interesse an den Kulturen der „Ersten Nationen" registriert. Inzwischen können Besucher in vielen Städten eine einzigartige Mahlzeit der „Native Canadian" (Ureinwohner) genießen. Die Gerichte der Ureinwohner Amerikas zeichnen sich vor allem durch die Verwendung von Wild und einheimischem Gemüse aus. Ausgefallene Delikatessen wie *fiddleheads* (Farnsprossen) bereiten einen überraschenden Genuß. In Kanada gibt es mehrere gute Mineralwasser, einige mit Obstgeschmack. Die bekannten internationalen Mineralwasser sind auch erhältlich.

Das kanadische Bier ist für den europäischen Geschmack zu dünn und wird als geschmacklich minderwertig empfunden. Viele Großstadtpubs folgen dem Trend, indem sie ihr eigenes „organisches" Bier brauen. Die Qualität ist viel höher, aber leider wird es eine Weile dauern, bis die Nachfrage nach Bier ohne Chemie eine allgemeine Verbesserung mit sich bringt.

Wein wird mit unterschiedlichem Erfolg in British Columbia, Ontario und Nova Scotia angebaut. Die billigsten kanadischen Weine kann man nicht empfehlen: Für ungefähr den gleichen Preis bekommt man einen ordentlichen importierten Wein. Alkoholische Getränke sind ausschließlich bei den staatlichen *liquor stores* erhältlich, deren Personal meist freundlich ist und über gute Fachkenntnisse verfügt. Wer die besseren kanadischen Weine kennenlernen möchte, sollte dort Empfehlungen einholen.

SHOPPING

Dank des schwachen Dollars werden diejenigen nicht enttäuscht, die ständig auf der Suche nach einem günstigen Kauf sind. Dies bedeutet nicht, daß Sie alles so billig wie in den Vereinigten Staaten finden werden: Viele Kanadier überqueren die Grenze, um in den USA Lebensmittel, Wäsche und Baumwollkleidung wie Jeans einzukaufen. Im allgemeinen sind jedoch nordamerikanische Markenartikel etwas billiger als in Europa, und wenn sie als Sonderangebot verkauft werden, kann man ein gutes Geschäft machen. Dies gilt auch für Musikkassetten, CDs und elektronische Geräte.

Praktische Souvenirs aus Kanada sind zum Beispiel karierte Holzfällerhemden, Hudson-Bay-Decken, Cowboystiefel und Wildwestkleidung. Manche Artikel findet man in den *Army and Navy surplus stores*, die Restposten aus Militärbeständen verkaufen und ein großes Angebot an günstiger Arbeits- und Allwetterkleidung führen.

Handgefertigte Artikel wie Eskimo-Parkas, *mukluks* (weiche Eskimo-Stiefel), von den Cowichan-Indianern handgearbeitete Pullover und Steppdecken sind häufig sehr preiswert. Ebenso *Native arts*: Bei Specksteinskulpturen, Holzschnitzereien und Silberschmuck mit Halbedelsteinen gibt es gute Qualitäten und vernünftige Preise.

Eßbare Souvenirs bekommt man an den Hauptflughäfen. Neben Ahornsirup, -butter und -süßigkeiten gibt es abgepackte Hummer im Osten und Räucherlachs im Westen.

Kleidergrößen

Men's clothing

Suits								
	Canada	36	38	40	42	44	46	48
	Europe	46	48	50	52	54	56	58
Shirts	Canada	14	14.5	15	15.5	16	16.5	17
	Europe	35/36	37	38	39	40/41	42	43
Shoes	Canada	6 ½	7 ½	8 ½	9 ½	10 ½		
	Europe	40	41	42	43	44		

Women's clothing

Dresses					
	Canada	10	12	14	16	18
	Europe	36	38	40	42	44
Stockings	Canada	8	8.5	9	9.5	10
	Europe	35	36	37	38	39
Shoes	Canada	5.5	6.5	7.5	8.5	9.5
	Europe	36	37	38	39	40

TOURIST-INFORMATION

Preparations

Getting Around

On the Road

Things to Know

PREPARATION

Since the former Soviet republics became independent in the early 1990s, Canada has enjoyed the status of the world's largest nation. The "true north strong and free", as it is referred to in the national anthem, has an area of 9,976,185 sq. km. It extends from the Atlantic Ocean in the east to the Pacific Ocean in the west, a distance of more than 7,000 km. Ellesmere Island, its northernmost point, is well within the Arctic Circle; its southern boundary – and border with its only neighbour, the United States – runs along the forty-ninth parallel.

Not surprisingly, the topography of this immense land varies greatly. From rocky uplands to lush forests, from vast prairies to the breathtaking peaks of the Rockies, Canada's natural diversity is renowned. Sportsmen, adventurers and the "civilization weary" come from all corners of the globe to refresh themselves by experiencing her great outdoors. Four distinct seasons and regional variations in temperature and humidity guarantee the right climate somewhere, at some time of year, for virtually every open-air activity.

Less well-known but equally fascinating is Canada's cultural diversity. Apart from the English and French, who spearheaded immigration starting in the 17th century, significant numbers of Germans, Italians, Eastern Europeans, Scandinavians, Chinese and East Indians have settled in Canada in the course of her history. Indigenous peoples (Indians, Inuit and Métis) comprise approximately 4% of the present population of 28 million. This unique ethnic heritage is reflected in Canada's art, music, literature, local traditions and, of course, cuisine.

Thanks to an extensive air and rail network, it is possible, with careful planning, to "sample" both East and West Canada in the course of one visit. To capture the Canadian atmosphere, though, you should keep the long distances in mind and "take it easy". Concentrate on the province or region that appeals to you most and leave yourself enough time to appreciate the spectacular scenery – and legendary hospitality – to their fullest.

VISA

Visitors from Great Britain (and all other EU countries except Portugal), Australia, and New Zealand do not need a visa in order to enter Canada for a period of up to 3 months.

A passport valid for the duration of their stay, sufficient funds, and proof of intent to leave Canada (e.g. a return ticket to their country of origin or an onward ticket and all documents required for the next destination) are necessary.

Adults travelling with children under 18 years of age should be able to provide proof of parenthood or legal guardianship. Youths under the age of 18 who are not accompanied by a parent must be in possession of a notarized letter from their parent or guardian stating that they have permission to travel to Canada, and giving an address and phone number at which the signor can be reached.

Minors up to the age of 16 can be named in an accompanying parent's passport or carry a children's pass. As of the age of 16, a passport is required.

Non-Canadians wishing to study or work in Canada must apply for student/employment authorization at the Canadian consulate in their country of origin. Visas will NOT be granted after entry into Canada.

Excursions to the USA

Citizens from Great Britain, Australia, and New Zealand who wish to enter the USA directly from Canada need only their valid passport and proof (a return/onward ticket) that the duration of their stay – including time spent in Canada – will not exceed 90 days.

Citizens or permanent residents of the United States do not require passports or visas and can usually cross the USA-Canada border without difficulty or delay. However, to assist officers in speeding the crossing, and particularly to re-enter the USA, native-born US citizens should carry some identification papers showing their citizenship, such as a birth, baptismal or voter's certificate. Proof of residence may also be required. Naturalized US citizens should carry a naturalization certificate or some other evidence of citizenship. Permanent residents of the United States who are not US citizens are advised to carry their Alien Registration Receipt Card (US Form I-151 or Form I-551).

HEALTH

Vaccinations
No vaccinations are currently required. Travellers coming from an area in which yellow fever or cholera is present will be asked to show proof of immunization. Canadian immigration authorities reserve the right to detain any visitor for a medical examination if deemed necessary.

HAZARDS

Travelling in Canada is not much different from travelling in Europe. As Canadian holidays tend to stress outdoor activities, however, the following hints may prove useful:

Campers, hikers, and those planning to drive through sparsely populated areas should be sure to pack a first aid kit. In addition to an antiseptic spray for minor cuts, it should contain bandages; scissors; tweezers; a pain killer, such as aspirin; insect repellent and a soothing lotion for bites; and sunscreen.

Hikers, skiers and those doing the driving need a good pair of sunglasses. A hat is also recommended for anyone planning to spend time outdoors in the height of summer or winter. Additional cold-weather precautions include dressing in layers, changing out of wet clothes as soon as possible, and packing a supply of light snacks and non-alcoholic drinks.

Mosquitoes can be a real problem after sundown in the summer months. A good repellent, long-sleeved shirts and long pants will discourage them. So will a smoking fire. The screens of tents and camper vans should be checked for holes before a night is spent in or near the woods. As a few bites are inevitable, a preparation to stop the itching (such as calamine lotion) is essential.

Always treat wild animals with due respect as they are potentially dangerous.

Canada's bears are generally shy and present no threat to tourists. Nevertheless, no attempt should ever be made to approach or feed one. Keep children nearby and in sight at all times. Food should not under any circumstances be stored in a tent in which campers are sleeping, and women should be aware that some perfumes seem to attract ursine attention. Store food so that bears cannot smell or reach it, such as in the trunk of your car. If you see bear signs (tracks or droppings) while hiking, leave the area.

Always slow down in areas where wildlife abounds. Watch for wildlife warning signs. Report any collision to the nearest park office or RCMP detachment.

Bison can be quite dangerous as they are unpredictable. They are extremely quick (50 km/h!) and sometimes attack without arning. Stay in your car and do not approach bison by the roadside.

HEALTH INSURANCE

It is highly recommended that you make arrangements before leaving home for a health insurance package covering the duration of your stay in Canada.

CUSTOM REGULATIONS

Duty-Free Articles
Customs declaration forms (E-311) are distributed on board vessels and planes en route to Canada and should be filled out before arrival.

The following articles may be imported duty free:

- personal effects such as clothing, jewellery and toilet articles
- sporting equipment such as tents, fishing rods, hunting rifles and up to 200 rounds of ammunition per person
- cameras, film, musical instruments, laptop computers, etc. intended for personal use
- a maximum of 50 cigars, 200 cigarettes and 800 g of pipe tobacco (persons 16 years of age and older only)
- 1.1 litres of wine or spirits or 8.5 l of canned or bottled beer (persons 18 years of age or over in Alberta, Manitoba and Québec; 19 in all other territories and provinces)
- a limited amount of food intended for personal consumption (as prerequisites for the import of food are complex, it is not recommended).
- gifts of up to Can$ 40 per recipient in value

Valuable objects such as video cameras and computers must be declared at customs upon entry and produced for inspection upon leaving the country. A deposit, which will be refunded to the visitor upon proof of export, is occasionally requested. Preparing a list of such items with photocopies of their original receipts is recommended.

United States residents returning to the US from Canada after more than 48 hours may bring back free of duty Can$ 400 worth of articles for personal or household use. If you are visiting Canada for less than 48 hours, you may bring back articles free of duty in the amount of Can$ 25.

Restricted Items
The import of many products is either strictly controlled or prohibited entirely. These include:
- fresh vegetables and fruits
- plants, including bulbs and seeds

For further information contact:
The Permit Office
Agriculture Canada
Plant Health Division
KW Neatby Bldg.
Central Experimental Farm
Ottawa, Ontario K1A OC6
Tel. (613) 998-9926

- meat, fish and poultry

For further information contact:
Animal Product & By-Products Imports
Agriculture Canada
Animal Health Division
2255 Carling Avenue, 3rd Floor
Ottawa, Ontario K1A OY9
Tel. (613) 995-5433

- firearms intended for self defense
- narcotics, including marijuana and hashish

In addition to their duty-free allowance, visitors may import up to 9 litres of alcoholic beverages upon payment of the import duty and beverage tax.

For information in Europe contact:
Canada Customs
2, Avenue de Tervuren
1040 Brüssel
Tel. (02) 741-0670

Pets
Cats and dogs over three months of age may be brought to Canada provided that they have been vaccinated against

PREPARATION

rabies. The vaccination must have taken place less than a year but more than 4 weeks before the date of entry. Animals without such certification will be placed in quarantine for a period of at least one month.

Other animals will only be admitted upon presentation of an import permit as well as a certificate of health issued by a qualified veterinarian.

For further information contact:
The Chief of Imports
Agriculture Canada
Animal Health Division
Ottawa, Ontario K1A OY9
Tel. (613) 995-4659

Motor Vehicles

Visitors may import a private vehicle – car, camper or motorcycle – provided it is registered to them or they have a letter from its owner authorizing its use. Customs permits will be issued at the time of entry, and a security deposit of Can$100 to Can$500 will be levied if deemed necessary by the responsible customs officer. Details as to how the deposit will be refunded should be obtained at the time it is paid.

In order to pass inspection by the Plant Health Division, it is imperative that the vehicle be thoroughly cleaned in its country of origin. The company shipping the vehicle should be able to recommend a steam or high-pressure cleaner who can certify that this requirement has been met.

Liability insurance is compulsory in all provinces of Canada and should be bought immediately upon arrival. A preferable rate will usually be granted to those who can provide written confirmation of accident-free driving in recent years. Information and advice is available from:

The Insurance Bureau of Canada
181 University Avenue
Toronto, Canada M5H 3M7
Tel. (416) 362-2031

The driver's national licence is valid in Canada for up to 3 months, but an international licence – in several languages and valid for a year – is also worth having.

The Canadian Automobile Association provides full membership services, including travel information, maps, accommodation reservations and help in case of emergencies to members of affiliated automobile clubs upon presentation of a valid membership card. Further details are available from:
Canadian Automobile Association
1775 Courtwood Crescent
Ottawa, Ontario
Canada K2C 3J2
Tel. (613) 226-7631

CURRENCY REGULATIONS

There is no limit to the amount of domestic or foreign currency that may be imported or exported. It is prohibited to export silver coins in excess of Can$5.00 per person.

As it is difficult to change foreign money (with the exception of American dollars) outside of the larger cities, Canadian funds should be bought prior to departure. Traveller's cheques in small denominations are recommended due to their convenience in case of loss or theft.

Eurocheques **cannot** be cashed in Canada. All major credit cards (Eurocard/Mastercard, Visa, American Express) are widely accepted. Carrying one is strongly recommended, as it may otherwise prove difficult to rent a car or reserve a hotel room.

HOW TO GET THERE

By Air
Canada's two official carriers, Canadian Airlines International and Air Canada, serve the main Canadian gateways from various central European hubs.

There are 13 international airports in Canada: Calgary (McCall Field), Edmonton, Gander, Halifax, Hamilton, Montréal (Dorval and Mirabel), Ottawa (Uplands), St. John's, Saskatoon, Toronto (Lester B. Pearson), Vancouver, and Winnipeg.

Flightime from London to Calgary is approximately 6 hours; from London to Montréal or Toronto approx. 7 hours; from London to Vancouver approx. 10 hours. From Sydney to Montréal or Toronto it is approx. 22 hours; from Sydney to Vancouver approx. 19 hours.

From London, for instance, Canadian offers daily flights to Toronto and Montréal; Air Canada serves Toronto twice daily and Montréal daily. Canadian also flies from Sydney to Toronto and Montréal 4 times/week in summer and 5 times/week in winter. Several private charter companies (Canada 3000, air transat) offer direct services in the summer months.

Thanks to an ongoing transatlantic fare war, air tariffs to Canada have sunk dramatically in the last years. While this is good news for the average tourist, it also means that flights in the high season (mid-June to mid-August and over Christmas) fill up well in advance. Those who wait until the last minute to book, anticipating further discounts, will probably be disappointed.

As always, planning carefully and shopping around are worthwhile. An airline will generally offer individual travellers only the official fare, but tour operators working with that carrier may well sell the same flights for considerably less. As the same applies to hotels and car rental firms, the price for an identical tour package can vary greatly depending upon the agency involved. It is almost always competitive, however, with what the traveller would pay should he buy the services individually.

In addition, travellers booking with a tour operator benefit from Europe's outstanding consumer protection laws.

Only in extremely rare cases is it worth the effort to contact a Canadian supplier directly.

Youths and students up to the age of 26 can take advantage of special fares; children normally pay fifty to sixty-seven percent of the adult fare. One infant per adult traveller is free of charge, but not entitled to a seat. A weekend surcharge may apply on Fridays and Saturdays westbound, Saturdays and Sundays eastbound.

Recent years have seen an increase in the demand for luxury travel. Many airlines have responded by introducing a business class surcharge for holiday travellers. As the difference in comfort will probably enhance your enjoyment of the first 48 hours of your trip, it is worth investigating.

Cancellation insurance is reasonably priced and strongly recommended.

For further information, consult your travel agent or contact:

Air Canada
7 Conduit Street
London W1R 9TG
Tel (071) 247-226

Canadian Airlines International
23-59 Staines Road, Hounslow
London TW3 3HE
Tel. (0181) 577-7722

By Sea

As Canada's major port in the east, Montréal is visited regularly by cruise ships and freighters from throughout the world. Other international seaports are Québec and Toronto in the east and Vancouver in the west. The latter, however, are not served by European passenger lines.

Well-heeled globetrotters who can afford to spend up to two weeks travelling between Europe and Canada will have several options to choose from. A good travel agency will have at least one catalogue from a tour operator specializing in cruises.

Finding a berth on a freighter is a little more complicated, but enquiring at a few shipping lines should get you the name of an agency that arranges such passages.

Season

Most visitors travel to Canada between June and September, when the mountain passes are free of snow and sleeping outdoors in a tent or motorhome is possible. This is definitely the best time of year for touring the national parks, with average lows varying between 3° (in Whitehorse) and 14° (in Toronto). April and May can also be pleasant, particularly on the west coast where Spring comes earliest. In October, many parts of Canada are still enjoying a spectacular Indian summer. These 3 months are ideal for a variety of sports, including golf and hiking.

Muddy slopes in Europe and Canada's guaranteed snowfalls have led to an increasing number of winter tourists. The ski season generally lasts from late December to mid-April.

WHAT TO TAKE WITH YOU

Airlines now tend to use the "piece concept" to limit baggage on international flights. Each passenger is allowed 2 checked bags, neither weighing more than 32 kg, and one carry-on bag. The carry-on bag must fit under the seat in front of you and consequently cannot be larger than 55 x 40 x 20 cm. Limited stowage is available for bulkier items that cannot be checked, but it is best not to count on taking advantage of it. In addition, a camera and purse may be carried. Mothers with infants are allowed to bring a diaper bag on board, although many airlines will provide both diapers and baby food upon request.

Make a complete list of everything you pack, regardless of its value, just in case your luggage is lost. For the same reason, be sure to have the essentials for an overnight in your carry-on bag.

Casual clothing is appropriate for most occasions in Canada. Slacks, sweaters, cotton shirts and blouses are practical attire and acceptable almost everywhere. Men should bring a sports jacket and tie, women a simple dress, if plans include eating out at better restaurants, visiting a casino, etc. Jewellery, as always, is best left at home. Good walking shoes are essential, as is a lightweight coat. Even in the height of summer, it can be chilly or wet.

Sunglasses are recommendable at all times of year, and those who need corrective lenses should pack a copy of their prescription. Any medicines taken on a regular basis should be brought along in their original package (this will help the pharmacist, should you need something similar), with a copy of the prescription, if applicable. A pocket French and/or English dictionary may prove useful.

A pouch for your valuables (passport, ticket, traveller's cheques, credit card, cash) that can be hung around your neck and concealed inside your clothing is advisable.

Check List

Passport, visa .... ☐
Tickets .... ☐
Reconfirm flight 48 hours before
   departure .... ☐
Traveller's cheques, Canadian
   dollars .... ☐
Credit card .... ☐
Driver's licences, national and
   international .... ☐
Insurance package (cancellation,
   health, luggage) .... ☐
Medication and prescriptions ..... ☐
Prescription for glasses or contact
   lenses .... ☐
Sunglasses .... ☐
Camera and film .... ☐
Sturdy footwear .... ☐
Light coat .... ☐
Hat .... ☐
Concealable pouch for valuables .. ☐
List of all valuables, copies of
   receipts .... ☐
Complete list of suitcase contents ☐

GETTING AROUND

Canada's infrastructure is sophisticated, and visitors will have no difficulty reaching the destination of their choice. Long distance buses and trains complement the extensive domestic air network, and the highways are conducive to exploring by car. Drivers used to the hectic pace of European roadways will be delighted to find them uncrowded and in good repair.

ARRIVAL

Luggage
Even Canada's major airports are relatively small and easy to navigate. Signs are in English (or English and French). Travellers who will need assistance upon arrival (those unable to walk long distances, mothers with small children, etc.) should request it at the time of booking their flight.

Luggage carts are readily available, but in most cases you will need coins to rent one. As "no change" is the norm here too, it is wise to arrive with about two dollars worth of quarters.

Customs
Canadian customs officers have the reputation of being friendlier than their counterparts elsewhere, if not necessarily less bureaucratic. Two questions are standard: "What is the purpose of your visit?", and "How long do you intend to stay?". Line-ups at Canada's main gateways tend to be short, and one can usually count on having completed all formalities within an hour of landing.

Accommodation
Most Canadian airports do not have a tourist information desk that can help you find accommodation upon arrival. A display board with descriptions of several larger hotels and a complimentary telephone is standard, but it won't help you much if you unwittingly arrive during a doctors" conference! Unless you are an extremely flexible and experienced traveller, you should book a hotel in advance for the first night.

Transfer Services
Convenient and reasonably-priced public transport from the airport to the city centre is unfortunately rare (Winnipeg is a notable exception). Shuttle buses are Everyman's alternative, while those who can afford it usually opt for a taxi or limousine. Most shuttles depart approximately every half hour and stop at several of the city's larger hotels. The driver can tell you how far it is from his stop to your particular lodging: ask before you buy your ticket, as you probably won't save money by taking the bus if you have to hire a taxi from the stop to your hotel.

AIR TRAVEL

In a country of such vast distances, air travel tends to be taken for granted. Many towns in which one would hardly expect to find even a bus depot have modest airports and citizens who jump onto a plane as readily as they jump into their cars. Some of these outposts are served by the international carriers and their commuter partners; many more belong to the "networks" of regional carriers with tiny fleets and exotic names like Aklak Air or Antler Aviation.

The average tourist will probably find that Canadian Airlines and Air Canada meet his/her travel needs. As these two are fierce competitors, "seat sales" on their shared routes frequently make flying an attractive alternative to long hours on the bus or train. Furthermore, both offer tourists reductions on normal one-way fares if purchased in their country of origin. These VUSA ("Visit USA") fares are popular with travellers needing just one or two flights because they have few restrictions: they are 100 % refundable, can be re-booked at no charge and are valid throughout the week.

Coupon Air Passes
Foreign visitors can also take advantage of economical air passes. There are several versions, but the basic conditions are always the same:

1) passengers must be in possession of an international return ticket;
2) one coupon is required per domestic flight;
3) a minimum number of coupons (3) must be purchased;
4) a maximum number of coupons (8) is stipulated;
5) the passes are valid for 60 days;
6) the entire routing must be selected before the ticket is issued, and the first flight must be booked before departure.

The savings represented by this kind of ticket are substantial. The normal economy fare from Toronto to Vancouver, for example, is Can$ 793; the VUSA Can$ 571. A 3-coupon air pass for Toronto – Vancouver plus 2 other flights can be had for as little as Can$ 570. During high season (01.07 – 31.08), the 3-coupon pass costs an additional Can$ 45. Travellers who don't fly transatlantic with Air Canada or Canadian also pay more: three domestic flights with the latter, for example, would then be Can$ 600 ... still a good deal! Air Canada's prices are similar.

BUS TRAVEL

Buses represent the Canadian alternative to Europe's highly-developed railway system. They are clean, safe, and provide relatively inexpensive, frequent service to pretty well everywhere. Advance booking is seldom required; just show up at the bus depot, buy a ticket and board. If more than one bus line is serving an area, they will share a central bus terminal. The address can usually be found in the phone book under "Greyhound Bus Lines" in western Canada, "Gray Coach" or "Voyageur Colonial" in the east.

Greyhound offers two bus passes good for unlimited travel in either eastern or western Canada The "International Canada Coach Pass" is valid for all routes between British Columbia and Ontario with connections to Quebec and several gateway cities. It costs Can$ 213/7 days, Can$ 278/15 days, Can$ 374/30 days, Can$ 481/60 days. The "International Canada Coach Pass Plus" in addition includes routes in the Atlantic Provinces: Can$ 348/15 days, Can$ 444/30 days, Can$ 551/60 days.

Services and Facilities

Travelling by bus tends to be a comparatively casual affair. Seats cannot be reserved in advance and you will be expected to drop off/pick up your own luggage at the side of the bus.

Only in rare cases is food served: generally you will have to make do with whatever the bus terminal cafeteria has to offer. Rest stops are scheduled every three hours on longer routes.

Most buses have panorama windows, reclining seats, footrests, air conditioning and lavatories.

Reading lamps are standard. Smoking is confined to the last few rows, and the consumption of alcoholic beverages is frowned upon. A pullover is recommended, even in summer, as buses tend to be drafty.

For further information contact:
Greyhound Bus Lines of Canada
877 16th Street S.W.
Calgary
Canada T3C 3V8
Tel. (403) 260-0871

TRAIN TRAVEL

The transcontinental railway system so integral to Canada's development as a nation now plays only a minor role in passenger transportation. Cutbacks in government funding over the past few years have resulted in comparatively high fares and limited service. Rather than representing an alternative to flying or travelling by bus, the train should be viewed as an experience in itself. For those with some leeway in terms of time and money, it can certainly be one of the most pleasant and nostalgic ways to see the country. Various accommodation (including some rooms with private toilets) is available, the dining car is generally complemented by a bar car and snack facilities, glass-domed lounge cars afford some stunning views, and the atmosphere is unique.

Most passenger trains are operated by government-owned VIA Rail. Foreign visitors can take advantage of their Canrailpasses. A pass valid for 12 days of systemwide, coach-class travel within a 30-day period costs Can$ 540 from June 1st to October 15th, Can$ 369 at other times. Senior citizens (60 years and older) and youths (up to the age of 24) pay somewhat less: Can$ 486 in the high season, Can$ 332 from January 15th to May 30th and October 16th to December 14th.

The Rail & Drive Pass is similar, but also includes 3 days use of a mid-size Hertz rental car. High season prices are Can$ 655 for youths and seniors, Can$ 710 regular. Low season rates are Can$ 475 and Can$ 510 respectively.

The best known VIA Rail train is the "Canadian", which runs from Toronto to Vancouver 3 times weekly.

Other popular trains include the independent "Rocky Mountaineer", which runs from Vancouver to Calgary via the resort towns of Jasper and Banff.

Fares include meals and non-alcoholic refreshments on board as well as 1 night in a hotel in Kamloops. The high season, one-way fare is currently about Can$ 675 (double room).

The Hudson Bay Railway's service from Winnipeg, Manitoba to Churchill is also famous, and well worth considering if a visit to the far north is planned.

Information is available from:
VIA RAIL
2 Place Ville Marie, Montréal, Québec Canada H3B 2C9, Tel. (514) 871-1331

TRAVEL BY CAR

Environmentally conscious Europeans tend to think that Canadians, like their neighbours to the south, are a little "car crazy". The fact of the matter is that public transportation in many places simply hasn't reached a level of development that would induce the average Canadian to rethink his primary means of locomotion. In any case, setting out on your own 4 wheels is the typically Canadian way to see Canada, and tourists who opt for this kind of travel will soon discover its seductive charms. Good secondary roads, ample service stations, picnic facilities and camp sites in idyllic settings, and abundant "drive-in" accommodation translate into the freedom to customize your vacation and experience Canada at your own pace.

While it is not difficult to bring a private vehicle into the country, such an expensive undertaking is not a viable alternative for most tourists. Transporting a car from Europe to Halifax, for example, would cost about Can$ 1,500.

Buying and reselling a car can also not be recommended unless the intention is to stay in North America for at least 6 months.

Rental cars are available in all shapes and sizes, and are more economical than might be expected. The standard categories and approximate high-season rental fees follow:

Economy models usually have 2 doors and a hatchback. They are suitable for longer trips (2 adults) as well as for zipping around town (4 adults). Their only drawback is the absence of a concealed trunk. Prices from April to October start at about Can$ 350/week.

GETTING AROUND

Compacts have 4 doors and are adequate even on longer stretches for 2 adults and 1 or 2 children. The trunk is separate, but rather small. Prices begin at Can$ 375/week.

Midsize cars have 4 doors and a relatively large trunk. Two adults and 2 children can tour comfortably in this class of car. Prices begin at Can$ 400/week.

Fullsize cars have 4 doors and spacious trunks. They can easily accommodate 4 adults or a family of five. Prices begin at Can$ 445/week.

Minivans have 4 doors and a hatchback, and are suitable for extended camping tours. They can seat 7, so even a large family will have plenty of room for their gear. Prices start at Can$ 570/ week.

Liability insurance, CDW and unlimited mileage are included in the prices quoted above. Gas, taxes and one-way drop-off charges are extra. A security deposit of Can$ 250 is mandatory, and the rental firm may demand up to one and a half times this amount in cash if the renter is not in possession of a valid credit card.

The driver must be at least 21 years of age; additional drivers sometimes have to pay an extra charge (depends from the car rental service). Safety seats are legally required for children under 3 years of age: they will be provided at no extra cost if requested at the time the booking is made.

Dependent on the car rental service, there exist different minimum rental periods (normally 4 to 7 days). Cars rented in the USA may only be brought into Canada if this is stipulated in the rental contract. Vehicles are generally equipped with power steering and brakes, automatic transmission, air conditioning and a radio.

By far the easiest – and usually the least expensive – way of renting a car is to book in advance through a travel agent.

Having done so, you arrive in Canada with a confirmed reservation, a payment voucher, and the full protection of your national consumer protection laws.

RECREATIONAL VEHICLES

Recreational vehicles make it possible to enjoy "camping out" without worrying about sudden rain showers, unseasonable cold spells and various other minor inconveniences. For many, they have proven to be the perfect way to tour Canada. There are three basic types of RVs – vans, campers and mobile homes – with so many variations that deciding which to opt for can be difficult. Like rental cars, they all have power steering and automatic transmission. The rental fee usually includes transfers to and from the airport, all taxes, CDW, liability insurance, a guide to RV campgrounds and about 100 free kilometres per day. Some firms provide camping gear (dishes, linen, etc.) at no extra cost; others have a one-time charge of Can$ 40 – Can$ 50 per person. The vehicle should be returned clean; ask what is expected when picking it up as the rental firm is entitled to a cleaning fee of up to Can$ 200 if they are not satisfied.

A security deposit is required. It varies between about Can$ 100 and Can$ 3,000, depending on whether additional insurance is taken out. Drivers must be at least 21 years of age (in some cases 25). Trips to Alaska, the Yukon, and the Northwest Territories are either prohibited or allowed only if an additional fee is paid. House pets may not be brought along.

A 4.6-metre *mini-camperhome*, suitable for 2 people (no toilet) runs about Can$ 155 a day in the absolute peak season (mid-July to mid-August), Can$ 129 in the shoulder season (mid-May to mid-July and mid-August to mid-October) and Can$ 90 in the off season.

A 9.4-metre *deluxe mobile home,* suitable for a family of six, costs around Can$ 320 a day in the peak season, Can$ 255 a day in the shoulder season, and Can$ 215 a day in the off season. Rates for vehicles of other sizes fall between these extremes.

Please note that it is prohibited to park an RV and spend the night anywhere except in a designated camping area. Depending on the facilities available, campgrounds charge between Can$ 5 and Can$ 35 per night.

BICYCLING

Bicycles represent a healthful alternative to motorized vacations. Many second and third time visitors to Canada choose to pedal at their leisure around a favourite region rather than whizz through a new one. For first-time visitors, a few operators offer organized tours which include all necessary bus transfers, a tour guide and mechanic, safety helmets, maps and accommodation. Some also provide meals.

BOATING

Canada's waterways have a long history as part of her transportation network. While their commercial importance has faded somewhat since the days of the coureurs de bois, tourists should not forget the many opportunities they offer.

Canoe tours are available in most regions, and vary greatly in the level of skill required. Beginners are sure to find one that will suit them in a popular canoeing area such as Algonquin Provincial Park (Ontario) or Bowron Lake Provincial Park (British Columbia). More experienced explorers may head for the wilder waters of the Northwest Territories and Yukon. A 18-day, advanced tour departing Whitehorse, including all meals and the services of an experienced guide, will run about Can$ 2,500 per person.

Visitors used to European traffic need not feel intimidated at the thought of driving in Canada. Thanks to a strictly enforced speed limit, the hair-raising pace of Europe's highways is unknown. Rules of the road are pretty much the same everywhere, and Canadian signs are easy to understand. An RV is not turned over until the driver has been given an explanation of its features – and a chance to ask questions. The same applies to touring bikes. Rush hour in Canada's cities can, admittedly, be nervewracking, though the natives tend to take it with aplomb. Visitors who find themselves caught in "a jam" should turn up the air conditioning, switch on the radio, and dream of the open road. No matter where they are in Canada, it won't be far away.

PUBLIC TRANSPORTATION

Public transportation in all major cities is up to European standards. The main difference visitors will notice is the predominance of diesel buses as opposed to subways and trams. It is worth noting that passengers generally pay as they board and drivers do not give change. A single ticket valid for travel in one direction within a reasonable time frame (about 90 minutes) will cost between Can$ 1,50 and Can$ 4, depending on the transit company and distance to be travelled. Transfers to connecting lines are usually allowed, but should be requested when paying the fare. Day passes good for unlimited travel run about Can$ 6 and are available in most cities, including Vancouver, Calgary and Toronto. A few places, such as Winnipeg, operate free shuttle buses in their downtown shopping areas.

SIGHTSEEING

In addition to the well-known Gray Line, dozens of regional and local bus companies offer sightseeing tours. All tourist information offices stock a variety of brochures and will generally accept bookings. The same applies to travel agencies and larger hotels. In the case of city tours and day trips, it is often not necessary to book in advance: just wait at the pick-up point and pay the driver.

The practice of "disguising" shopping trips as sightseeing is not common in Canada. Nevertheless, it is wise to find out exactly what you are paying for. Are meals included, or should you bring extra cash? Will the tour be conducted in a language you can understand, even if only a few people request it? How many other languages will the guide be using? If it is more than one, you may be getting the explanation you need in order to know what's going on long after the "sight" in question has disappeared from view!

As a rule, tours representing a major expenditure should be booked through your travel agent before leaving home. The consumer protection laws of your country of origin will then apply should something go wrong.

TRAFFIC REGULATIONS

Clubs affiliated with the Canadian Automobile Association can provide their members with comprehensive information about driving in Canada. Foreign drivers should be aware of the following facts:

– The speed limit in Canada is strictly enforced. If no sign to the contrary is posted, it is 100 km/h on the highway, 80 km/h on secondary roads and 50 km/h in built-up areas.

– Around schools and playgrounds, the speed limit is 30 km/h: be on the alert for signs depicting children or reading "School". It is illegal and dangerous to pass a school bus in either direction while it is stopped with its blinkers on. The children being picked up or dropped off expect traffic from both directions to come to a halt so that they can cross the street if necessary.

– Radar detectors are illegal in some provinces and may be confiscated even if not in use. Check with the CAA before purchasing such a device.

– If a police car behind you has its light flashing or siren on, pull over as soon as safely possible and turn off the motor of your car. Remain seated, roll down the window, and leave both hands where they are clearly visible.

Fire hydrants in Canada are often the object of artistic creativity. Remember, however, that it is prohibited to park in front of one.

– As in Europe, it is prohibited to overtake in intersections, on curves or near the top a hill.

– The use of seat belts is compulsory in most provinces.

– Motorcyclists and their passengers are required to wear a helmet. In some provinces, motorcycles must be driven with their lights on.

Stop · No left turn · Railroad crossing · Road narrows · One-way street

Keep to the right · Playground · School · Ninety-degree turn right · 100 km/h on highway

Curves ahead · Yield right of way · Curve right · Sharp turn right · 80 km/h on secondary roads · 50 km/h in built-up areas

- Railroad crossings frequently have no bars, only a round sign with a diagonal cross reading "RR". Bring your vehicle to a complete stop and look in both directions before continuing.

- The sequence of traffic lights is: red, yellow, green, red. A flashing yellow light means "proceed with caution"; a flashing red light means "come to a complete stop and then proceed with caution".

- Except in Québec, it is permitted to turn right on a red light after coming to a complete stop and checking for traffic from the left.

- Some intersections are 4-way stops, i.e. there is a stop sign on every corner and whoever arrives first, drives through first.

- Parking in urban areas is highly regulated, and pulling up onto the sidewalk is not allowed. Public parking is inexpensive, but finding an empty spot next to a metre can be difficult. Leaving your car in a "No Parking" zone, too close to an intersection, or blocking access to a fire hydrant can result in a fine and some hefty towing charges. Privately-owned parking lots abound, but their rates are exorbitant. Under normal circumstances, your best bet in every major city is to leave your vehicle in the hotel's garage and use the public transport.

ACCOMMODATION

Hotels

Canadian hotels are much the same as their counterparts elsewhere. Most international chains have properties here, and all categories of comfort – from 2-storey presidential suites to simple rooms with no amenities – exist. Mid-price hotels catering to tourists tend to be comfortably furnished. Rooms are large by European standards, often having two double beds. Private bathrooms are the norm; towels, soap and shampoo are provided. Except in rare cases, rooms are equipped with a telephone, radio, colour television and air conditioning. Mini-bars are common, but the key is generally handed out only upon presentation of a valid credit card. Ice machines are found in the hall. A crib or cot will usually be provided free of charge if desired.

Most hotels have a coffee shop and a beer parlour or lounge. Beer parlours basically serve only beer. Their characteristic rough-and-tumble atmosphere is hinted at by the fact that they traditionally have two entrances – one for "Ladies and Escorts", one for "Gents". Since everyone ends up in the same room, the intended effect of this separation is a mystery. A good beer parlour has at least one pool table and a couple of other games.

Lounges are dimly lit, and serve both beer and cocktails. Snacks, such as peanuts and nachos, can also be ordered. Nowadays, one or more wide-screen TVs broadcasting music videos or sports seems to be *de rigueur*. Hotel lounges can be quite pleasant and – as they frequently have a "happy hour", during which two drinks are served for the price of one – *bon marche*.

In addition to a lounge and coffee shop, larger hotels usually have at least one restaurant and a disco. Swimming pools, long since taken for granted, have been complemented by saunas and other fitness facilities. A gift shop, a beauty salon, and a newsstand stocking necessities like toothpaste and "Kleenex" are other common features.

Reservations will be held until about 6 p.m. Be sure to notify the hotel if you intend to arrive later.

Motels
The motel came into being as a result of the North American's legendary love affair with his automobile. Thanks to their abundance, it is possible to drive off into the sunset everywhere except in the far north without giving a second thought to accommodation for the night. Even the smallest town has a "motor hotel". If there isn't enough traffic to warrant its existence, it will be combined with a trailer park, operate a drive-in hamburger stand, or open its pool to the public in summer. Overheads are minimal: the majority of motels are family businesses employing only a receptionist (often the owner), and a cleaning lady (often the owner's wife).

Motels are prominently situated at the side of the road. Large signs enable motorists to see at a glance what comforts they have to offer (cable TV, a coffee shop, a heated pool, etc.) and if they have "vacancies". After checking in at the reception, it is usually possible to drive to the unit rented and park right in front of it. Lobbies and shared hallways are seldom encountered. Each unit has a private bathroom (towels and soap provided) and, traditionally, a kitchenette. A telephone, carpet, and air conditioning are standard. In some cases, "motel" simply designates an inexpensive, family-oriented hotel with limited amenities. Room service and laundry service, for example, may not be available, but facilities for making coffee and coin-operated washing machines may be. Such establishments are also referred to as "motor inns".

Several reputable motor inn chains participate in a "Canada Hotel Pass" programme marketed by Guest International, Inc. The rates are reasonable (Can\$ 60-90 per room, including tax) and unused vouchers may be refunded.

Guesthouses
"Guesthouse" refers to several types of accommodation suitable to those on a limited budget. It may mean a private dwelling, in which one or more rooms are rented by the night, a small unpretentious hotel, or a cottage available by the week or month. In the East, in particular, many stately old houses have been converted into "tourist homes". Baths and toilets are usually shared, rooms are simple, and breakfast is sometimes included.

Bed and Breakfast
In recent years, B&B associations have sprung up all over the country. Their members rent rooms in their own homes and provide guests with a full breakfast. Bathrooms may be private or shared. The various associations monitor standards and match prospective guests with the most suitable accommodation. B&Bs are generally approved and licensed by the municipal authorities. Apart from the cost factor, they appeal to many because of their location in residential areas and their informal atmosphere.

The YMCA/YWCA
The Young Men's/Women's Christian Association is an international service organization geared towards students and young travellers. In addition to operating a variety of recreational facilities, such as swimming pools and gyms, "the Y" has reasonably priced, centrally located residences in many cities throughout the world. Single and double rooms, as well as dormitory accommodation, are usually available; shared bathrooms are the norm. An inexpensive cafeteria is an additional benefit in most complexes.

The "Y" has residences in Victoria, Vancouver, Yellowknife, Calgary, Edmonton, Toronto, Ottawa, Québec City, Montréal, St. John and Halifax. Prices range from about Can\$ 25/night for the dorm to Can\$ 60/night for a double room. Some accept only women and couples, others only men, so it's wise to investigate and reserve in advance.

For further information contact:

YMCA of Greater Toronto
15, Breadalbane Street
Toronto, Ontario
Canada M4Y 1C2
Tel. (416) 324-4221

Youth Hostels
Hostels across Canada provide dormitory accommodation for as little as Can\$ 12 per night. Self-service kitchens and laundry facilities are standard; many also boast a convenient, central location. Most are operated by the Canadian Hostelling Association; privately-run hostels offer similar facilities for about the same price.

The CHA belongs to the International Youth Hostelling Federation. IYHF members are entitled to preferential overnight rates at affiliated hostels throughout the world. A one-year membership costs about Can\$ 30 and can be purchased in Canada or your country of origin. The latter is recommended. As some Canadian hostels are not open year round and others tend to be full in the high season, it is wise to study the IYHF directory and contact the hostels that interest you before leaving home.

Further information is available from:

Youth Hostel Association
8 St. Stephen's Hill
St. Albans, Herts AL 1 2DY
Tel. (1727) 855215
Fax (1727) 844126

Hostelling International – Canada
205 Catherine Street, Suite 400
Ottawa, Ontario, Canada K2P 1C3
Tel. (613) 237-7884
Fax (613) 237-7868

University Residences

During the summer holiday – from about mid-May to the end of August – many Canadian universities make their student residences available to visitors at a reasonable cost. The accommodation is simple, but certainly adequate. Rooms are small and have single beds, desks and ample cupboard space. They will, of course, be clean and warm. Not to be expected are carpets, TVs and radios. Coin-operated public telephones are generally found on every floor, and guests can often make use of the university's cafeterias and sports facilities.

For further information contact the provincial or municipal tourism authority of the city you plan to visit, or look in the phone book.

Farms and Ranches

Farming and ranching have been mainstays of the Canadian economy since the country was founded in 1867. Despite the economic diversification that has occurred in recent decades, they continue to play an important role. The farmer and his cowpunching counterpart also figure prominently in Canadian mythology. Less famous abroad than their American cousins (having appeared in fewer TV shows), they are nevertheless an essential part of Canada's self-image.

In many parts of the country, working farms and ranches have now opened their doors to visitors. In addition to experiencing a unique way of life, guests can enjoy a relaxing atmosphere, home-cooked meals, and a variety of outdoor activities. Depending on where the property is located, these may include swimming, fishing, hiking, riding, cross-country skiing and skating. Organized events such as hay rides, sleigh rides, barbeques and hoe-downs are also usual.

The type of accommodation varies from rooms in the host's home, to cabins, to tents or trailer sites.

Guest ranches are dedicated solely to the needs of their guests. They feature many of the same outdoor activities, plus some jazzier ones, such as heli-hiking, snowmobiling and golf. Cow milking and cattle drives are out of the question: as compensation, the resort ranches offer licensed dining rooms, hot tubs and deluxe accommodation. Some ranches conduct special courses in wilderness survival and nature awareness. Others organize workshops (in writing or photography, for example) or "murder mystery weekends".

Farms and ranches that accept guests must meet the standards of the provincial tourist authorities or hotel associations.

Camping

Some tourists arrive in Canada with a distorted picture of the country they are visiting. If they think about the populace at all, they imagine a friendly simple folk divided into two groups. One group is clustered along the 49th parallel, and strongly reminiscent of natives they met while exploring New York, California or Florida. The darker countenance of the second group is hidden by the fur of their parkas. Between these two boundaries, tourists of this sort imagine a vast, spectacular wilderness in which they are alone. They can see themselves, vividly, walking on the shore of a pristine lake, gazing at the stars as the campfire dies, waking in the clear light of dawn to the mournful cry of a loon. These tourists don't regard camping as an inexpensive way to see the country; camping, to them, is the essence of Canada. These tourists are in luck!

Canada has literally hundreds of campgrounds, many of which are situated in stunning natural settings. In most of the national and provincial parks, camping is allowed and facilities of some sort are provided. Wooden picnic tables, cooking grills, and toilets are the basic version. Depending on the popularity and suitability of the site, these may be expanded to include shelters, change houses, showers, electrical hook-ups, sewage dumping facilities, public telephones, and so on. Many parks have boat launches and groomed cross-country ski trails. Interpretive programmes, featuring talks and guided hikes, are also common.

Government-run campgrounds, with a few exceptions, operate on a "first come, first served" basis, so it is wise to arrive some time in the afternoon. If there is no visitor's centre at the entrance, you can choose your own site. A ranger will generally come around to collect the fee (anywhere from Can$ 5 to Can$ 20 per night). In the off season, it can happen that no-one shows up. A lot of parks close around the middle of September, or are available for day use only from October to May.

Private campgrounds are more expensive (Can$ 15 to Can$ 25 per night for 2 people, plus Can$ 2 per additional person), but almost always have such luxuries as electricity and hot showers. Thanks to the fact that they tend to have dumping facilities, they are favoured by RVs. Some are actually referred to as "RV Parks". Rental companies provide a camping guide with most vehicles. If the campground you wanted to stay at is full, remember that the next one is probably less than 100 kilometres away. Setting up camp on the side of the road is definitely not approved of.

For most European travellers the Canadian way of life will seem quite familiar. Since Canadians also tend to be a friendly and hospitable people, visitors should encounter few problems during their sojourn here. Nevertheless, the following practical information may prove useful.

MONEY MATTERS

Legal tender throughout Canada is the Canadian dollar (Can$), which is worth 100 cents. Five dollar, $10, $20 and $50 bills are commonly encountered. A $1 bill exists but is rare, as it is being replaced by a gold-coloured $1 coin. Bills in higher denominations ($100 and $1000) are difficult to change due to the fear of counterfeit and consequently seldom seen.

Unlike their American cousins, Canadian bills vary in colour. Older versions of some denominations also circulate, so you'll end up with a motley collection in your wallet.

Pennies (1 cent), nickels (5 cents), dimes (10 cents), quarters (25 cents) and "loonies" (1 dollar) are the usual coins. The last depicts the common loon, a waterfowl whose distinctive cry is heard in the Canadian wilderness. It is typical of the Canadian sense of humour that this coin was irreverently dubbed the "loonie" – or do they mean loony? – immediately after it appeared. Quarters are often referred to as "two bits".

Tourists should carry the bulk of their currency in the form of low denomination, Canadian dollar travellers' cheques. These can be cashed at banks and hotels, and are an accepted form of payment in most restaurants, gas stations and stores. Banking hours are generally 9:00 a.m. to 4:00 p.m.

All major credit cards, including VISA, MasterCard (Eurocard), Diner's Club and American Express are well known.

TAXES

Taxes of one kind or another are added to the price of most items and services bought in Canada. A provincial sales tax is common, although its applicability and amount vary. In some cases, non-residents can submit a request for partial reimbursement, but this is generally not worth the trouble unless a major purchase has been made. Several provinces do not collect sales tax on goods that are shipped directly from the store to the visitor's home address.

The 7% Goods and Services Tax (GST) is almost universally applied. Although this unpopular federal tax undoubtedly contributed to the downfall of the last Conservative government, it is unlikely to be revoked now. Tourists are encouraged to claim a rebate for short-term accommodation (less than one month) and goods bought to be used outside the country. GST paid on the following items will not be refunded: meals, alcoholic beverages, tobacco products, services (such as dry cleaning), automotive fuels and car rentals. The application for a rebate may be mailed to Revenue Canada within a year after the date of purchase or taken into one of several participating Canadian Duty Free shops. It must be accompanied by original receipts; credit card slips and photocopies are not acceptable. A pamphlet produced by the government in both French and English includes a "Visitors Application for Rebate" form and all necessary details. Further information is available from Revenue Canada, Customs and Excise, Visitors' Rebate Program, Ottawa, Canada K1A 1J5. Within Canada, the toll-free number 1-800-668-4748 can also provide information.

TIPPING

Canadian service personnel are not as well paid as their European counterparts and consequently depend on tips for a significant part of their income. In restaurants, it is customary to leave 10 – 15% of the meal's price (excluding taxes) on the table for the person who served you. While this is voluntary, it is so normal that not leaving a tip is a clear expression of dissatisfaction.

Taxi drivers expect about 10 – 15% of the fare, and bellboys should be given at least a dollar per bag. No tipping is necessary in motels, but a modest gratuity may be left for a hotel chambermaid. Any special services, such as laundry or room service, should also be recognized. Hairdressers generally receive a dollar or two, as does the driver and/or guide on an organized bus tour.

ELECTRICAL SUPPLY

The electrical supply in Canada is 110 V, 60 Hz alternating current. Since transformers are too heavy to carry around, only appliances that can operate with this voltage should be taken. Department stores usually stock adapter plugs: ask in the electrical or hardware section.

TELEPHONE

Canada's telephone system is extensive and easy to use. Coin-operated public phones are found in hotel lobbies, restaurants, bars, gas stations, shopping malls and department stores. Phone booths are situated on the street corner at busy intersections and at regular intervals on major arteries. The one place not to look is at the post office: federally-run Canada Post has nothing to do with the privately-owned telecommunication companies.

Local calls cost 25 cents at public phones, and long-distance charges vary depending on the type of call made. It is possible to dial direct virtually anywhere in the world if the country and city codes for the desired number are known. Operator-assisted long-distance calls are more expensive, but give you the option of calling collect (the other

THINGS TO KNOW

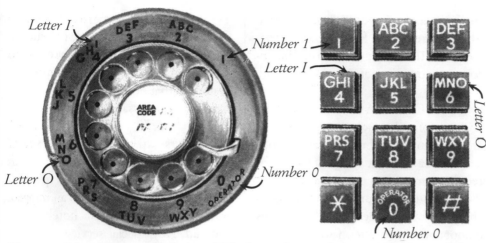

Please remember: do not mistake the letter "I" for the number 1, or the letter "O" for the number 0.

party pays for the call) or person-to-person (there is no charge if the person you wish to speak to cannot be reached). Directions for making calls and the number to dial for assistance are posted next to all public phones, as are various emergency numbers.

Long-distance rates are much lower at night and over the weekend. Details and exact times can be found in the information section at the front of the phone book. The use of telephone calling cards is not yet as widespread in Canada as it is in Central Europe. An increasing number of public phones – at airports, for example – do accept credit cards.

Many businesses and government agencies publish toll-free numbers. Any number beginning with "1-800" will be charged as a local call.

POSTAL SERVICES

Canadian postal services are reasonably priced and reliable. Stamps can be bought at the reception of any large hotel, from coin-operated machines, or at one of the many "mini" post offices located primarily in drugstores.

A first-class letter or postcard weighing up to 30 g costs 45 cents within Canada, 52 cents to the US and 92 cents as international airmail. For an additional charge of Can$ 5.15, letters may be registered. The express (special delivery) charge is Can$ 7. Reduced rates apply for printed matter.

Packages weighing up to 500 grams may be mailed first-class as "Petits Paquets". Anything heavier is classified as parcel post. A parcel weighing one kilo (2.2 lbs.) can be sent to Europe by surface mail for Can$ 6.80, or by air for Can$ 15.20.

Visitors who don't know where they will be staying in Canada can have mail held for them at the main post office in any city. It should be addressed c/o General Delivery, Main Post Office, in the city where they intend to pick it up.

TELEGRAMMES

Telegramme services are provided by a number of private companies, rather than the post office. Local contacts will be listed in the yellow pages. "Unitel" has an international network and can be reached from anywhere in Canada under the following toll-free number: 1-800-361-1872.

LAUNDRY SERVICES

Most hotels have a valet service that will wash and press laundry in 24 hours or less.

Numerous coin-operated laundries, known as laundromats, present an economical alternative. Using them is simple, but time consuming. Bring about 2 hours and plenty of quarters! Private campgrounds usually have a couple of washers and dryers for their

tenants. At the very least, a large sink is provided. Campers will find that a line to string between two trees and a few clothes pegs come in handy.

PUBLIC HOLIDAYS

On the following national holidays in 1994, banks, government agencies and most businesses will remain closed.

New Year's Day (January 1), Good Friday (April 1), Easter Monday (April 4), Victoria Day (May 23), Canada Day (July 1), Labour Day (September 5), Thanksgiving (October 10), Remembrance Day (November 11), Christmas (December 25/26).

In addition, B.C., Alberta, Saskatchewan, Manitoba, Ontario, New Brunswick, the Yukon and the Northwest Territories celebrate a provincial heritage day some time in August. Saint-Jean Baptiste (Québec National Holiday), June 24, is a public holiday in Québec. Newfoundland observes St. Patrick's Day (mid-March), St. George's Day (end-April), Discovery Day (end-June), Memorial Day (early July) and Orangeman's Day (mid-July).

TIME ZONES

Travellers who cross Canada will pass through 6 time zones. At 12 noon Pacific Standard Time (Vancouver), it is 1 p.m. Mountain Standard Time (Calgary), 2 p.m. Central Standard Time (Winnipeg), 3 p.m. Eastern Standard Time (Ottawa), 4 p.m. Atlantic Standard Time (Halifax) and 4:30 p.m. Newfoundland Standard Time.

Canada is "behind" Europe: watches must be set back on the way over, forward on the way home. Daylight saving time is in effect from the first Sunday in April to the last Sunday in October.

Except in a military context, the 24-hour clock is not used. Between 0001 and 1200, times are ante meridiem (a.m.); from 1201 to midnight, they are post meridiem (p.m.).

CLIMATE

Obviously a country of such vast size cannot have a uniform climate. While it is true that all regions experience four distinct seasons, their severity and duration vary greatly. The same applies to levels of precipitation.

June, July and August are warm and dry pretty well everywhere, with daily highs ranging between 17 and 27 C. September is warm in many parts of the country, but daily highs in the north are already hovering around 11. In October, the wooded areas of Ontario and Québec are ablaze with turning leaves, and Hudson's Bay is starting to freeze over. From November to February, winter reigns.

Daily highs range between -25 and 9 C, lows between -33 and 3 C. In February, spring arrives on the west coast. Daffodils and golfers emerge from their winter's sleep. As the warm weather penetrates the heartland, summer at the Pacific has already begun.

EATING AND DRINKING

Canada doesn't have one cuisine, but many. "Authentic" Canadian meals reflect both the ethnic diversity of the population and the natural wealth of the land. Unfortunately, few of the really unique dishes, such as "Reindeer Stroganoff" and "Fried Saskatoons", are available commercially. This doesn't mean that there is a lack of good, affordable restaurant food… just that visitors sometimes come away with the wrong impression of Canadian gastronomy. Eating establishments range from fast-food outlets to exclusive restaurants serving *haute cuisine*. Tourists will recognize some of the former, but may be pleased to know that fast food in Canada also includes scallop burgers, Caesar salads, and take-away sushi.

Coffee shops are widespread and relatively inexpensive. They usually serve breakfast until about 11 a.m. Bacon, fried sausages, eggs and toast are the norm; also popular are muffins, cereal and pancakes. Some hotel coffee shops serve continental breakfasts as well as more sophisticated dishes such as Eggs Benedict or omelette with smoked salmon. Lunch usually means soup (often home-made), salads, and a variety of sandwiches. Canadian bread has few fans in Europe, but most agree that ordering sandwiches on wholewheat toast is a big improvement. Burgers, fish and chips, goulash and other light meals are available all day in a traditional coffee shop.

Cafés and bistros are more fashionable versions of the old standard. Their menus will feature trendier dishes, such as linguini with clams or curry. More importantly, they serve up espresso, cappuccino and other strong Italian-style coffees.

Chinese, Vietnamese, Greek and Italian restaurants are reasonably priced and found almost everywhere. Indian food is downright cheap by European standards, but not as readily available outside of the major cities. The same applies to Mexican food. Japanese restaurants are plentiful and tend to be excellent, if pricey.

Canadian specialities include Alberta grain-fed beef, famous the world over. Steakhouses abound, but prime rib is what the connoisseurs order. Thanks to its marbling, Canadian beef is also excellent barbequed.

Seafood naturally dominates in coastal regions. Many varieties of Pacific salmon – including the flavourful sockeye – are not known in Europe and should definitely be sampled. For an unforgettable culinary experience, campers might try wrapping a whole fresh salmon in tin foil and baking it over an open fire. In the Maritime provinces of the east, shellfish is delicious and affordable. Steamed lobster, dipped in drawn butter and served with fresh rolls, is a feast. A lot of restaurants catering to tourists have placemats that explain with diagrams how a cooked lobster is eaten.

Fruit and berries play an important role in Canadian cookery. Desserts, in particular, tend to feature them. Home-made pies of all description, strawberry shortcake, and cheesecake with fruit topping are only a few examples.

Typically Canadian and hard to beat is a breakfast consisting of hot, buttered fresh blueberry muffins.

Farmers in many areas set up roadside stands to sell their produce throughout the summer. Travellers can refresh themselves with a glass of apple cider while browsing over a selection of sun ripened fruits.

A couple of Canada's cheeses, notably Cheddar and Oka, are deservedly known worldwide. The latter owes its name to the region in Québec where it was first produced by French Trappist monks.

Québec's cuisine naturally exhibits greater French influence than that of the rest of the country. Visitors to the *belle province* should sample some of the more than 100 cheeses produced there, green pea soup, *tourti* (pork pie), johnny cake, *bouillabaisse*, and anything made with maple syrup that they can get their hands on.

Recent years have witnessed increasing interest in the cultures of the First Nations. As a result, visitors to many cities can now have the unique experience of dining on Native Canadian dishes. Game and indigenous vegetables feature prominently; unusual delicacies such as fiddleheads (fern shoots) will prove a pleasant surprise.

Canada has several good mineral waters, some of which come in a variety of fruit flavours. All well-known international brands are also sold.

Domestic beer is weak by European standards, and generally thought to be inferior in taste. It has become fashionable for city pubs to produce their own – much better – "organic" brew, but it will be a while before the demand for beer without chemicals results in an overall improvement in quality.

Wine is produced with varying degrees of success in British Columbia, Ontario and Nova Scotia. The cheapest domestic wines cannot be recommended: for about the same price, a modest import is better value. Alcoholic beverages are available exclusively at government-run liquor stores, most of which boast a friendly and knowledgable staff. Anyone interested in getting to know the better Canadian wines should ask for their recommendation.

SHOPPING

Thanks in part to the weak dollar, bargain hunters will not be disappointed in Canada. This doesn't mean that they will find everything as inexpensive as in the US: many Canadians actually cross the border to stock up on groceries, linens, and cotton clothing such as jeans. In general, though, North American brand-name items are somewhat cheaper than in Europe, and when "on sale" can be a super deal. The same applies to music cassettes, CDs, and all kinds of electronic equipment. Practical Canadian souvenirs include checkered lumberjack shirts, Hudson's Bay blankets, cowboy boots and western attire. Some of these can be found in Army & Navy surplus stores, which carry a large selection of inexpensive work and outdoor clothing.

Handcrafted items, such as "Eskimo" parkas, mukluks, Cowichan Indian sweaters and patchwork quilts are often good value for the money. The same applies to various Native arts. Soapstone sculptures, wood carvings, jewellery of silver and semiprecious stones – reasonably-priced, high-quality examples of all can be found.

Apparel Sizes
Men's clothing

Suits								
	Canada	36	38	40	42	44	46	48
	Europe	46	48	50	52	54	56	58
Shirts	Canada	14	14.5	15	15.5	16	16.5	17
	Europe	35/36	37	38	39	40/41	42	43
Shoes	Canada	6 ½	7 ½	8 ½	9 ½	10 ½		
	Europe	40	41	42	43	44		

Women's clothing

Dresses						
	Canada	10	12	14	16	18
	Europe	36	38	40	42	44
Stockings	Canada	8	8.5	9	9.5	10
	Europe	35	36	37	38	39
Shoes	Canada	5.5	6.5	7.5	8.5	9.5
	Europe	36	37	38	39	40

Edible souvenirs can be bought at the major airports. In addition to maple syrup, maple butter, and maple sugar candy, lobster packed for travel is available in the east, smoked salmon in the west. To combat the long hard winter, Canadian retailers build covered walkways and huge indoor shopping malls. In many cities it is possible to browse around the downtown area for hours without setting foot outside.

"Normal" supermarkets are constructed on the same oversized scale, and are fascinating to stroll through even if you don't need groceries! Opening hours are not standard throughout the country. In general, stores are open from about 9 a.m. to 6 p.m. Monday, Tuesday, Wednesday and Saturday; 9 a.m. to 9 p.m. Thursday and Friday. With the exception of food stores, most businesses are shut on Sunday.

MASS MEDIA

All metropolitan areas have at least one daily paper. The Toronto *Globe & Mail*, Canada's largest newspaper, is also available throughout the country six days a week.

Maclean's, a weekly news magazine, is well written and covers world events from a Canadian perspective. A wide variety of American magazines is sold everywhere, and a few foreign language periodicals can be found at international newsstands in most cities.

The Canadian Broadcasting Corporation (CBC) is publicly owned and has a mandate to promote Canadian culture. It broadcasts on radio and television nationwide in both French and English. An additional shortwave radio network serves northern communities with programmes in Indian and Inuit as well as the two official languages. The CBC's standards are high, thanks in part to strict guidelines about Canadian content.

CTV is a privately owned, national television network. The major American television networks (ABC, NBC, CBS) can be picked up in most parts of Canada.

WEIGHTS AND MEASURES

Canada has officially been metric for many years. While old-timers may still "watch" their weight in pounds and ounces, shopkeepers deal with kilos and grams. All road signs are in kilometres and petrol (gas) is sold in litres. The temperature in Canada is measured in degrees Celsius.

INFORMATIONS TOURISTIQUES

Préparations

A travers le pays

Sur la route

Choses à savoir

PREPARATION

Depuis que les anciennes républiques soviétiques sont devenues indépendantes au début de 1990, le Canada jouit du statut de la plus grande nation du monde. Le »vrai nord fort et libre« auquel se réfère l'hymne national, a une superficie de 9 976 185 km². Il s'étend de l'océan Atlantique, à l'est, à l'océan Pacifique, à l'ouest sur une distance de plus de 7000 km. L'île Ellesmere, la plus au nord, est située dans le cercle polaire; sa frontière au sud avec son seul voisin, les Etats-Unis, longe le quarante-neuvième parallèle.

Il n'est pas surprenant que la topographie de cet immense territoire soit d'une grande variété. Des hautes-terres rocheuses aux forêts luxuriantes, des vastes prairies aux sommets ahurissants des Rockies, la diversité naturelle du Canada est renommée. Sportifs, aventuriers et »las de la civilisation« viennent de tous les coins du globe pour se détendre en plein air. Quatre saisons distinctes et des variations régionales de température et d'humidité garantissent un climat opportun à un certain endroit et une certaine période de l'année, pour vraiment n'importe quelle activité en plein air.

La diversité culturelle du Canada est moins connue mais aussi fascinante. En dehors des Anglais et Français qui furent les pionniers des immigrations à partir du 17e siècle, un nombre important d'Allemands, Italiens, Européens de l'Est, Scandinaves, Chinois et Indiens de l'Est se sont installés au Canada au cours de l'histoire. Les indigènes (Indiens, Inuits et Métis) représentent environ 4 % de la population actuelle de 28 millions d'habitants. Cet héritage ethnique unique se fait sentir dans l'art, la musique, la littérature, les traditions locales et, bien entendu, la cuisine canadienne.

Grâce au large réseau aérien et de chemins de fer, il est possible, en organisant soigneusement le voyage, d'avoir un aperçu à la fois du Canada oriental et occidental. Pour saisir l'atmosphère du Canada, cependant, n'oubliez-pas que les distances à parcourir sont longues et »ne vous en faites pas«. Concentrez-vous sur la province ou la région qui vous attire le plus et prenez le temps d'apprécier profondément l'extraordinaire paysage et la légendaire hospitalité des Canadiens.

VISA

Un visa n'est pas nécessaire aux visiteurs français pour entrer au Canada pour une période jusqu'à 3 mois. Ils doivent être munis d'un passeport valide pour la durée du séjour, suffisamment de moyens de paiement et de la preuve de l'intention de quitter le pays (par exemple un billet de retour dans le pays d'origine ou un billet et tous les documents nécessaires pour la destination suivante).

Les adultes voyageant avec des enfants de moins de 18 ans doivent être munis d'une preuve de leur parenté ou de leur tutelle légale. Les jeunes de moins de 18 ans, non accompagnés de leurs parents, doivent être en possession d'une lettre notariée de leurs parents ou de leur tutelle les autorisant à voyager au Canada et indiquant l'adresse et le numéro de téléphone où le signataire peut être joint.

Les mineurs de moins de 16 ans peuvent être soit mentionnés sur le passeport de leurs parents, soit avoir une carte d'identité propre. A partir de 16 ans un passeport individuel est obligatoire.

Les français désirant étudier ou travailler au Canada doivent en faire la demande auprès du consulat canadien dans leur pays d'origine. AUCUN visa ne sera fourni après l'entrée au Canada.

Excursions aux USA

Les citoyens français désirant aller aux USA du Canada doivent seulement être en possession d'un passeport valide et de la preuve (billet de retour ou d'autre destination) que la durée de leur séjour – y compris celui au Canada – ne dépassera pas 90 jours.

SANTE

Vaccinations

Aucune vaccination n'est exigée. Les visiteurs venant d'une région où il y a encore la fièvre jaune ou le choléra doivent présenter un certificat d'immunisation. Les autorités d'immigration canadiennes se réservent le droit de garder un visiteur pour examen médical si jugé nécessaire.

Risques

Il n'y a pas de grande différence entre voyager au Canada ou en Europe centrale. Les vacances au Canada étant souvent liées à des activités en plein air, les conseils suivants peuvent être utiles:

Campeurs, auto-stoppeurs et ceux qui désirent se rendre en voiture dans des régions peu peuplées doivent se munir d'une trousse de premier secours. En plus d'un spray antiseptique contre les coupures mineures, elle doit contenir des bandages, une paire de ciseaux, une petite pince, un antalgique comme l'aspirine, un répulsif et un beaume contre les piqûres d'insectes, un produit antisolaire.

Les randonneurs à pied, skieurs et conducteurs ont besoin d'une bonne paire de lunettes de soleil. Un chapeau est aussi recommandé à ceux qui projettent de passer beaucoup de temps en plein air, en été comme en hiver. Des précautions supplémentaires sont à prendre en cas de froid: changer les vêtements humides rapidement et emporter un repas léger et des boissons non alcoolisées.

Les moustiques peuvent être un problème pendant les mois d'été après la tombée de la nuit. Un bon répulsif, une chemise à manches longues et un pantalon long les décourageront. Un feu de camp en fera autant. Avant de camper dans ou près d'une forêt, vérifiez si la toile de tente ou de caravane n'a pas de trous. Comme il est inévitable d'attraper quelques piqûres, il faut absolument avoir un produit contre les démangeaisons (par exemple une lotion calmante).

Les ours du Canada sont généralement peureux et ne présentent aucun danger pour les touristes. Mais il ne faut pas essayer de les approcher ou de les nourrir. Gardez vos enfants près de vous et toujours dans votre vue. Ne laissez jamais de vivres sous la tente où vous couchez. Placez vos provisions de telle sorte que les ours ne peuvent ni les flairer ni les gagner, ainsi p.e. dans le compartiment à bagages de votre voiture. Les femmes doivent aussi savoir que certains parfums attirent les ours.

Les élans peuvent être agressifs et attaquent quelquefois sans crier gare, particulièrement pendant le temps du rut (d'août jusqu'à septembre). Au printemps pendant le temps de vêlagement (de mai jusqu'à juin) les élans femelles ont tendance de défendre leurs petits contre toute menace. Gardez toujours une distance sûre. Les bisons peuvent être très dangereux, surtout à cause de l'impossibilité de calculer leurs intentions. Ces animaux sont extrêmement rapides (50 km/h!) et parfois attaquent sans crier gare. Demeurez dans votre voiture et ne faites pas des avances aux bisons de par le bord de la route.

Les bêtes fauves quelquefois sont à la recherche de la nourriture se trouvant de temps en temps chez les campeurs et les pique-niqueurs. S'il vous plaît, évitez de donner à manger ou de faire des avances à ces animaux.

En général il serait absolument expédient de limiter la vitesse dans les régions où il y a des animaux sauvages en grand nombre. Faites attention aux panneaux de signalisation spéciaux. En cas de collision avec un tel animal en rapportez toujours au bureau du parc le plus proche ou dans le détachement correspondant au RCMP.

Assurance maladie

Il est vivement recommandé de contacter une assurance avant le départ pour la durée du séjour.

REGLEMENT DOUANIER

Articles exempts de droits de douane

Les formulaires de déclaration en douane (E-311) sont distribués sur les paquebots ou dans les avions en route vers le Canada et doivent être dûment remplis avant l'arrivée.

Les articles suivant peuvent être importés en franchise:
- effets personnels comme vêtements, bijoux et articles de toilette;
- équipement sportif comme tentes, cannes à pêche, carabines de chasse et jusqu'à 200 cartouches de munition;
- appareils photo, instruments de musique, ordinateurs portables etc. pour utilisation personnelle;
- maximum 50 cigares, 200 cigarettes et 800g de tabac pour pipes (seulement pour les personnes âgées de plus de 16 ans);
- 1,1l de vin ou d'alcool ou 8,5l de bière en bouteille ou en boîte (personnes de plus de 18 ans en Alberta, au Manitoba et au Québec; 19 ans dans toutes les autres régions et provinces);
- un montant limité d'aliments comestibles pour la consommation personnelle. Le règlement pour l'importation de denrées alimentaires étant très complexe, elle n'est pas recommandée. Des renseignements supplémentaires sont fournis par:

Canada Customs
2, avenue de Tervuren
1040 Bruxelles
Tel. (02) 741-0670

- cadeaux d'un montant n'excédant pas Can$ 40 par cadeau.

Les objets de valeur comme appareils vidéo et ordinateurs doivent être déclarés à la douane à l'arrivée et soumis à un contrôle à la sortie. Une caution, remboursable au visiteur sur présentation de la preuve d'exportation, est parfois requise. Il est donc recommandé de faire une liste de tels appareils avec photocopies des factures.

Restrictions

L'importation d'un certain nombre de produits est, ou strictement contrôlée, ou entièrement prohibée, parmi lesquels:
- légumes et fruits frais;
- plantes, y compris oignons et graines; de plus amples renseignements sont fournis par:

The Permit Office
Plant Health Division
Agriculture Canada
Ottawa, Ontario K1A 0C6
Tel. (613) 998-9926

- viande, poisson, volaille; de plus amples renseignements sont fournis par:

Animal Product and
By-Product Imports
Agriculture Canada
2255 Carling Avenue, 3rd Floor
Ottawa, Ontario K1A 0Y9
Tel. (613) 995-5433

- armes à feu pour se défendre;
- stupéfiants, y compris marihuana et hachisch.

En plus des produits exempts de droits, les visiteurs peuvent importer jusqu'à 9 litres de boissons alcoolisées contre paiement d'une taxe d'importation de boisson.

Animaux domestiques

Les chats et les chiens de plus de trois mois peuvent être emmenés au Canada s'ils sont vaccinés contre la rage. La vaccination doit avoir eu lieu moins d'un an mais plus de 4 semaines avant la date d'entrée. Les animaux sans certificat seront mis en quarantaine pour une période d'au moins un mois.

PREPARATION

D'autres animaux ne seront admis que sur présentation d'un permis d'importation et d'un certificat de vaccination établi par un vétérinaire qualifié. Pour de plus amples renseignements, contactez:

The Chief of Imports
Animal Health Division
Agriculture Canada
Ottawa, Ontario K1A 0Y9
Tel. (613) 995-4659

Véhicules automobiles

Les visiteurs peuvent importer un véhicule privé – automobile, camping-car ou motocyclette – à condition qu'il soit enregistré à leur nom ou de posséder une lettre du propriétaire autorisant leur utilisation. Un permis de douane sera établi à l'entrée et une caution de Can$ 100 à Can$ 500 sera exigée si jugé nécessaire pour le douanier responsable.

Vous pourrez obtenir des détails concernant le remboursement de la caution lors de son paiement.

Pour passer l'inspection de la Plant Health Division, il est indispensable que le véhicule ait été bien nettoyé dans le pays d'origine. Votre compagnie de navigation devrait être en mesure de vous recommander une entreprise de nettoyage par haute-pression ou à vapeur qui attestera que cette formalité a été effectuée.

Une assurance de responsabilité civile est obligatoire dans toutes les provinces du Canada et il faut se la procurer à l'arrivée. Un tarif plus avantageux est généralement accordé à toute personne ayant une attestation écrite de conduite sans accident dans les dernières années. Renseignements et conseils peuvent être obtenus de:

The Insurance Bureau of Canada
181 University Avenue
Toronto, Canada M5H 3M7
Tel. (416) 362-2031

Le permis de conduire national est valable au Canada pour 3 mois, mais il vaut mieux avoir un permis international – en différentes langues et valable un an.

La Canadian Automobile Association assure tous les services garantis à ses membres, y compris renseignements pour voyager, cartes, réservations d'hébergement et aide en cas d'urgence à toute personne affiliée à un club automobile sur présentation d'une carte d'adhésion valable. Vous pouvez vous procurer des renseignements supplémentaires à:

Canadian Automobile Association
1775 Courtwood Crescent
Ottawa, Ontario
Canada K2C 3J2
Tel. (613) 226-7631

MONNAIE

Le montant de monnaie courante ou devises n'est pas limité, à l'entrée comme à la sortie. Mais il est interdit d'exporter des pièces en argent d'un montant supérieur à Can$ 5 par personne.

Comme il est difficile de changer des devises (sauf le dollar américain) en dehors des grandes villes, il est conseillé d'acheter des dollars canadiens avant le départ. Des chèques de voyage en petits coupons sont recommandés car ils sont pratiques en cas de perte ou vol.

Les eurochèques ne peuvent pas être encaissés au Canada.

COMMENT S'Y RENDRE

En Avion

Il y a 13 aéroports internationaux au Canada: Calgary (McCall Field), Edmonton, Gander, Halifax, Hamilton, Montréal (Dorval et Mirabel), Ottawa (Uplands), St John's, Saskatoon, Toronto (Lester B. Pearson), Vancouver et Winnipeg.

La durée de vol de Paris à Toronto est environ 8 heures, de Paris à Vancouver environ 12 heures.

Les deux compagnies canadiennes officielles, Canadian Airlines International et Air Canada, relient différentes villes d'Europe centrale aux principaux aéroports canadiens. Canadian Airlines assure des vols journaliers de Paris à Toronto et Montréal en pleine saison et trois fois par semaine le reste de l'année. De Paris, Air Canada dessert également les aéroports de Toronto et Montréal tous les jours.

Grâce à une continuelle guerre de tarifs transatlantiques, les billets d'avion pour le Canada ont diminué drastiquement les cinq dernières années. C'est une bonne nouvelle pour le touriste moyen, mais cela signifie aussi que les vols de pleine saison (de mi-juin à mi-août et à Noël) sont complets très longtemps à l'avance. Ceux qui attendent le dernier moment pour réserver en comptant avoir des réductions supplémentaires seront certainement déçus.

Comme toujours, bien organiser le voyage et se renseigner un peu partout en vaut la peine. Une compagnie aérienne offre en général un billet officiel à un voyageur individuel, mais il est possible qu'une agence de voyage travaillant avec cette même compagnie offre les mêmes vols à des prix plus avantageux. Il en est de même pour les hôtels et agences de location de voitures: le prix d'un voyage à forfait peut beaucoup varier suivant l'agence de voyage concernée. Mais il sera presque toujours moins cher que si le voyageur paie ces services individuellement. En plus, les touristes passant par une agence de voyage européenne bénéficient des lois de protection du consommateur. Il est donc rarement rentable de réserver directement au Canada.

Les jeunes et étudiants âgés de moins de 26 ans peuvent profiter d'un tarif spécial; les enfants paient en général 50% à 67% du prix adulte. Un enfant par voyageur adulte est graduit mais il n'a pas droit à une place assise. Il peut y avoir une surcharge le week-end, le vendredi et samedi en direction de l'ouest, le samedi et dimanche en direction de l'est.

Au cours des dernières années la demande en voyages de luxe a augmenté. De nombreuses compagnies aériennes ont répondu par l'introduction d'une surcharge en *business class* pour les touristes. En choisissant cette catégorie, vous aurez plus de confort et pourrez donc jouir de votre voyage dès les premières 48 heures.

Une assurance voyage, en cas de résiliation de contrat, est vivement recommandée; les prix sont généralement modérés.

Par mer

Des paquebots de croisière et cargos du monde entier font régulièrement escale au port principal du Canada oriental, Montréal. Il y d'autres ports de mer internationals comme celui de Québec ou de Toronto dans l'est et celui de Vancouver dans l'ouest.

Cependant des paquebots ne font pas escale à ces ports cités en dernier lieu. Les globetrotters fortunés qui peuvent se permettre de passer deux semaines en mer entre l'Europe et le Canada, pourront choisir entre plusieurs options. Une bonne agence de voyage a le catalogue au moins d'une entreprise spécialisée dans ces croisières.

Trouver une couchette sur un cargo est déjà plus difficile mais en se renseignant auprès de quelques agences maritimes, vous obtiendrez certainement le nom et l'adresse d'une ligne maritime offrant de tels services de passagers.

Saison

La plupart des visiteurs viennent au Canada entre juin et septembre quand les cols de montagne sont libres et qu'il est possible de dormir en plein air sous une tente ou dans une caravane.

C'est vraiment la meilleure période de l'année pour traverser les parcs nationaux, les températures les plus basses étant en moyenne 3°C (à Whitehorse) et 14°C (à Toronto).

Avril et mai peuvent également être agréables, en particulier sur la côte ouest où le printemps est le plus tôt. En octobre de nombreuses régions du Canada jouissent encore d'un été indien. Ces trois mois sont idéals pour une gamme de sports, y compris le golf et la randonnée pédestre.

Les pentes bourbeuses européennes d'une part, et la garantie d'avoir de la neige d'autre part, ont conduit de plus en plus de touristes à aller aux sports d'hiver au Canada. La saison dure en général de fin décembre à mi-avril.

QUE PRENDRE AVEC VOUS

Les compagnies aériennes ont tendance à pratiquer maintenant le »concept par pièce« pour limiter les bagages sur les vols internationaux. Deux bagages contrôlés ne pesant pas plus de 32 kg et un bagage à main sont autorisés par passager. Le bagage à main doit pouvoir tenir sous le siège devant vous et ne doit donc pas dépasser 55 x 40 x 20 cm. Un espace limité est disponible pour les marchandises (objets encombrants qui ne peuvent pas être contrôlés) mais il vaut mieux ne pas compter sur cet avantage. En plus, vous pouvez avoir avec vous un appareil photo et une bourse. Les mères de jeunes bébés sont autorisées à emporter un sac de couches bien que de nombreuses compagnies aériennes fournissent couches et aliments pour les bébés sur demande.

Faites une liste complète de ce que vous emportez, indépendamment de la valeur, en cas de perte de vos bagages. Pour la même raison assurez-vous d'avoir le nécessaire pour une nuit dans votre bagage à main.

Des vêtements sportifs sont appropriés dans la plupart des cas au Canada. Pantalons, pulls, chemises en coton, tee-shirts sont pratiques et peuvent être portés presque partout. Une veste sportive et une cravatte pour les hommes, une robe simple pour les femmes sont à prévoir pour aller dans un restaurant chic, au casino etc... Comme partout ailleurs, il est préférable de ne pas emporter de bijoux. De bonnes chaussures de marche et une veste légère sont indispensables. Même en plein été il peut faire frais ou humide.

Il est conseillé toute l'année d'avoir des lunettes de soleil et une copie de l'ordonnance pour ceux portant des verres correctifs ou lentilles de contact. Tout médicament pris régulièrement doit être emporté dans son emballage original (ce qui aidera le pharmacien en cas de besoin d'un produit similaire) avec la copie de l'ordonnance.

Un dictionnaire de poche anglais-français peut être utile.

Une pochette-organisateur pour vos papiers de valeur (passeport, billet d'avion, chèques de voyage, carte de crédit, argent liquide), qui peut être pendue au cou et mise sous les vêtements, est conseillée.

Liste de contrôle

passeport, visa .... ☐
billets .... ☐
reconfirmer le vol 48 heures avant
   le départ .... ☐
chèques de voyage, dollars
   canadiens .... ☐
carte de crédit .... ☐
permis de conduire, national et
   international .... ☐
assurance (voyage, santé, bagages) ☐
médicaments et ordonnance ...... ☐
ordonnance pour verres correctifs
   ou lentilles de contact .... ☐
lunettes de soleil .... ☐
appareil photo et films .... ☐
chaussures robustes .... ☐
veste légère .... ☐
chapeau .... ☐
pochette pour papiers de valeur ... ☐
liste des objets de valeur, copie
   des factures .... ☐
liste complète du contenu des
   valises .... ☐

A TRAVERS LE PAYS

L'infrastructure du Canada est très perfectionnée et les touristes n'auront aucune difficulté à atteindre la destination de leur choix. Des autobus longs-parcours et trains complètent le vaste réseau aérien intérieur et les routes sont bien aménagées pour des excursions en voiture. Les conducteurs habitués à la vive allure sur les routes européennes seront ravis de trouver des routes peu empreintées et en bon état.

ARRIVEE

Bagages

Même les principaux aéroports du Canada sont relativement petits et l'orientation y est facile. Les inscriptions sont en anglais (ou en anglais et français). Les voyageurs qui désirent être assistés à l'arrivée (ceux qui ne peuvent marcher longtemps ou les mères de jeunes enfants etc.) doivent le signaler en réservant le vol.

Un caddie est disponible mais vous aurez certainement besoin d'une pièce pour en louer un. Comme »PAS DE CHANGE« est aussi la règle là-bas, il est conseillé d'arriver avec au moins deux dollars de pièces de 25 cents. Sinon, les banques refusant les pièces étrangères, il faut avoir de la patience et de la chance. Si vous n'arrivez pas à en trouver, achetez au moins quelques billets en petites coupures (Can$ 2, Can$ 5), ils sont plus faciles à changer.

Douanes

Les douaniers canadiens ont la réputation d'être plus aimables que leurs confrères de partout ailleurs, mais pas obligatoirement moins bureaucrates. Voici les deux questions habituelles: *What is the purpose of your visit* (Quel est le but de votre visite?). *How long do you intend to stay* (Combien de temps avez-vous l'intention de rester?). La queue aux principaux aéroports canadiens est plutôt courte et les formalités sont généralement réglées une heure après l'atterrissage.

Hébergement

La plupart des aéroports canadiens n'ont pas de bureau touristique d'information pouvant aider à réserver un hébergement à l'arrivée. Il y a habituellement un tableau d'affichage avec la liste détaillée de nombreux grands hôtels et le n° de téléphone; cette liste est toutefois inutile si vous arrivez sans le savoir pendant une conférence de médecins! A moins d'être un voyageur flexible et expérimenté, réservez un hôtel à l'avance pour la première nuit.

Services de transfert

Les services de transports publics de l'aéroport au centre-ville, appropriés et à un prix modéré sont malheureusement rares (Winnipeg est une exception notable). En alternative, il y a un service de navette, mais ceux qui peuvent choisiront de prendre un taxi ou une limousine. Le départ de la navette est environ toutes les demi-heures et elle s'arrête à la plupart des grands hôtels de la ville. Le chauffeur peut vous indiquer le chemin de l'arrêt à votre lieu d'hébergement particulier. Mais demandez avant d'acheter votre billet, vous pourrez ainsi économiser l'autobus au cas où vous seriez ensuite obligé de prendre un taxi de l'arrêt à votre hôtel.

Distances et emplois du temps approximatifs du transfert des principaux aéroports canadiens:

Calgary	19 km – 20 min
Edmonton	28 km – 45 min
Gander	3 km – 10 min
Halifax	42 km – 30 min
Hamilton	10 km – 20 min
Montréal (Dorval)	21 km – 25 min
Montréal (Mirabel	55 km – 60 min
Ottawa	18 km – 25 min
St John's	8 km – 15 min
Saskatoon	7 km – 10 min
Toronto	28 km – 20 min
Vancouver	15 km – 20 min
Winnipeg	7 km – 20 min

VOYAGER PAR AVION

Dans un pays aux si vastes distances, voyager par avion est chose courante. De nombreuses villes où on ne s'attendrait même pas à trouver une gare routière ont un petit aéroport et les gens montent aussi facilement en avion que dans leur voiture. Certaines localités éloignées sont désservies par les compagnies internationales et leurs partenaires, mais un grand nombre font partie du »réseau« des compagnies régionales avec de minuscules flottes aériennes et des noms exotiques comme Aklak Air ou Antler Aviation.

Le touriste moyen trouvera probablement que Canada Airlines et Air Canada conviennent à ses besoins. Comme se sont de féroces concurrents »la vente de places« sur les lignes désservies par les deux compagnies font souvent de l'avion une alternative attrayante aux longues heures d'autobus ou de train. De plus, elles offrent toutes les deux des réductions aux touristes sur les billets aller s'ils ont été achetés dans leur pays d'origine. Ces billets dits VUSA (Visitez les USA) sont populaires parmi les voyageurs désirant seulement un ou deux vols en raison de leurs avantages: ils sont remboursables à 100 %, peuvent être réservés à nouveau sans charge et sont valables toute la semaine.

Les Coupons Air Pass

Les voyageurs étrangers peuvent aussi bénéficier d'une formule économique, »l'Air Pass«. Il y en a différentes versions, mais les conditions de base sont les mêmes:

1) les passagers doivent être en possession d'un billet de retour international

2) un coupon est obligatoire par vol intérieur

3) nombre minimum de coupons: 3

4) nombre maximum de coupons: 8

5) l'Air Pass a une validité de 60 jours

6) l'itinéraire complet doit être fixé avant l'achat du billet et le premier vol doit être réservé avant le départ

Les économies faites par l'achat d'un tel billet sont considérables. Le billet en classe économique de Toronto à Vancouver coûte, par exemple Can$ 793, le VUSA CAN$ 571.

Un Air Pass de 3 coupons pour Toronto-Vancouver plus 2 autres vols coûte seulement Can$ 570; pendant la pleine saison (01-07 – 31-08), il faut ajouter un supplément de Can$ 45. Les voyageurs qui n'empreintent pas Air Canada ou Canadian Airlines pour venir d'Europe au Canada doivent aussi payer un supplément:

trois vols intérieurs avec Canadian Airlines coûtent alors Can$ 600 ... malgré tout une bonne affaire ! Les prix d'Air Canada sont similaires.

Pour des renseignements complémentaires, consultez votre agence de voyage ou contactez:

Canadian Airlines International
109, Rue du Faubourg St. Honoré
75373 Paris
Tel. (1) 42999930 et
(1) 69327300

Air Canada
10, Rue de la Paix
75002 Paris
Tel. (1) 44502020

Il y a environ 75 compagnies de navigation aérienne régionales au Canada. Les plus grandes sont:

– la région atlantique:
Air Nova, Air Atlantic

– la région occidentale:
Time Air, Air BC

– la région centrale:
Nordair Ltd, Québecair

VOYAGER EN AUTOBUS

Les autobus sont le pendant canadien au système de chemins de fer hautement développé en Europe. Ils sont propres, assurent une certaine sécurité et offrent des services peu coûteux presque partout. Il est rarement nécessaire de réserver; allez tout simplement à la station d'autobus, achetez un billet et montez.

Si plusieurs lignes desservent la même zone, elles se partagent une gare routière centrale. L'adresse est généralement indiquée dans l'annuaire sous la rubrique »Greyhound Bus Lines« à l'ouest du Canada, »Gray Coach« ou »Voyageur Colonial« à l'est.

Greyhound offre deux formules-voyageur, valables sur un parcours illimité, soit à l'est, soit à l'ouest du Canada. Le »International Canada Coach Pass« est valable sur toutes les routes entre British Columbia et Ontario et correspondance avec Québec et quelques villes frontières américaines. Les prix sont: Can$ 213/7 jours, Can$ 278/15 jours, Can$ 374/30 jours, Can$ 481/60 jours. Avec le »International Canada Coach Pass Plus« vous pouvez utilisez les mêmes routes qu'avec le »International Canada Coach Pass« y compris celles des provinces atlantiques. Les prix sont: Can$ 348/15 jours, Can$ 444/30 jours, Can$ 551/60 jours.

Services et aménagements
Voyager en autobus relève un peu du hasard. Les places ne peuvent être réservées à l'avance et vous êtes obligés de mettre ou retirer vous-même vos bagages dans la soute à bagages sur le côté du bus (vous êtes encouragé à ne pas prendre plus de 2 bagages d'un poids total maximum de 45 kg). Il est rare qu'on vous serve un repas: en général vous devrez vous contenter de ce qu'offre la caféteria de la gare routière. Sur les longs itinéraires une halte est prévue toutes les trois heures.

La plupart des autobus ont des vitres panoramiques, des appuis-pieds, des sièges inclinables, l'air conditionné et des toilettes. L'absence de possibilités de dormir ne signifie pas que vous serez le seul à se rouler en boule, fermez les yeux et profitez du voyage de nuit pour économiser une note d'hôtel (essayez de prendre un autobus express si c'est votre intention). Des lampes de lecture font également partie de l'équipement. Les derniers rangs sont réservés aux fumeurs et la consommation de boissons alcoolisées est désapprouvée. Un pull est recommandé, même en été, car il y a toujours des courants d'air dans les autobus.

Pour de plus amples renseignements contactez:

Greyhound Bus Lines of Canada
877 16th Street S.W.
Calgary
Canada T3C 3V8
Tel. (403) 260-0877

Voyageur Colonial
505 East De Maisonneuve
Montreal, Quebec H2L 1Y4
Tel. (514) 842-2281

VOYAGER PAR LE TRAIN

Le réseau de chemins de fer transcontinental, partie entière du développement d'une nation comme le Canada, joue aujourd'hui un rôle mineur dans le transport des passagers. La régression des fonds gouvernementaux au cours des dernières années ont conduit à l'augmentation des prix pour des services limités.

Le train ne doit pas être considéré comme une alternative à l'avion ou à l'autobus, mais comme une expérience en soi. Pour ceux qui ont assez de temps et d'argent, cela peut être une façon très agréable et nostalgique de découvrir le pays. Des aménagements divers (y compris cabines avec toilettes particulières) sont disponibles, la voiture-restaurant est généralement complétée par un bar et un snack-bar, et les voitures-salons aux vitres bombées permettent d'avoir une vue magnifique, le tout contribuant à un atmosphère unique.

La plupart des trains de passagers font partie des chemins de fer publics VIA Rail. Les voyageurs étrangers peuvent bénéficier de leur formule »Canrail«. Le billet est valable pendant 12 jours sur tout le réseau en train de voyageurs (»coach-class«) dans un délai de 30 jours et coûte Can$ 540 du 1er juin au 15 octobre, Can$ 369 le reste de l'année.

Les personnes de plus de 60 ans et de moins de 24 ans bénéficient d'un tarif réduit: Can$ 486 en pleine saison, Can$ 332 du 15 janvier au 30 mai et du 16 octobre au 14 décembre.

Le »Rail & Drive Pass« est semblable mais il comprend l'utilisation d'une voiture de location Hertz de classe moyenne durant 3 jours. Le prix en pleine saison s'élève à Can$ 655 pour les jeunes et retraités, Can$ 710 régulièrement, le reste de l'année Can$ 475 et Can$ 510 respectivement.

Le plus connu des trains de la compagnie VIA Rail est le »Canadian« qui relie Toronto à Vancouver 3 fois par semaine.

Parmi les autres trains populaires il y a le »Rocky Mountaineer«, privé, qui relie Vancouver à Calgary par Jasper et Banff. Le prix du billet comprend des repas et boissons non alcoolisées ainsi qu'une nuit dans un hôtel de Kamloops. En pleine saison un billet aller coûte environ Can$ 675 (chambre double).

Le »Hudson Bay Railway« de Winnipeg, Manitoba à Churchill est aussi renommé et à prendre en considération si un voyage au nord est prévu.

Des renseignements sont fournis par:

VIA RAIL
2, Place Ville Marie
Montréal, Québec
Canada H3B 2C9
Tel. (514) 871-1331

VOYAGER EN VOITURE

Les Européens conscients de leur environnement ont tendance à penser que les Canadiens, comme leurs voisins du sud, sont un peu »fous de voitures«. En vérité, les transports publics ne sont pas assez bien développés dans différentes régions pour que les Canadiens envisagent un éventuel changement de moyen de locomotion.

Se mettre au volant pour voir le Canada est évidemment typiquement canadien, mais les touristes qui opteront pour ce mode de voyager en découvriront bientôt les charmes séducteurs. De bonnes routes secondaires, un vaste réseau de stations essence, des aires de pique-nique et de camping dans un cadre idyllique et de multiples restoroutes et motels vous donneront la liberté d'organiser vos vacances librement et de parcourir le Canada à votre propre rythme.

Il est facile de prendre un véhicule privé avec soi, mais une telle entreprise est très chère et n'est donc pas rentable pour la plupart des touristes. Le coût du transport d'une voiture d'Europe à Halifax, par exemple, s'élève à environ Can$ 1500.

Il n'est pas non plus conseillé d'acheter une voiture pour la revendre, à moins de rester en Amérique du Nord au moins 6 mois.

Des voitures de toutes tailles et formes peuvent être louées facilement et à des prix bien plus bas qu'on pourrait le penser. Le prix de location approximatif des catégories standards en pleine saison est le suivant:

Les modèles economy ont en général 2 portes, plus une porte arrière. Ils conviennent à de longs trajets (2 adultes) ou pour faire une excursion aux environs d'une ville (4 adultes). Leur seul inconvénient est l'absence de malle indépendante. Prix d'avril à octobre: à partir de Can$ 350 par semaine.

La catégorie compact a 4 portes et est appropriée pour 2 adultes et 1 ou 2 enfants, même pour de longues distances. La malle est séparée mais plutôt petite. Prix à partir de Can$ 375 par semaine.

Les voitures midsize ont 4 portes et une malle assez grande. 2 adultes et 2 enfants peuvent voyager confortablement dans cette catégorie de voiture. Prix à partir de Can$ 400 par semaine. Les voitures fullsize ont 4 portes et une malle spacieuse. 4 adultes ou une famille de 5 personnes peuvent tenir facilement. Prix à partir de Can$ 445 par semaine.

Les minivans (petits bus) ont 4 portes plus une porte arrière et sont idéals pour de longues excursions avec camping. Ils ont 7 sièges, même une grande famille aura assez de place pour tous les bagages. Prix à partir de Can$ 570 par semaine.

Assurance et un kilométrage illimité sont compris dans les prix indiqués. Essence, taxes et les frais de restitution de la voiture au retour sont en supplément. Une caution de Can$ 250 est exigée et une agence de location peut demander une fois et demi ce prix si le locataire n'a pas de carte de crédit valide. Le conducteur doit avoir au moins 21 ans; d'autres conducteurs éventuelles quelquefois doivent payer une taxe additionelle (cela depend de la location de voiture). Des sièges de sécurité sont obligatoires pour les enfants de moins de 3 ans; ils sont fournis gratuitement si la demande en est faite en même temps que la réservation.

Les périodes minimums de location varient selon le loueur (normalement à partir de 4 jours). Les voitures louées aux USA peuvent être utilisées au Canada si une telle clause est stipulée dans le contrat de location.

Les véhicules sont généralement équipés d'une direction assistée, d'un embrayage automatique, air conditionné et radio.

Les visiteurs habitués à la circulation européenne ne doivent pas être intimidés par la pensée de conduire au Canada. Grâce à la vitesse strictement limitée, l'allure horrifiante des routes européennes y est inconnue. Le règlement de la circulation est à peu près le même partout et la signalisation canadienne est facile à comprendre. Un véhicule de loisir n'est pas remis à son conducteur qu'après lui avoir expliqué ses caractéristiques – une occasion de poser des questions. C'est la même chose pour les bicyclettes. Les heures de pointe dans les villes canadiennes sont, il est vrai, parfois éprouvantes, mais les gens gardent leur sang-froid. Les touristes pris dans un embouteillage n'auront qu'à mettre en marche l'air conditionné, brancher la radio et rêver d'une route libre: elle n'est pas loin, où qu'ils soient au Canada.

TRANSPORTS PUBLICS

Les transports publics dans toutes les villes principales ont un niveau européen. La seule différence que le touriste remarquera est la prédominance des autobus diesel sur le tramway et le métro. Il est aussi intéressant de noter que les passagers paient généralement une fois montés et que les chauffeurs ne rendent pas la monnaie. Un ticket simple, valable pour un trajet dans une seule direction pour une assez longue période de temps (environ 90 minutes) coûte entre Can$ 1,50 et Can$ 4, dépendant de la compagnie de transport et de la distance à parcourir. Le changement de ligne pour avoir la correspondance avec une autre est habituellement permis, mais il faut le signaler en achetant le ticket. Les tickets à la journée pour un trajet illimité coûtent environ Can$ 6 et sont en vente dans la plupart des villes, y compris Vancouver, Calgary et Toronto. Dans quelques endroits comme Winnipeg, les autobus font la navette gratuitement jusqu'aux centres commerciaux de la ville.

CURIOSITES

En plus de la célèbre Gray Line, des douzaines de compagnies d'autobus régionales et locales organisent des visites guidées. Tous les bureaux d'information touristique ont un choix de brochures et se chargent généralement des réservations. Il en est de même pour les agences de voyage et grands hôtels.

Pour la visite d'une ville ou excursion à la journée, une réservation à l'avance n'est pas nécessaire: attendez seulement au point de ramassage et payez le chauffeur.

La pratique abusive d'arranger une excursion à but commercial pour une visite touristique n'est pas commune au Canada. Cependant, il vaut mieux vous renseigner exactement à l'avance de ce que vous aurez pour votre argent. Est-ce que les repas sont compris ou devez-vous avoir de l'argent en plus? Est-ce que l'excursion est guidée dans une langue que vous comprenez, même si seulement une minorité l'a demandé? En combien d'autres langues parlera le guide? S'il parle en plusieurs langues, vous risquez d'avoir une réponse à votre question, afin de savoir de quoi il s'agit, longtemps après que la »curiosité« soit disparue!

En règle générale, il est conseillé de réserver les excursions d'un prix élevé par votre agence de voyage avant le départ. Les lois de protection du consommateur de votre pays d'origine seront alors appliquées si tout ne se déroule pas comme prévu.

REGLEMENT DE LA CIRCULATION

Les clubs affiliés à la Canadian Automobile Association peuvent fournir à leurs membres des renseignements précis sur la conduite au Canada. L'Automobile-Club de France (A.C.F.) en fait partie.

Ce que les conducteurs étrangers doivent savoir:

– La limite de vitesse est strictement appliquée au Canada. Si aucun signal n'indique le contraire, 100 km/h sur route principale, 80 km/h sur route secondaire et 50 km/h en agglomération.

– Près des écoles et aires de jeux, la limite est de 30 km/h. Soyez prudents si vous voyez un signal représentant des enfants ou indiquant *School*. Il est interdit et dangereux de dépasser un car scolaire dans les deux sens lorsqu'il est à l'arrêt et clignote. Les enfants qui sont ramassés ou déposés s'attendent à ce que la circulation venant des deux directions s'arrête pour les laisser traverser la rue, si nécessaire.

– Les détecteurs de radars sont interdits dans certaines provinces et peuvent être confisqués, même s'ils ne sont pas branchés. Adressez-vous à la CAA avant d'acheter un tel appareil.

– Si une voiture de police derrière vous a ses feux clignotants ou sa sirène en marche, rangez-vous prudemment dès que vous pouvez et arrêtez le moteur de votre voiture. Restez assis, baissez la vitre, et laissez vos mains bien visibles.

– Comme en Europe, il est interdit de dépasser aux croisements, dans les virages et en haut des côtes.

– La ceinture de sécurité est obligatoire dans la plupart des provinces.

– Les motocyclistes et leurs passagers doivent porter un casque. Dans certaines provinces, ils doivent conduire phares allumés.

– Les passages à niveau sont souvent sans barrière, seul un signal rond avec barre diagonale indique »RR«. Arrêtez-vous complètement et regardez dans les deux sens avant de passer.

– La succession des feux de signalisation est: rouge, jaune, vert, jaune. Le feu clignotant jaune signifie »passez mais prudence«, le feu clignotant rouge »arrêtez-vous et passez prudemment«.

SUR LA ROUTE

Arrêt
obligatoire

Interdiction de
tourner à gauche

Passage
à niveau
(attention)

Chausseé
rétrécie

Sens unique

Vitesse limitée à 100 km/h
sur routes agglomération
principales

Passez
à droite

Aire de jeux

Ecole

Virage à droite
de 90 degrés

Vitesse limitée à 80 km/h
sur routes secondaires

Succession de
virages

Cédez le
passage

Virage à droite
simple

Virage
dangereux

Vitesse limitée à 50 km/h
en villes

- Il est permis de tourner à droite à un feu rouge en s'arrêtant complètement et vérifiant qu'aucun véhicule vient de la gauche, sauf au Québec.
- A certains carrefours il y a quatre stops, c'est-à-dire un stop à chaque route et celui qui arrive le premier passe le premier.
- Le stationnement dans les zones urbaines est sévèrement réglementé et il est interdit de stationner sur le trottoir. Les parkings publics ne sont pas chers mais trouver une place libre à proximité peut être difficile. Si vous laissez votre voiture dans une zone de stationnement interdite (*no parking*), à proximité d'une intersection, ou bloquant l'accès d'une bouche d'in-

cendie, vous risquez une amende et des frais de fourrière considérables. Les parkings privés abondent mais leur prix est exorbitant. Dans les grandes villes, le mieux est de laisser votre véhicule sur le parking de votre hôtel et d'utiliser les transports publics.

HEBERGEMENT

Hôtels
Les hôtels canadiens sont à peu près les mêmes que partout ailleurs. De nombreuses chaînes internationales y ont des concessions et toutes les catégories de confort, des suites présidentielles à 2

étages aux chambres simples sans charmes, existent. Les hôtels de catégorie moyenne pour touristes ont un confort standard. Les chambres sont grandes, comparées au niveau européen et ont souvent deux grands lits et une salle de bain individuelle; serviettes de bain, savon et shampoing sont fournis. A quelques exceptions près, toutes les chambres sont équipées d'un téléphone, radio, téléviseur couleur et air conditionné. Les mini-bars sont courants mais on ne peut se procurer généralement la clé que sur présentation d'une carte de crédit valide. On trouve des machines à glaçons dans le hall des hôtels. Couchette ou lit d'enfant sont habituellement fournis gratuitement en cas de besoin.

La plupart des hôtels ont une caféteria et un bar ou un salon. Les bars (*beer parlour*) servent exclusivement de la bière. Leur atmosphère typique mouvementé vient du fait qu'ils ont deux entrées, une pour les »dames et leurs accompagnateurs«, l'autre pour les »hommes«. Comme tout le monde se retrouve au même endroit, l'effet à produire par cette séparation est un mystère. Un tel bar doit au moins avoir un billard et quelques autres jeux.

Les salons ont une lumière tamisée et servent à la fois de la bière et des cocktails et aussi des cacahuètes, *nachos* (maïs chips) etc. De nos jours, un ou plusieurs téléviseurs diffusant de la musique vidéo ou des sports semblent être »de rigueur«. Les salons des hôtels peuvent être agréables, et, comme ils ont fréquemment une *happy hour,* heure pendant laquelle deux boissons sont servies pour le prix d'une, bon marché. En plus du salon et de la caféteria, les grands hôtels ont habituellement au moins un restaurant et une discothèque. Aux piscines, faisant partie depuis longtemps des aménagements de base, se sont ajoutés saunas et autres activités physiques. Une boutique de cadeaux, un salon de beauté et un kiosque à journaux, pourvu d'un assortiment de produits utiles comme le dentifrice ou les »kleenex«, sont courants.

Les réservations sont retenues jusqu'à environ 18 heures. Prévenez l'hôtel si vous avez l'intention d'arriver plus tard.

Motels

Les motels sont le résultat de l'histoire d'amour légendaire des Nord-Américains avec leur automobile. Comme ils abondent, il est possible de conduire jusqu'au crépuscule n'importe où, sauf dans les régions éloignées du nord, sans se soucier d'un hébergement pour la nuit. Même les plus petites villes possèdent un *motor hotel.* Si la circulation n'est pas assez dense pour assurer son existence, le motel sera combiné à un camping, un snack-bar en bordure de route ou une piscine ouverte au public en été. Les frais généraux sont minimisés: la majorité des motels sont des entreprises familiales employant seulement un réceptionniste (souvent le propriétaire lui-même) et une femme de ménage (souvent la femme du propriétaire).

Les motels sont situés bien en vue au bord des routes. De grands panneaux signalent aux automobilistes quels conforts sont offerts (télévision par câble, caféteria, piscine chauffée etc.) et si des chambres sont libres. Après enregistrement à la réception, il est généralement possible de stationner juste devant l'unité réservée. Chaque unité a une salle de bain individuelle (avec serviettes de bain et savon) et, traditionnellement, un coin cuisine. L'aménagement standard comprend téléphone, moquette et air conditionné.

Dans certains cas, le motel désigne simplement un hôtel bon marché pour familles aux aménagements succincts. Il ne peut pas y avoir de service de chambre et de pressing, par exemple, mais par contre la possibilité de faire du café et une machine à laver fonctionnant par pièces. De tels établissements sont aussi connus sous le nom de *motor inns.*

Plusieurs chaînes renommées de ce type d'auberges participent au programme du »Canada Hotel Pass« lancé par Guest International Inc. Les prix sont raisonnables (Can$ 60-90 par chambre, toutes taxes comprises) et les bons non utilisés peuvent être remboursés.

Guesthouses

Le terme *guesthouses* désigne différents types d'hébergement convenant aux personnes d'un budget modéré. Il peut s'agir d'une habitation privée dans laquelle une ou plusieurs chambres (chambres d'hôtes) sont louées à la nuit, un petit hôtel sans prétentions (pension) ou un cottage loué à la semaine ou au mois. A l'est du pays, en particulier, de nombreuses anciennes villas ont été transformées en *tourist homes.* Elles sont semblables aux pensions européennes: salle de bain et toilettes sont habituellement communes, les chambres sont simples, le petit déjeuner est parfois compris.

Bed and Breakfast

Au cours des dernières années des associations de *Bed & Breakfast* (gîte du passant) ont surgi dans tout le pays. Leurs membres louent des chambres dans leurs maisons particulières avec un petit déjeuner complet. Les salles de bain sont soit individuelles, soit communes. Les différentes associations contrôlent l'aménagement et offrent aux touristes intéressés l'hébergement qui leur convient le mieux. Les B&B sont généralement agréés et patentés par les autorités municipales. Outre le facteur coût, ils attirent par leur situation dans des zones résidentielles et leur atmosphère familial.

La YMCA/YWCA

Young Men's/Women's Christian Association est une organisation internationale de services s'adressant aux étudiants et jeunes voyageurs. En plus de fournir des distractions variées comme piscine et gymnase, la »Y« a des prix modérés et des résidences centrales dans de nombreuses villes à travers le monde. Elle dispose habituellement de chambres d'une ou deux personnes ou de dortoirs; les salles de bain sont en commun. La plupart des résidences ont, en plus, une caféteria bon marché.

La »Y« a des résidences à Victoria, Vancouver, Yellowknife, Banff, Calgary, Demonton, Toronto, Ottawa, Québec City, Montréal, St. John et Halifax. Les prix vont de Can$ 25 par nuit en dortoir à Can$ 60 par nuit en chambre de deux personnes. Certaines n'acceptent que les femmes et couples, d'autres que les hommes; il est donc conseillé de réserver à l'avance. Pour de plus amples renseignements, contactez:

YMCA of Greater Toronto
15, Breadalbane Street
Toronto, Ontario
Canada M4Y 1C2
Tel. (416) 324-4221

SUR LA ROUTE

Auberges de jeunesse

Les auberges de jeunesse offrent un hébergement en dortoir à travers le Canada pour seulement Can$ 12 par nuit. Cuisines en self-service et pressing sont usuels; de nombreuses auberges de jeunesse peuvent aussi se vanter d'un autre avantage: leur situation centrale. La plupart sont gérées par la Canadian Hostelling Association; les auberges de jeunesse privées offrent les mêmes services à peu près au même prix.

La CHA fait partie de l'International Youth Hostelling Federation. Ses membres ont droit à des tarifs d'hébergement préférentiels dans toutes les auberges affiliées du monde entier. L'adhésion coûte environ Can$ 30 par an et peut s'effectuer au Canada ou dans votre pays d'origine.

Cette dernière est recommandée. Comme certaines auberges de jeunesse canadiennes ne sont pas ouvertes toute l'année, d'autres complètes en pleine saison, il est conseillé de consulter la liste d'adresses de l'IYHF et contacter les auberges qui vous intéressent avant votre départ.

De plus amples renseignements sont fournis par:

Fédération Unie des Auberges de Jeunesse
27 Rue Pajol
75018 Paris
Tel. (1) 44898727
Fax (1) 44898710

Hostelling International – Canada
205 Catherine Street, Suite 400
Ottawa, Ontario, Canada K2P 1C3
Tel. (613) 237-7884
Fax (613) 237-7868

Fermes et ranchs

Les fermes et les ranchs ont été le soutien de l'économie canadienne depuis la fondation du pays en 1867. Malgré la diversification économique intervenue au cours des dernières décennies, ils jouent toujours un rôle important. Le fermier et le cowboy sont des personnages éminents de la mythologie canadienne. Moins célèbres à l'étranger que leurs cousins américains (ayant moins parus sur le petit écran), ils sont cependant une partie essentielle de l'image en soi du Canada.

Dans de nombreuses régions du pays, les fermes et ranchs ont ouvert leurs portes aux visiteurs. En plus de découvrir un mode de vie nouveau et unique en son genre, les hôtes peuvent jouir d'un atmosphère de détente, de repas maison et d'une gamme d'activités en plein air. Suivant l'endroit où la propriété est située, la natation, les randonnées pédestres, la pêche, l'équitation, le ski de fond et le patinage sont possibles.

Des promenades en traîneau ou en chariot à foin, des barbecues et des danses folkloriques en soirée sont aussi habituellement proposés.

Le type d'hébergement varie, de la chambre dans l'habitation du propriétaire, aux huttes, tentes et caravanes de camping.

Les ranchs accueillant des hôtes sont uniquement aménagés pour les besoins de leurs visiteurs. Ils offrent des activités semblables en plein air et en plus quelques unes plus spectaculaires comme les excursions en hélicoptère, en motoneige (*skidoo*) ou le golf. Traire les vaches et chasser les troupeaux est hors de question: en compensation le propriétaire du ranch dispose de salles de restaurants, de bains thermaux et d'un hébergement de luxe.

Certains ranchs proposent des cours spéciaux de survie dans les contrées sauvages et d'exploration de la nature. D'autres organisent des séminaires (en écriture et en photographie, par exemple) ou des »week-ends policiers«.

Les fermes et ranchs acceptant des hôtes doivent se conformer aux normes des autorités provinciales de tourisme ou aux associations d'hôtels.

Camping

Le Canada a des centaines de terrains de camping dont certains d'entre eux sont situés dans un cadre naturel idyllique. Le camping est autorisé dans la plupart des parcs nationaux et provinciaux et certains aménagements sont fournis.

Des tables de pique-nique en bois, des grils pour cuisiner et des toilettes sont la version de base auquelle peut s'ajouter, suivant la popularité et l'endroit, des abris, vestiaires, douches, prises électriques, téléphone public, radio, téléviseur, service d'enlèvement des ordures, etc... De nombreux parcs ont des jetées pour les petites embarcations et des pistes pour ski de fond. Des ateliers, conférences et randonnées guidées sont souvent organisés.

Les terrains de camping gérés par le gouvernement, à quelques exceptions près, partent du principe »le premier venu, le premier servi«; il est donc conseillé d'arriver dans la matinée. S'il n'y a pas de réception pour les visiteurs à l'entrée, vous pouvez choisir votre place. Un gardien passera généralement collecter l'argent (entre Can$ 5 et Can$ 20 par nuit). En dehors de la saison, il peut arriver que personne ne vienne. De nombreux parcs ferment vers mi-septembre ou sont seulement ouverts la journée d'octobre à mai.

Les terrains de camping privés sont plus chers (Can$ 15 à Can$ 25 par nuit pour 2 personnes, plus Can$ 2 par personne supplémentaire), mais ont presque toujours des aménagements de luxe comme l'électricité ou les douches chaudes. Comme ils ont souvent un service d'enlèvement des ordures, ils ont la préférence des touristes en véhicules de camping. Certains sont connus comme *RV Parks*. Un guide des campings est fourni par les agences de location de la plupart des véhicules.

Si le terrain de camping où vous vouliez séjourner est plein, rappelez-vous que le prochain est probablement à moins de 100 km. Dresser sa tente au bord de la route n'est vraiment pas autorisé.

La plupart des voyageurs se rendant au Canada connaissent déjà la signification de *way of life* canadien. Les Canadiens sont dotés d'un caractère ouvert, sont aimables et les étrangers ne rencontreront guère de problèmes dans la communication. Il existe pourtant quelques particularités que vous devez connaître avant d'entreprendre votre voyage.

MONNAIE

La monnaie courante dans tout le Canada est le dollar canadien (Can$) qui vaut 100 cents. Il y a en général des billets de $ 5, $ 10, $ 20 et $ 50. Il existe aussi un billet de $ 1 mais il est rare et est actuellement remplacé par une pièce de $ 1 de couleur d'or. Les plus grandes coupures de billets ($ 100 et $ 1 000) sont difficiles à changer à cause des risques de falsification et sont donc rarement en circulation. Contrairement à leurs cousins américains, les billets canadiens ont des couleurs variées. L'ancienne version de certaines coupures circulent encore, vous aurez donc à la fin de votre voyage une gamme de billets multicolores dans votre portefeuille.

Les pièces habituelles sont les *pennies* (1 cent), *nickels* (5 cents), *dimes* (10 cents), *quarters* (25 cents) et *loonies* (1 dollar). Ces dernières doivent leur nom au plongeon commun, un oiseau aquatique au cri bien particulier qu'on entend dans les contrées sauvages du Canada. Que cette pièce ait été irrespectueusement qualifiée de *loonie* dès son apparition montre bien le sens de l'humour typiquement canadien – ou est-ce qu'ils ont voulu dire *loony* (fou)? Les quarters sont souvent appelés *two bits*.

Il est conseillé aux touristes d'emporter comme devises des chèques de voyage en petites coupures de dollars canadiens. Ils peuvent être encaissés par les banques et les hôtels et sont un moyen de paiement accepté dans la plupart des restaurants, stations essence et magasins. Les banques sont généralement ouvertes de 9 à 16 heures.

Les principales cartes de crédit comme VISA, MasterCard (Eurocard), Diner's Club et American Express sont courantes.

TAXES

Des taxes d'une sorte ou d'une autre sont ajoutées au prix de la plupart des produits et services canadiens. Une taxe de vente régionale est courante, mais son application et son montant varient.

Dans certains cas, les non-résidents peuvent faire une demande de remboursement partiel, mais cela n'en vaut pas souvent la peine, à moins d'avoir fait un achat important. De nombreuses provinces ne prélèvent pas de taxe de vente sur les marchandises qui sont expédiées directement d'un magasin à l'adresse du pays natal du visiteur.

La taxe de 7% sur les marchandises et services est appliquée presque universellement. Bien que cette taxe fédérale impopulaire ait contribué à la chute du dernier gouvernement conservateur, il est peu probable qu'elle soit abolie maintenant. Les touristes sont encouragés à réclamer une exonération fiscale sur un hébergement à court-terme (moins d'un mois) et sur les marchandises achetées pour utilisation en dehors du pays. La taxe sur les marchandises et services n'est pas remboursable sur les articles suivants: repas, boissons alcoolisées, tabacs, services (comme nettoyage à sec), essence, location de voiture. La demande d'exonération fiscale doit être envoyée au Trésor public canadien dans l'année de la date d'achat ou déposée dans une des nombreuses boutiques canadiennes en duty free. Elle doit être accompagnée de l'original des factures; reçus de carte de crédit et photocopies ne sont pas valables. Un formulaire et tous les détails nécessaires sont joints à une brochure publiée par le gouvernement, à la fois en anglais et en français. Elle est disponible à: Revenue Canada, Customs and Excise, Visitors« Rebate Program, Ottawa, Canada K1A 1J5. Au Canada, en composant le numéro de téléphone gratuit 1-800-668-4748, on peut aussi avoir des renseignements.

POURBOIRES

Le personnel des services canadiens n'est pas si bien payé que ses confrères européens et une partie de son salaire dépend des pourboires. Au restaurant il est d'usage de laisser 10 à 15 % du prix du repas (taxes exclues) pour la personne qui vous sert. Ne rien laisser est un geste volontaire qui exprime un signe de désatisfaction.

Pour les chauffeurs de taxi il faut compter 10 à 15 % de la course et les porteurs de bagages au moins 1 dollar par bagage. Aucun pourboire est nécessaire dans les motels, mais une petite gratification peut être laissée à la femme de chambre. Tous services spéciaux comme pressing ou service de chambre doivent être aussi gratifiés. Les coiffeurs reçoivent généralement 1 ou 2 dollars, il en est de même pour le chauffeur et/ou le guide d'une excursion organisée en autobus.

COURANT ELECTRIQUE

Le courant électrique est un courant alternatif à 110 volts, 60 Hz. Comme un transformateur est trop lourd à transporter avec soi, il est conseillé d'emporter seulement les appareils fonctionnant avec ce voltage. On trouve généralement des adapteurs dans les grands magasins: demandez au rayon électricité ou quincaillerie.

TELEPHONE

Le réseau téléphonique canadien est vaste et facile à utiliser. On trouve des appareils téléphoniques publics à pièces dans le hall des hôtels, restaurants, bars, stations essence, centres commerciaux

CHOSES A SAVOIR

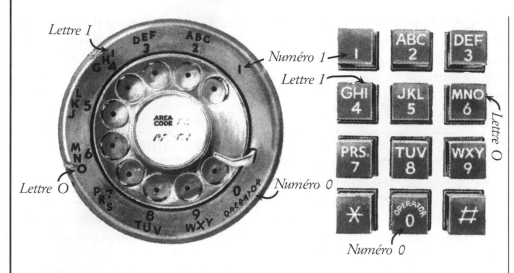

Faîtes attention à ne pas confondre la lettre I avec le chiffre 1 et la lettre O avec le chiffre 0!

et grands magasins. Les cabines téléphoniques sont situées au coin des rues, à des carrefours importants et à intervalles réguliers des artères principales. Le seul endroit où il ne faut pas en chercher est le bureau de poste: les bureaux de poste canadiens fédéraux sont indépendants des compagnies de télécommunication à propriété privée.

Les communications téléphoniques locales coûtent 25 cents dans une cabine publique, le prix d'un appel interurbain varie suivant la distance de l'abonné. Il est possible de composer un numéro directement vraiment n'importe où dans le monde en connaissant le code du pays et de la ville. Les communications interurbaines sont plus chères en passant par une standardiste mais vous donne la possibilité que l'abonné paie (*calling collect*) ou que vous n'ayez aucune charge si la personne à qui vous désirez parler ne peut être jointe (*person-to-person*). Les instructions pour effectuer un appel et le numéro à composer pour assistance, de même que les différents numéros de secours sont affichés près des cabines téléphoniques.

Les communications téléphoniques interurbaines sont moins chères la nuit et pendant le week-end. Détails et heures exactes sont indiqués dans la partie informations générales au début de l'annuaire.

L'utilisation de télécartes n'est pas si courante au Canada qu'en Europe centrale. Mais un nombre grandissant de téléphones publics – aux aéroports par exemple – sont aménagés pour ces cartes.

De nombreuses agences d'affaires et gouvernementales publient des numéros à communication gratuite. Tout numéro commençant par »1-800« compte pour un appel local.

SERVICES POSTAUX

Les services postaux canadiens sont sérieux et ont des prix modérés. On peut acheter des timbres à la réception de n'importe quel grand hôtel, aux distributeurs automatiques ou à l'un des nombreux »mini« bureaux de poste qui se trouvent principalement dans les *drugstores*.

Une lettre de première classe ou une carte postale pesant jusqu'à 30 g coûte 45 cents à l'intérieur du Canada, 52 cents à destination des Etats-Unis et 90 cents pour tout courrier international par avion. Pour un montant supplémentaire de Can$ 5,15 les lettres peuvent être recommandées. Les lettres exprès (distribution spéciale) coûtent Can$ 7. Des tarifs réduits sont appliqués pour les imprimés.

Les paquets pesant jusqu'à 500 g peuvent être expédiés en première classe comme »petits paquets«. Tout ce qui pèse plus lourd entre dans la catégorie des paquets. Un paquet pesant 1 kilo peut être envoyé en Europe en courrier de surface pour Can$ 6,80 ou par avion pour Can$ 15,20.

Les visiteurs qui ne savent pas à l'avance où ils séjourneront au Canada peuvent se faire envoyer le courrier en poste restante dans n'importe quelle ville. Il doit être adressé c/o General Delivery, Main Post Office dans la ville de leur choix.

TELEGRAMMES

Les services de télégrammes sont assurés par des entreprises privées plutôt que par les bureaux de poste. Ces entreprises locales sont indiquées dans les pages jaunes de l'annuaire. Unitel a un réseau international et peut être joint de n'importe où au Canada sous le numéro gratuit suivant: 1-800-361-1872

PRESSING

La plupart des hôtels ont un service de pressing lavant et repassant le linge en 24 heures ou moins. De nombreux pressings fonctionnant par pièces (*landromats*), sont une alternative économique. Les utiliser est facile mais prend du temps. Comptez environ 2 heures et plein de quarters!

Les terrains de camping privés ont habituellement quelques machines à laver et à sécher pour leurs locataires. En cas extrême, un grand bac est fourni. Les campeurs trouveront qu'une corde entre deux arbres et quelques épingles à linge sont très commodes.

JOURS FERIES

Les banques, agences gouvernementales et la plupart des commerces seront fermés les jours fériés officiels suivants:

New Year's Day (1er janvier), *Good Friday* (Vendredi Saint), *Easter Monday* (Lundi de Pâques), *Victoria Day* (23 mai 1994), *Canada Day* (1er juillet), *Labour Day* (5 septembre), *Thanksgiving* (10 octobre 1994), *Remembrance Day* (11 novembre), *Christmas* (Noël).

En plus, la Colombie britannique, l'Alberta, le Saskatchewan, le Manitoba, l'Ontario, le Nouveau-Brunswick, le Yukon et les Territoires du Nord-Ouest célèbrent la Fête du Patrimoine Provincial en août. La Saint-Jean Baptiste (Fête Nationale du Québec) est jour férié au Québec. Terre-Neuve fête la Saint-Patrick (mi-mars), la Saint-Georges (fin avril), le Jour de la Découverte (fin juin), la Fête Commémorative (début juillet) et la Fête des Orangistes (mi-juillet).

ZONES HORAIRES

Les voyageurs qui traversent le Canada passeront par 6 zones horaires. A midi à Vancouver (Horaire Standard du Pacifique), il est 13 heures à Calgary (Horaire Standard des Montagnes), 14 heures à Winnipeg (Horaire Standard Central), 15 heures à Ottawa (Horaire Standard Oriental), 16 heures à Halifax (Horaire Standard d'Atlantique) et 16 heures 30 à l'Horaire Standard de Terre-Neuve. Le Canada est »derrière« l'Europe: les montres doivent être retardées en y allant. L'horaire d'été est du premier dimanche d'avril au dernier dimanche d'octobre.

Excepté dans un contexte militaire, les 24 heures ne sont pas d'usage. Entre 0001 et 1200, c'est l'heure ante meridiem (*a.m.*); de 1201 à minuit l'heure post meridiem (*p.m.*).

CLIMAT

Il est bien évident qu'un pays d'une si vaste étendue ne peut avoir un climat uniforme. Les régions ont toutes quatre saisons distinctes, mais d'une durée et d'une rigueur très variables. Il en est de même pour les précipitations.

Juin, juillet et août sont chauds et secs à peu près partout et la journée les températures atteignent 17°C à 27°C. Septembre est chaud dans de nombreuses régions du pays, mais au nord les températures descendent déjà autour de 11°C. En octobre les régions boisées de l'Ontario et du Québec s'enflamment d'un tourbillon de feuilles d'érables et la baie d'Hudson commence à geler à la surface. De novembre à février l'hiver règne. Les températures journalières les plus hautes varient de − 25°C à 9°C et les plus basses de − 33°C à 3°C. En février le printemps arrive sur la côte ouest. Les jonquilles et les golfeurs émergent de leur sommeil hivernal. Quand le temps chaud pénètre dans le coeur du pays, l'été a déjà commencé sur la côte Pacifique.

GASTRONOMIE

Le Canada n'a pas une cuisine mais plusieurs. Les repas canadiens »authentiques« reflètent à la fois la diversité ethnique de la population et la richesse naturelle du pays. Malheureusement peu de plats vraiment typiques comme le *Reindeer Stroganoff* ou *Fried Saskatoons* sont servis. Cela ne signifie pas que les bons restaurants abordables manquent... mais que les visiteurs repartent souvent avec une fausse impression de la gastronomie canadienne.

Les établissements gastronomiques vont de la restauration rapide (*fast food*) aux restaurants exclusifs où on sert de la haute cuisine. Les touristes reconnaîtrons souvent les premiers indiqués mais doivent savoir que la *fast food* au Canada comprend aussi des escalopes-burgers, des salades vertes *ceasar* et des sushis à emporter.

Les cafés-restaurants sont très répandus et assez bon marché. Ils servent généralement le petit déjeuner jusqu'à 11 heures: il est composé de bacon, saucisses grillées, oeufs et toasts; typiques aussi sont les muffins, céréales et crêpes. Les cafétérias de certains hôtels servent un petit déjeuner continental de même que des plats plus sophistiqués comme les oeufs bénédictine ou l'omelette au saumon fumé. Le déjeuner signifie d'ordinaire une soupe (souvent faite maison), des salades et une variété de sandwichs.

Le pain canadien a peu d'adeptes en Europe, mais la plupart reconnaîtrons que commander des sandwichs de toasts à la farine complète est déjà un grand progrès. Dans un café-restaurant traditionnel on peut acheter toute la journée burgers, poisson et frites, goulasch et autres mets légers.

Les cafés et bistros sont la version plus moderne des anciens établissements. Leurs menus comportent des mets nouveaux comme les *linguini* (pâtes italiennes) aux palourdes ou un plat complet au curry. Ils servent aussi express, cappuccino et autres cafés forts, style italien.

Les restaurants chinois, vietnamiens, grecs et italiens ont des prix moyens et on en trouve presque partout. La nourriture indienne est tout à fait bon marché, mais peu fréquente en dehors des grandes villes. C'est la même chose pour les restaurants mexicains. Les restaurants japonais, par contre, sont nombreux et d'une qualité plutôt excellente mais chers.

Parmi les spécialités canadiennes le boeuf nourri au grain de l'Alberta est renommé dans le monde entier. Les *steakhouses* abondent et les connaisseurs commanderont une côte de boeuf de surchoix. Le boeuf canadien est aussi excellent en barbecue.

Les produits de mer dominent dans les régions côtières. De nombreuses variétés de saumon du Pacifique très savoureuses, inconnues en Europe, doivent absolument être goûtées. Les campeurs peuvent faire une expérience culinaire inoubliable en enroulant un saumon frais entier dans une feuille d'aluminium et le faisant cuire au feu de bois. Dans les

TABLEAU DU CLIMAT

Province/Territory City	High Temp. Low Temp.	JAN	FEB	MAR	APR	MAY	JUN	JUL	AUG	SEP	OCT	NOV	DEC
British Columbia (Victoria)	H	6	8	10	13	17	19	22	21	19	14	9	7
	L	0	1	2	4	7	9	11	11	9	6	3	1
Alberta (Edmonton)	H	−11	−6	−1	9	17	21	22	22	17	11	0	−8
	L	−22	−17	−12	−3	3	7	9	8	3	−2	−11	−19
Saskatchewan (Regina)	H	−13	−8	−2	9	18	23	26	25	19	12	0	−8
	L	−23	−19	−13	−3	4	9	12	10	5	−2	−10	−18
Manitoba (Winnipeg)	H	−14	−10	−3	9	18	23	26	25	18	12	0	−9
	L	−24	−21	−14	−2	5	11	13	12	6	1	−9	−19
Ontario (Toronto)	H	−1	−1	4	12	18	24	27	26	21	15	8	1
	L	−8	−7	−3	3	9	14	17	17	13	7	2	−5
Québec (Québec City)	H	−8	−6	0	8	17	22	25	23	18	11	3	−5
	L	−17	−16	−9	−2	5	10	13	12	7	2	−4	−13
Nova Scotia (Halifax)	H	1	1	4	9	14	19	23	23	20	14	9	3
	L	−7	−7	−4	1	5	10	14	14	12	7	2	−4
Prince Edward Island (Charlottetown)	H	−3	−3	1	7	14	20	23	23	18	12	7	0
	L	−11	−11	−6	−1	4	10	14	14	10	5	0	−7
Newfoundland (St. John's)	H	0	0	2	5	11	17	21	20	17	11	7	2
	L	−7	−8	−5	−1	2	7	11	12	8	4	0	−4
New Brunswick (Fredericton)	H	−4	−3	3	9	17	23	26	25	20	13	6	−2
	L	−15	−14	−8	−1	4	10	13	12	7	2	−3	−11
N.W.T. (Yellowknife)	H	−25	−20	−13	−1	10	18	21	18	10	1	−10	−20
	L	−33	−30	−25	−13	0	8	12	10	4	−4	−18	−28
Yukon (Whitehorse)	H	−16	−8	−2	6	13	18	20	18	12	4	−5	−13
	L	−25	−18	−14	−5	1	6	8	7	3	−3	−12	−21

provinces maritimes de l'est, les crustacés sont délicieux et d'un prix modéré. Du homard à la vapeur, servi dans du beurre fondu avec des petits pains frais est un festin. De nombreux restaurants touristiques ont des sets de table imprimés d'un schéma expliquant comment manger le homard.

Les fruits et baies jouent un rôle important dans la cuisine canadienne, en particulier dans les desserts. Des tourtes maison aux multiples variations, des biscuits sablés aux fraises, des tartes au fromage blanc garnies de fruits en sont seulement quelques exemples typiques. Un petit déjeuner composé de muffins chauds, beurrés et fourrés d'airelles est délicieux et aussi typiquement canadien.

Dans de nombreuses régions les fermiers se mettent au bord de la route pour vendre leurs produits pendant l'été. Les voyageurs se rafraîchiront avec un verre de cidre tout en savourant des fruits mûris au soleil d'une grande variété.

Un certain nombre de fromages canadiens, en particulier le cheddar et l'oka, sont connus à juste titre dans le monde entier. L'oka doit son nom à une région du Québec où il fut fabriqué pour la première fois par des moines trappistes français.

La cuisine québécoise a subi, bien entendu, une influence française plus marquée que celle du reste du pays. Les visi-

teurs de la »belle province« doivent goûter à quelques uns des plus de 100 espèces de fromages qui y sont fabriqués, à la soupe aux petits pois, tourtière de porc, gâteau johnny, bouillabaisse et à tous les mets à base de sirop d'érable qu'ils rencontreront.

Au cours des dernières années, un intérêt grandissant s'est développé pour la culture des premières nations. Les visiteurs pourront donc faire l'expérience unique de dîner à la manière des indigènes américains. Cette cuisine est caractérisée par le gibier et les légumes.

Des délicatesses inhabituelles comme les pousses de fougère (fiddleheads) seront une surprise agréable.